Mometrix
TEST PREPARATION

I0868264

CSET®

English Language Development Exam Secrets Study Guide

Dear Future Exam Success Story

First of all, **THANK YOU** for purchasing Mometrix study materials!

Second, congratulations! You are one of the few determined test-takers who are committed to doing whatever it takes to excel on your exam. **You have come to the right place.** We developed these study materials with one goal in mind: to deliver you the information you need in a format that's concise and easy to use.

In addition to optimizing your guide for the content of the test, we've outlined our recommended steps for breaking down the preparation process into small, attainable goals so you can make sure you stay on track.

We've also analyzed the entire test-taking process, identifying the most common pitfalls and showing how you can overcome them and be ready for any curveball the test throws you.

Standardized testing is one of the biggest obstacles on your road to success, which only increases the importance of doing well in the high-pressure, high-stakes environment of test day. Your results on this test could have a significant impact on your future, and this guide provides the information and practical advice to help you achieve your full potential on test day.

Your success is our success

We would love to hear from you! If you would like to share the story of your exam success or if you have any questions or comments in regard to our products, please contact us at **800-673-8175** or **support@mometrix.com**.

Thanks again for your business and we wish you continued success!

Sincerely,
The Mometrix Test Preparation Team

Need more help? Check out our flashcards at:
http://MometrixFlashcards.com/CSET

Printed in the United States of America

TABLE OF CONTENTS

Introduction

Thank you for purchasing this resource! You have made the choice to prepare yourself for a test that could have a huge impact on your future, and this guide is designed to help you be fully ready for test day. Obviously, it's important to have a solid understanding of the test material, but you also need to be prepared for the unique environment and stressors of the test, so that you can perform to the best of your abilities.

For this purpose, the first section that appears in this guide is the **Secret Keys**. We've devoted countless hours to meticulously researching what works and what doesn't, and we've boiled down our findings to the five most impactful steps you can take to improve your performance on the test. We start at the beginning with study planning and move through the preparation process, all the way to the testing strategies that will help you get the most out of what you know when you're finally sitting in front of the test.

We recommend that you start preparing for your test as far in advance as possible. However, if you've bought this guide as a last-minute study resource and only have a few days before your test, we recommend that you skip over the first two Secret Keys since they address a long-term study plan.

If you struggle with **test anxiety**, we strongly encourage you to check out our recommendations for how you can overcome it. Test anxiety is a formidable foe, but it can be beaten, and we want to make sure you have the tools you need to defeat it.

Secret Key #1 – Plan Big, Study Small

There's a lot riding on your performance. If you want to ace this test, you're going to need to keep your skills sharp and the material fresh in your mind. You need a plan that lets you review everything you need to know while still fitting in your schedule. We'll break this strategy down into three categories.

Information Organization

Start with the information you already have: the official test outline. From this, you can make a complete list of all the concepts you need to cover before the test. Organize these concepts into groups that can be studied together, and create a list of any related vocabulary you need to learn so you can brush up on any difficult terms. You'll want to keep this vocabulary list handy once you actually start studying since you may need to add to it along the way.

Time Management

Once you have your set of study concepts, decide how to spread them out over the time you have left before the test. Break your study plan into small, clear goals so you have a manageable task for each day and know exactly what you're doing. Then just focus on one small step at a time. When you manage your time this way, you don't need to spend hours at a time studying. Studying a small block of content for a short period each day helps you retain information better and avoid stressing over how much you have left to do. You can relax knowing that you have a plan to cover everything in time. In order for this strategy to be effective though, you have to start studying early and stick to your schedule. Avoid the exhaustion and futility that comes from last-minute cramming!

Study Environment

The environment you study in has a big impact on your learning. Studying in a coffee shop, while probably more enjoyable, is not likely to be as fruitful as studying in a quiet room. It's important to keep distractions to a minimum. You're only planning to study for a short block of time, so make the most of it. Don't pause to check your phone or get up to find a snack. It's also important to **avoid multitasking**. Research has consistently shown that multitasking will make your studying dramatically less effective. Your study area should also be comfortable and well-lit so you don't have the distraction of straining your eyes or sitting on an uncomfortable chair.

The time of day you study is also important. You want to be rested and alert. Don't wait until just before bedtime. Study when you'll be most likely to comprehend and remember. Even better, if you know what time of day your test will be, set that time aside for study. That way your brain will be used to working on that subject at that specific time and you'll have a better chance of recalling information.

Finally, it can be helpful to team up with others who are studying for the same test. Your actual studying should be done in as isolated an environment as possible, but the work of organizing the information and setting up the study plan can be divided up. In between study sessions, you can discuss with your teammates the concepts that you're all studying and quiz each other on the details. Just be sure that your teammates are as serious about the test as you are. If you find that your study time is being replaced with social time, you might need to find a new team.

Secret Key #2 – Make Your Studying Count

You're devoting a lot of time and effort to preparing for this test, so you want to be absolutely certain it will pay off. This means doing more than just reading the content and hoping you can remember it on test day. It's important to make every minute of study count. There are two main areas you can focus on to make your studying count.

Retention

It doesn't matter how much time you study if you can't remember the material. You need to make sure you are retaining the concepts. To check your retention of the information you're learning, try recalling it at later times with minimal prompting. Try carrying around flashcards and glance at one or two from time to time or ask a friend who's also studying for the test to quiz you.

To enhance your retention, look for ways to put the information into practice so that you can apply it rather than simply recalling it. If you're using the information in practical ways, it will be much easier to remember. Similarly, it helps to solidify a concept in your mind if you're not only reading it to yourself but also explaining it to someone else. Ask a friend to let you teach them about a concept you're a little shaky on (or speak aloud to an imaginary audience if necessary). As you try to summarize, define, give examples, and answer your friend's questions, you'll understand the concepts better and they will stay with you longer. Finally, step back for a big picture view and ask yourself how each piece of information fits with the whole subject. When you link the different concepts together and see them working together as a whole, it's easier to remember the individual components.

Finally, practice showing your work on any multi-step problems, even if you're just studying. Writing out each step you take to solve a problem will help solidify the process in your mind, and you'll be more likely to remember it during the test.

Modality

Modality simply refers to the means or method by which you study. Choosing a study modality that fits your own individual learning style is crucial. No two people learn best in exactly the same way, so it's important to know your strengths and use them to your advantage.

For example, if you learn best by visualization, focus on visualizing a concept in your mind and draw an image or a diagram. Try color-coding your notes, illustrating them, or creating symbols that will trigger your mind to recall a learned concept. If you learn best by hearing or discussing information, find a study partner who learns the same way or read aloud to yourself. Think about how to put the information in your own words. Imagine that you are giving a lecture on the topic and record yourself so you can listen to it later.

For any learning style, flashcards can be helpful. Organize the information so you can take advantage of spare moments to review. Underline key words or phrases. Use different colors for different categories. Mnemonic devices (such as creating a short list in which every item starts with the same letter) can also help with retention. Find what works best for you and use it to store the information in your mind most effectively and easily.

Secret Key #3 – Practice the Right Way

Your success on test day depends not only on how many hours you put into preparing, but also on whether you prepared the right way. It's good to check along the way to see if your studying is paying off. One of the most effective ways to do this is by taking practice tests to evaluate your progress. Practice tests are useful because they show exactly where you need to improve. Every time you take a practice test, pay special attention to these three groups of questions:

- The questions you got wrong
- The questions you had to guess on, even if you guessed right
- The questions you found difficult or slow to work through

This will show you exactly what your weak areas are, and where you need to devote more study time. Ask yourself why each of these questions gave you trouble. Was it because you didn't understand the material? Was it because you didn't remember the vocabulary? Do you need more repetitions on this type of question to build speed and confidence? Dig into those questions and figure out how you can strengthen your weak areas as you go back to review the material.

Additionally, many practice tests have a section explaining the answer choices. It can be tempting to read the explanation and think that you now have a good understanding of the concept. However, an explanation likely only covers part of the question's broader context. Even if the explanation makes perfect sense, **go back and investigate** every concept related to the question until you're positive you have a thorough understanding.

As you go along, keep in mind that the practice test is just that: practice. Memorizing these questions and answers will not be very helpful on the actual test because it is unlikely to have any of the same exact questions. If you only know the right answers to the sample questions, you won't be prepared for the real thing. **Study the concepts** until you understand them fully, and then you'll be able to answer any question that shows up on the test.

It's important to wait on the practice tests until you're ready. If you take a test on your first day of study, you may be overwhelmed by the amount of material covered and how much you need to learn. Work up to it gradually.

On test day, you'll need to be prepared for answering questions, managing your time, and using the test-taking strategies you've learned. It's a lot to balance, like a mental marathon that will have a big impact on your future. Like training for a marathon, you'll need to start slowly and work your way up. When test day arrives, you'll be ready.

Start with the strategies you've read in the first two Secret Keys—plan your course and study in the way that works best for you. If you have time, consider using multiple study resources to get different approaches to the same concepts. It can be helpful to see difficult concepts from more than one angle. Then find a good source for practice tests. Many times, the test website will suggest potential study resources or provide sample tests.

Practice Test Strategy

If you're able to find at least three practice tests, we recommend this strategy:

Untimed and Open-Book Practice

Take the first test with no time constraints and with your notes and study guide handy. Take your time and focus on applying the strategies you've learned.

Timed and Open-Book Practice

Take the second practice test open-book as well, but set a timer and practice pacing yourself to finish in time.

Timed and Closed-Book Practice

Take any other practice tests as if it were test day. Set a timer and put away your study materials. Sit at a table or desk in a quiet room, imagine yourself at the testing center, and answer questions as quickly and accurately as possible.

Keep repeating timed and closed-book tests on a regular basis until you run out of practice tests or it's time for the actual test. Your mind will be ready for the schedule and stress of test day, and you'll be able to focus on recalling the material you've learned.

Secret Key #4 – Pace Yourself

Once you're fully prepared for the material on the test, your biggest challenge on test day will be managing your time. Just knowing that the clock is ticking can make you panic even if you have plenty of time left. Work on pacing yourself so you can build confidence against the time constraints of the exam. Pacing is a difficult skill to master, especially in a high-pressure environment, so **practice is vital**.

Set time expectations for your pace based on how much time is available. For example, if a section has 60 questions and the time limit is 30 minutes, you know you have to average 30 seconds or less per question in order to answer them all. Although 30 seconds is the hard limit, set 25 seconds per question as your goal, so you reserve extra time to spend on harder questions. When you budget extra time for the harder questions, you no longer have any reason to stress when those questions take longer to answer.

Don't let this time expectation distract you from working through the test at a calm, steady pace, but keep it in mind so you don't spend too much time on any one question. Recognize that taking extra time on one question you don't understand may keep you from answering two that you do understand later in the test. If your time limit for a question is up and you're still not sure of the answer, mark it and move on, and come back to it later if the time and the test format allow. If the testing format doesn't allow you to return to earlier questions, just make an educated guess; then put it out of your mind and move on.

On the easier questions, be careful not to rush. It may seem wise to hurry through them so you have more time for the challenging ones, but it's not worth missing one if you know the concept and just didn't take the time to read the question fully. Work efficiently but make sure you understand the question and have looked at all of the answer choices, since more than one may seem right at first.

Even if you're paying attention to the time, you may find yourself a little behind at some point. You should speed up to get back on track, but do so wisely. Don't panic; just take a few seconds less on each question until you're caught up. Don't guess without thinking, but do look through the answer choices and eliminate any you know are wrong. If you can get down to two choices, it is often worthwhile to guess from those. Once you've chosen an answer, move on and don't dwell on any that you skipped or had to hurry through. If a question was taking too long, chances are it was one of the harder ones, so you weren't as likely to get it right anyway.

On the other hand, if you find yourself getting ahead of schedule, it may be beneficial to slow down a little. The more quickly you work, the more likely you are to make a careless mistake that will affect your score. You've budgeted time for each question, so don't be afraid to spend that time. Practice an efficient but careful pace to get the most out of the time you have.

Secret Key #5 – Have a Plan for Guessing

When you're taking the test, you may find yourself stuck on a question. Some of the answer choices seem better than others, but you don't see the one answer choice that is obviously correct. What do you do?

The scenario described above is very common, yet most test takers have not effectively prepared for it. Developing and practicing a plan for guessing may be one of the single most effective uses of your time as you get ready for the exam.

In developing your plan for guessing, there are three questions to address:

- When should you start the guessing process?
- How should you narrow down the choices?
- Which answer should you choose?

When to Start the Guessing Process

Unless your plan for guessing is to select C every time (which, despite its merits, is not what we recommend), you need to leave yourself enough time to apply your answer elimination strategies. Since you have a limited amount of time for each question, that means that if you're going to give yourself the best shot at guessing correctly, you have to decide quickly whether or not you will guess.

Of course, the best-case scenario is that you don't have to guess at all, so first, see if you can answer the question based on your knowledge of the subject and basic reasoning skills. Focus on the key words in the question and try to jog your memory of related topics. Give yourself a chance to bring the knowledge to mind, but once you realize that you don't have (or you can't access) the knowledge you need to answer the question, it's time to start the guessing process.

It's almost always better to start the guessing process too early than too late. It only takes a few seconds to remember something and answer the question from knowledge. Carefully eliminating wrong answer choices takes longer. Plus, going through the process of eliminating answer choices can actually help jog your memory.

Summary: Start the guessing process as soon as you decide that you can't answer the question based on your knowledge.

How to Narrow Down the Choices

The next chapter in this book (**Test-Taking Strategies**) includes a wide range of strategies for how to approach questions and how to look for answer choices to eliminate. You will definitely want to read those carefully, practice them, and figure out which ones work best for you. Here though, we're going to address a mindset rather than a particular strategy.

Your odds of guessing an answer correctly depend on how many options you are choosing from.

Number of options left	5	4	3	2	1
Odds of guessing correctly	20%	25%	33%	50%	100%

You can see from this chart just how valuable it is to be able to eliminate incorrect answers and make an educated guess, but there are two things that many test takers do that cause them to miss out on the benefits of guessing:

- Accidentally eliminating the correct answer
- Selecting an answer based on an impression

We'll look at the first one here, and the second one in the next section.

To avoid accidentally eliminating the correct answer, we recommend a thought exercise called **the $5 challenge**. In this challenge, you only eliminate an answer choice from contention if you are willing to bet $5 on it being wrong. Why $5? Five dollars is a small but not insignificant amount of money. It's an amount you could afford to lose but wouldn't want to throw away. And while losing $5 once might not hurt too much, doing it twenty times will set you back $100. In the same way, each small decision you make—eliminating a choice here, guessing on a question there—won't by itself impact your score very much, but when you put them all together, they can make a big difference. By holding each answer choice elimination decision to a higher standard, you can reduce the risk of accidentally eliminating the correct answer.

The $5 challenge can also be applied in a positive sense: If you are willing to bet $5 that an answer choice *is* correct, go ahead and mark it as correct.

Summary: Only eliminate an answer choice if you are willing to bet $5 that it is wrong.

Which Answer to Choose

You're taking the test. You've run into a hard question and decided you'll have to guess. You've eliminated all the answer choices you're willing to bet $5 on. Now you have to pick an answer. Why do we even need to talk about this? Why can't you just pick whichever one you feel like when the time comes?

The answer to these questions is that if you don't come into the test with a plan, you'll rely on your impression to select an answer choice, and if you do that, you risk falling into a trap. The test writers know that everyone who takes their test will be guessing on some of the questions, so they intentionally write wrong answer choices to seem plausible. You still have to pick an answer though, and if the wrong answer choices are designed to look right, how can you ever be sure that you're not falling for their trap? The best solution we've found to this dilemma is to take the decision out of your hands entirely. Here is the process we recommend:

Once you've eliminated any choices that you are confident (willing to bet $5) are wrong, select the first remaining choice as your answer.

Whether you choose to select the first remaining choice, the second, or the last, the important thing is that you use some preselected standard. Using this approach guarantees that you will not be enticed into selecting an answer choice that looks right, because you are not basing your decision on how the answer choices look.

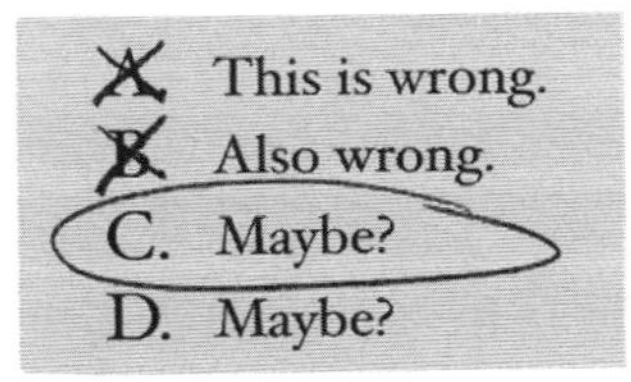

This is not meant to make you question your knowledge. Instead, it is to help you recognize the difference between your knowledge and your impressions. There's a huge difference between thinking an answer is right because of what you know, and thinking an answer is right because it looks or sounds like it should be right.

Summary: To ensure that your selection is appropriately random, make a predetermined selection from among all answer choices you have not eliminated.

Test-Taking Strategies

This section contains a list of test-taking strategies that you may find helpful as you work through the test. By taking what you know and applying logical thought, you can maximize your chances of answering any question correctly!

It is very important to realize that every question is different and every person is different: no single strategy will work on every question, and no single strategy will work for every person. That's why we've included all of them here, so you can try them out and determine which ones work best for different types of questions and which ones work best for you.

Question Strategies

Read Carefully

Read the question and the answer choices carefully. Don't miss the question because you misread the terms. You have plenty of time to read each question thoroughly and make sure you understand what is being asked. Yet a happy medium must be attained, so don't waste too much time. You must read carefully and efficiently.

Contextual Clues

Look for contextual clues. If the question includes a word you are not familiar with, look at the immediate context for some indication of what the word might mean. Contextual clues can often give you all the information you need to decipher the meaning of an unfamiliar word. Even if you can't determine the meaning, you may be able to narrow down the possibilities enough to make a solid guess at the answer to the question.

Prefixes

If you're having trouble with a word in the question or answer choices, try dissecting it. Take advantage of every clue that the word might include. Prefixes can be a huge help. Usually, they allow you to determine a basic meaning. *Pre-* means before, *post-* means after, *pro-* is positive, *de-* is negative. From prefixes, you can get an idea of the general meaning of the word and try to put it into context.

Hedge Words

Watch out for critical hedge words, such as *likely, may, can, often, almost, mostly, usually, generally, rarely*, and *sometimes*. Question writers insert these hedge phrases to cover every possibility. Often an answer choice will be wrong simply because it leaves no room for exception. Be on guard for answer choices that have definitive words such as *exactly* and *always.*

Switchback Words

Stay alert for *switchbacks*. These are the words and phrases frequently used to alert you to shifts in thought. The most common switchback words are *but, although*, and *however*. Others include *nevertheless, on the other hand, even though, while, in spite of, despite*, and *regardless of.* Switchback words are important to catch because they can change the direction of the question or an answer choice.

⊘ Face Value

When in doubt, use common sense. Accept the situation in the problem at face value. Don't read too much into it. These problems will not require you to make wild assumptions. If you have to go beyond creativity and warp time or space in order to have an answer choice fit the question, then you should move on and consider the other answer choices. These are normal problems rooted in reality. The applicable relationship or explanation may not be readily apparent, but it is there for you to figure out. Use your common sense to interpret anything that isn't clear.

Answer Choice Strategies

⊘ Answer Selection

The most thorough way to pick an answer choice is to identify and eliminate wrong answers until only one is left, then confirm it is the correct answer. Sometimes an answer choice may immediately seem right, but be careful. The test writers will usually put more than one reasonable answer choice on each question, so take a second to read all of them and make sure that the other choices are not equally obvious. As long as you have time left, it is better to read every answer choice than to pick the first one that looks right without checking the others.

⊘ Answer Choice Families

An answer choice family consists of two (in rare cases, three) answer choices that are very similar in construction and cannot all be true at the same time. If you see two answer choices that are direct opposites or parallels, one of them is usually the correct answer. For instance, if one answer choice says that quantity *x* increases and another either says that quantity *x* decreases (opposite) or says that quantity *y* increases (parallel), then those answer choices would fall into the same family. An answer choice that doesn't match the construction of the answer choice family is more likely to be incorrect. Most questions will not have answer choice families, but when they do appear, you should be prepared to recognize them.

⊘ Eliminate Answers

Eliminate answer choices as soon as you realize they are wrong, but make sure you consider all possibilities. If you are eliminating answer choices and realize that the last one you are left with is also wrong, don't panic. Start over and consider each choice again. There may be something you missed the first time that you will realize on the second pass.

⊘ Avoid Fact Traps

Don't be distracted by an answer choice that is factually true but doesn't answer the question. You are looking for the choice that answers the question. Stay focused on what the question is asking for so you don't accidentally pick an answer that is true but incorrect. Always go back to the question and make sure the answer choice you've selected actually answers the question and is not merely a true statement.

⊘ Extreme Statements

In general, you should avoid answers that put forth extreme actions as standard practice or proclaim controversial ideas as established fact. An answer choice that states the "process should be used in certain situations, if…" is much more likely to be correct than one that states the "process should be discontinued completely." The first is a calm rational statement and doesn't even make a definitive, uncompromising stance, using a hedge word *if* to provide wiggle room, whereas the second choice is far more extreme.

✓ Benchmark

As you read through the answer choices and you come across one that seems to answer the question well, mentally select that answer choice. This is not your final answer, but it's the one that will help you evaluate the other answer choices. The one that you selected is your benchmark or standard for judging each of the other answer choices. Every other answer choice must be compared to your benchmark. That choice is correct until proven otherwise by another answer choice beating it. If you find a better answer, then that one becomes your new benchmark. Once you've decided that no other choice answers the question as well as your benchmark, you have your final answer.

✓ Predict the Answer

Before you even start looking at the answer choices, it is often best to try to predict the answer. When you come up with the answer on your own, it is easier to avoid distractions and traps because you will know exactly what to look for. The right answer choice is unlikely to be word-for-word what you came up with, but it should be a close match. Even if you are confident that you have the right answer, you should still take the time to read each option before moving on.

General Strategies

✓ Tough Questions

If you are stumped on a problem or it appears too hard or too difficult, don't waste time. Move on! Remember though, if you can quickly check for obviously incorrect answer choices, your chances of guessing correctly are greatly improved. Before you completely give up, at least try to knock out a couple of possible answers. Eliminate what you can and then guess at the remaining answer choices before moving on.

✓ Check Your Work

Since you will probably not know every term listed and the answer to every question, it is important that you get credit for the ones that you do know. Don't miss any questions through careless mistakes. If at all possible, try to take a second to look back over your answer selection and make sure you've selected the correct answer choice and haven't made a costly careless mistake (such as marking an answer choice that you didn't mean to mark). This quick double check should more than pay for itself in caught mistakes for the time it costs.

✓ Pace Yourself

It's easy to be overwhelmed when you're looking at a page full of questions; your mind is confused and full of random thoughts, and the clock is ticking down faster than you would like. Calm down and maintain the pace that you have set for yourself. Especially as you get down to the last few minutes of the test, don't let the small numbers on the clock make you panic. As long as you are on track by monitoring your pace, you are guaranteed to have time for each question.

✓ Don't Rush

It is very easy to make errors when you are in a hurry. Maintaining a fast pace in answering questions is pointless if it makes you miss questions that you would have gotten right otherwise. Test writers like to include distracting information and wrong answers that seem right. Taking a little extra time to avoid careless mistakes can make all the difference in your test score. Find a pace that allows you to be confident in the answers that you select.

✓ Keep Moving

Panicking will not help you pass the test, so do your best to stay calm and keep moving. Taking deep breaths and going through the answer elimination steps you practiced can help to break through a stress barrier and keep your pace.

Final Notes

The combination of a solid foundation of content knowledge and the confidence that comes from practicing your plan for applying that knowledge is the key to maximizing your performance on test day. As your foundation of content knowledge is built up and strengthened, you'll find that the strategies included in this chapter become more and more effective in helping you quickly sift through the distractions and traps of the test to isolate the correct answer.

Now that you're preparing to move forward into the test content chapters of this book, be sure to keep your goal in mind. As you read, think about how you will be able to apply this information on the test. If you've already seen sample questions for the test and you have an idea of the question format and style, try to come up with questions of your own that you can answer based on what you're reading. This will give you valuable practice applying your knowledge in the same ways you can expect to on test day.

Good luck and good studying!

English Learners in California and the United States

General Language Acquisition Theory

Krashen's Monitor Hypothesis

Stephen Krashen argues that individuals who acquire languages know inherently what is correct in that language, even if they have not formally studied the grammatical or syntactical rules of that language. However, learning continues to play a role even for individuals who have acquired a language: once they learn explicit rules, they can use them to **monitor** and correct their language use. Monitoring one's language, however, takes time and conscious attention and, thus, is more feasible when writing than speaking. As Krashen points out, it is difficult to speak fluently and simultaneously attend to what one is saying—attempting to do so usually leads to interrupted speech. Critics of the monitor hypothesis include both those who argue that children may monitor their speech before they have learned language rules and those who argue that, as defined, the hypothesis does not apply to the vast majority of speech and thus is of limited use.

Krashen's Acquisition/Learning Hypothesis

Stephen Krashen distinguishes between acquiring a language and learning a language. **Acquisition** is an unconscious, natural process that occurs when a learner uses the language for a variety of real-life purposes and interacts extensively with native speakers. **Learning**, by contrast, is a conscious process during which a student is likely to study parts of a language in sequence, as when they study vocabulary lists or learn to conjugate verbs. Krashen argues that only acquisition leads to fluency, and he further claims that learning cannot be transformed into acquisition. Unlike some theorists, Krashen does not deny that adults can acquire (rather than learn) a new language but argues that doing so would require them to immerse themselves in that language. Krashen's distinction is widely used in language theory. Critics, however, have disputed his claim that learned languages cannot subsequently be acquired and say that the distinction is difficult to define in some contexts.

Review Video: Second Language Learning
Visit mometrix.com/academy and enter code: 795047

Krashen's Natural Order

Stephen Krashen argues that people acquire aspects of language in a **natural order**, regardless of which language they are acquiring or which language is their primary language. That is, certain grammatical structures are acquired early in the language process and others later. For example, research shows that individuals acquiring English will master the use of the "-ing" form of verbs before they learn to add an "-s" to the third person singular form of regular verbs. Research since Krashen's formulation of the hypothesis has weakened his findings but not overturned them. Critics have argued that, in fact, one's first language does influence the order in which elements of a second language are acquired.

Krashen's Input Hypothesis

Stephen Krashen argues that language acquisition takes place most efficiently when students are presented with **input** that is slightly beyond their current mastery level. In other words, students should be able to understand most of what they hear or read, but not all. If used correctly, students will be able to understand this **comprehensible input** through the use of context, their background knowledge, or non-linguistic cues. If comprehensible input is used effectively, it eliminates the need for explicit explanation of new structures or meanings; students will be able to deduce the meaning without explanation. Merrill Swain answered one of the principal criticisms of this hypothesis—that it only treated comprehension, not speech production—by coining the term "**output hypothesis**." In Swain's view, students will be motivated to improve their speech production when they notice, in conversation, that they are unable to express themselves fully.

KRASHEN'S AFFECTIVE FILTER HYPOTHESIS

Stephen Krashen's affective filter hypothesis states that students learn most effectively in **low-stress learning environments**. Affective factors such as boredom or anxiety, Krashen argues, create **affective filters** that interfere with the learning process. Krashen and collaborator Tracy Terrell are credited with developing the natural approach to second-language learning around this idea. This approach emphasizes that students should not be forced to speak until they feel comfortable doing so, in order to avoid affective interference in the learning process. Krashen argued that children are less influenced by affective factors than adults, providing children with an advantage in language acquisition. This assertion has subsequently been challenged. Krashen's hypothesis remains useful, however, in drawing attention to the importance of non-linguistic factors in language acquisition.

SEQUENTIAL BILINGUALISM, SIMULTANEOUS BILINGUALISM, AND MULTILINGUALISM

Bilingualism is the ability to use two languages fluently, while **multilingualism** is the ability to use more than one language fluently. **Simultaneous bilingualism** occurs when a child is raised bilingually from birth or is introduced to the second language before the age of three. **Sequential bilingualism** occurs when a child obtains fluency in a second language after the first language is well established—usually around the age of three.

Recent research has demonstrated that children can readily learn more than one language at a time. This research overturns the limited capacity hypothesis—the assertion that children exposed to more than one language at a time experience delayed and incomplete proficiency in either—that influenced the field for decades. Current research suggests bilingual learners may experience slight delays in speech production, but the variance is small and within the range of normal development. Further, bilingual children often possess smaller vocabularies in either language than their monolingual peers, but their combined vocabulary is on par with that of their peers.

CODE-SWITCHING

Code-switching is a phenomenon in which speakers switch from one language to another in the same conversation, often in the same sentence. **Code-switching** among bilingual Spanish-English speakers is so common that a name for it has been coined: "Spanglish." One reason people code-switch is that they are unable to think of a word in the language they are speaking, and so they resort to a word from their native language. However, in conversation with other bilinguals, code-switching may signal solidarity or familiarity, or it may be used to convey associative, technical, or figurative meanings not available in the primary language. Bilingual speakers often use their native language to talk about their daily life and use their learned language when discussing academic or job-related topics.

Code-switching can also refer to alterations in discourse undertaken in a single language—for example, when one speaker changes accent to match that of his or her interlocutor, or when an English speaker drops the final "-g" on progressive-tense verbs to project an informal, working-class form of speech.

Interlanguage

An interlanguage is the version of a learned language produced at any given moment by a language learner. An **interlanguage** contains elements and structures of both L1 and L2 but may differ substantially from either, leading some linguists to refer to the interlanguage as an entirely separate language. Interlanguage is often referred to as a strategy adopted by a learner to compensate for his or her limited proficiency in L2. While interlanguage is considered a normal part of language learning, it risks becoming **fossilized** if a learner lacks the opportunity or motivation to improve upon it. Fossilization often occurs when a learner achieves a level of proficiency that allows for effective, albeit limited, communication.

Various **cognitive tendencies** contribute to the formation of an interlanguage. The linguist Larry Selinker, who first developed the concept of interlanguage in the 1970s, identified five such tendencies, including language transfer, which occurs when a learner applies knowledge or rules from L1 to L2. A second tendency, overgeneralization, occurs when a learner extends a language rule beyond its actual scope—for example, when an ELL universally adds "-ed" to create a past-tense verb, resulting in errors like "swimmed."

The Basic Word Order of English

The grammars of nearly all languages have **subjects** (S), **verbs** (V), and **objects** (O). This is an example of a non-absolute language universal. Of the possible ordering of those three components in a standard sentence, only three are frequently found—S-V-O (as in English), S-O-V (as in Japanese), and V-S-O (as in Malagasy).

Both Spanish and English rely overwhelmingly on the **S-V-O ordering**, though Spanish does allow for frequent subject-verb inversion in cases where English does not. Many Spanish sentences do not have a stated subject at all—because Spanish verbs are conjugated differently for each person (unlike in English), the subject of a sentence can be inferred from the verb. In English, adjectives typically precede nouns; in Spanish, the opposite is more common. In Spanish, nouns cannot modify nouns, so possession is indicated after an object, contrary to English: "John's car" versus "el coche de John" ("the car of John").

Universals

A language universal is a characteristic that is shared by all the world's languages. In 1966, the linguist Joseph Greenberg published a list of 45 allegedly universal characteristics of language, but modern linguists, with much more language data and computer analysis available to them, are much more cautious. The few agreed-upon **absolute universals** (those with no known exceptions) are relatively uninteresting—for example, all languages have syllables, consonants, and vowels. Linguists work more fruitfully with **non-absolute universals**—that is, features that are found with a high degree of statistical regularity but also have exceptions.

Implicational universals are language properties that occur together—in other words, they fit the logical form of "If a language has A, it will also have B." An example of a non-absolute implicational universal is "If verb-subject-object is the dominant syntax form in a language, the adjective will follow the noun."

First Language Acquisition Theory

Model of First-Language Acquisition

Developmental psychologists have created approximate timelines for both first-language acquisition and second-language learning. The following are typical stages and landmarks in first-language acquisition:

1. **Pre-speech stage (0-6 months)**: Babies may produce what are called comfort signs (grunts and sighs) while paying attention to spoken language and beginning to distinguish phonemes.
2. **Babbling stage (6-8 months)**: Babies begin to babble, or produce rhythmic sounds with syllable-like stops, often with repeated patterns. Babbling allows infants to practice essential motor skills and learn how to produce basic sounds.
3. **One-word stage (10-18 months)**: Children produce their first words, usually in reference to people, objects, or actions that produce desired outcomes. Overextension and underextension (using words too broadly or too narrowly) are common.
4. **Two-word or telegraphic stage (18-24 months)**: Children produce two-word phrases using lexical rather than functional or grammatical morphemes.
5. **Multiword stage (30 months)**: Children speak in complete sentences, adding functional and grammatical elements, though often making errors.

Pivot Grammar

The cognitive psychologist Martin Braine created the **pivot grammar model** in the 1960s to explain how children first structure language when moving from the one-word to the two-word speaking phase. Braine noticed children create many utterances anchored by a single word (the **pivot**) used in combination with a larger variety of words (which he termed **open-class words**). For example, children commonly use the anchor "all" to create oft-repeated variations: "all gone," "all done," "all eat," etc. "More" is another typical anchor: "more milk," "more TV," etc. Researchers noticed that children use certain pivot words first and others second, suggesting that in this phase they have begun to understand differences in word class and function. While some scholars suggest that pivot grammar is compatible with universal grammar (UG) models, others argue that with pivot grammars children are not building upon *syntactic* regularities, but rather upon *lexical* regularities—a direct challenge to the UG model of how children acquire languages.

Holophrase

A holophrase is a single word used to express complex thought. For example, a toddler who utters the **holophrase** "up" may be intending the more complex thought "pick me up." Consistent with the idea that children understand more language than they can produce, holophrastic conversations with adults often consist of the adult trying to interpret the meaning of a holophrastic phrase, offering alternatives to which the child responds with body-language affirmations or rejections. For example, a toddler may say "mommy," leaving the adult to guess "where's mommy?" or "you want mommy's bag?"—one of which will eventually trigger the toddler's assent.

Some holophrases may consist of unanalyzed combinations of two or more words—for example, "allgone." According to development theory, children pass into the subsequent, **telegraphic stage** of language development when they begin to produce two-word utterances, many of which are structured around pivot words as elaborated in the pivot grammar model.

The Behaviorist Theory of First-Language Acquisition

Behaviorist theories of language learning propose that humans learn language through a process of **reinforcement**. In response to a stimulus, children offer a spoken response, usually a repetition of something they've just heard, and then receive either positive or negative feedback. This feedback creates what founder B.F. Skinner (1904–1990) coined the term **operant conditioning**—a change in behavior in response to feedback. (In contrast, his so-called classical conditioning involves learning to associate two events but does not entail any behavioral change.) Through this back-and-forth inductive process, children learn the rules and patterns of language.

The behaviorist theory has intuitive appeal, as we often use variations of the repetition/feedback model in teaching. However, critics point out that the model completely excludes any **theory of the mind**, reducing the complexity of language to a rudimentary input-output model. Critics also challenged the behaviorists to explain how children could produce novel, and often complex, utterances that they had never heard—these utterances could not have been acquired through imitation, repetition, or reinforcement.

The Innate or Universal Grammar Theory of First-Language Acquisition

The universal grammar theory, developed by the linguist Noam Chomsky in the 1960s, posits that humans are born with **innate language abilities**, which include general grammatical categories and constraints that can be adapted to or activated by any language a child is exposed to. Chomsky gave the name "**language activation device**" to this hypothetical region of the brain devoted to language acquisition and production. Chomsky developed his theory in response to the behaviorists' suggestion that language competence is built through a process of trial and error.

The **universal grammar theory** helps explain several key features of languages and language learning: that all languages share certain properties; that children who are exposed to a common language will all converge in their competence, despite receiving different input; and that children will learn linguistic forms for which they have received no specific input. Chomsky also turned theoretical attention to the brain and its adaptive capacities. Critics of innateness theories suggest that it privileges syntax over semantics, pragmatics, and discourse and, further, that it focuses on developmental aspects of language acquisition at the expense of social and psychological aspects.

The Cognitive Constructivist Model of First-Language Acquisition

The cognitive constructivist model of L1 acquisition is derived from the work of the Swiss psychologist Jean Piaget (1896–1980). Piaget hypothesized that **cognitive development** (and thus language development) occurs in universal, identifiable stages. **Learning** occurs when a child's experiences challenge his or her current understanding of the world, driving the child to a new, more complex stage of cognitive/linguistic development. Thus, language learning is a form of adaptation to one's environment.

Proponents of cognitive models of language learning point to the fact that language learning does appear to proceed according to certain **stages of complexity**—for example, learners in all languages master functional morphemes in similar order. Critics argue that there is little merit in Piaget's four-stage model, as the stages themselves cannot be empirically identified. Further, critics argue that the theory undervalues the influence of both culture and social interaction on language development.

Cognitive constructivism differs from social constructivism in its suggestion that learners create representations of their world largely through their own inquiries and activities rather than through social interaction.

The Social Constructivism Theory of First-Language Acquisition

The social constructivism theory, attributed to the Soviet psychologist Lev Vygotsky (1896–1934), emphasizes the importance of social interaction in language theory. According to this model, children learn primarily from adults ("more experienced others" to Vygotsky) who model new language patterns and also correct errors. Vygotsky coined the influential term "**zone of proximal development**" to explain how learning occurs: according to Vygotsky, children best learn when presented with tasks or challenges that they can accomplish with the help of others but not alone. The set of challenges that a child can accomplish with assistance or scaffolding fall within his or her zone of proximal development.

Social constructivism theory is often credited with giving proper attention to **discourse**, or actual language use. In this view, language is developed in a specific context rather than in accordance with universal structures or dispositions. Critics point to the fact that not all cultures prioritize interaction between children and "more experienced others," and yet children in these cultures still become competent language users.

Review Video: Instructional Scaffolding
Visit mometrix.com/academy and enter code: 989759

Review Video: Zone of Proximal Development (ZPD)
Visit mometrix.com/academy and enter code: 555594

Discovery Learning Theory

Discovery learning theory posits that students learn best when they **construct their own knowledge** through a process of inquiry, investigation, and problem-solving ("discovery") rather than when a teacher or parent tells them explicitly what they are expected to know. Bruner's theory has been very influential in the modern movement away from lecture-based teaching and toward methods that guide students in various **inquiry-based activities**.

Like Piaget, Bruner argued that children learn in different ways as they develop, moving from mere physical manipulation of objects to the creation of mental images to the use of language. However, unlike Piaget, Bruner believed these stages to be continuous and that children can speed up their progression through the stages. He also theorized that it is language that causes cognitive development rather than vice versa. Like Piaget, Bruner is a **constructivist**, emphasizing the active role of the learner in building understanding through successively more complex engagements with the world. Chomsky, by contrast, prioritizes the importance of innate cognitive potentials.

The Critical Period Hypothesis

The critical period hypothesis argues that there is an **optimal age for learning a language** and that the ease with which a person can learn languages declines over time.

The hypothesis was first formulated by neurologist Wilder Penfield and then elaborated by Eric Lenneberg, who argued that language learning is dependent on **brain plasticity**, which in humans is at an optimal level for learning during a critical period extending from roughly age two until puberty.

The hypothesis has been extended to L2 learning based on the claim that adults rarely achieve full fluency in a second language learned later in life, failing most often to master complex grammatical structures or achieve a native accent. Critics of the hypothesis point to the fact that some adult learners do fully master a second language. They also point out that factors other than brain development could explain the difference in L2 learning, as adults and children learn in different motivational and social contexts.

The hypothesis privileges the explanatory framework of developmental biology by positing the existence of certain biological potentials for and limitations to language learning. It shares this orientation with Noam Chomsky and the universal grammar school of language acquisition.

Connectionist Theories of Language Acquisition

Connectionist theories attempt to apply insights from neuroscience and computer science to explain language acquisition. Proponents look to advances in knowledge of how neurons function in order to explain how learning occurs. For example, the more frequently a given set of neurons fires in tandem, the more established that neuron network becomes—a feature that helps explain memory and is seen as a mechanism by which a language learner comes to associate words with objects or events. In more general terms, learning is seen as the development of specific **connections** in an otherwise general network in response to environmental stimuli. Computer scientists working in the field of artificial intelligence attempt to build learning networks with silicon chips playing the role of simplified neurons. Computer scientists have built models that simulate many language-acquisition activities, including how to break a continuous auditory stream into words and how to correctly form both regular and irregular verbs. These models rely primarily on statistical, inferential learning rather than on the symbol- and rule-based learning typically advanced by non-computational models. Critics of the existing computational models point to their unrealistic initial assumptions and abstractions from human reality, whereas proponents see these as weaknesses that can be overcome in time.

The Emergentist Theory of Language Acquisition

The emergentist theory suggests that children learn language by using a simple but adaptable set of **neural networks** to process and understand the complex linguistic environment they are immersed in. The theory differs from the innate theories of scholars such as Noam Chomsky in that it doesn't suggest that children are born with an expansive universal grammar hard-wired in the brain—rather, children are born with a **pattern extraction ability** that arises from the growth and strengthening of neural networks. Emergentist theory shares with social constructivism the idea that social interaction is critical for language development but differs in its focus on the brain's ability to find patterns and extract meaning from what is potentially an overwhelming linguistic environment. The theory suggests that the brain narrows the field of possible meanings through the use of contextual, phonological, and morphological cues and by applying a type of statistical analysis of frequent language forms. While the brain is inherently capable of narrowing the field of possible meanings and finding patterns, parents and teachers can help the process by providing rich, structured, patterned linguistic input.

The Competition Model of Language Acquisition

The competition model of language learning or acquisition attributed to Brian MacWhinney and Elizabeth Bates argues that there is no fundamental difference in how people acquire a first language or learn subsequent languages—in both cases, various cognitive processes compete to offer the best **interpretation of the language cues** offered to the language learner by the surrounding environment. The cognitive processes that make the best interpretations of the language—those that lead to the learner having successful interactions and speech acts—are reinforced as neural networks eventually get consolidated as permanent features of the brain. With its focus on the development and consolidation of neural networks in the brain, the competition model is a type of connectionist theory of language learning.

The competition model rejects the idea of innate *linguistic* structures in the brain. Rather, it posits that language develops through the interaction of generalized *cognitive* structures in the brain (those responsible for all aspects of thought, not just language) with the environment.

Second Language Acquisition Theory

Acquisition of First and Second Languages

The following chart outlines some of the differences in the acquisition of first and second languages:

First Language	Second Language
Is acquired without conscious effort	Is acquired with conscious effort
Is a natural, integrated part of daily life	May be acquired primarily in a classroom
Is based on a universal grammar	Is affected by first-language grammar
Doesn't require instruction	Requires instruction
Needed to function in life and satisfy desires	May be acquired for various reasons
Is less influenced by cognitive and affective factors	Is critically influenced by cognitive and affective factors

There are many similarities in the acquisition of L1 and L2: both occur in predictable stages, mistakes are normal, learners of both rely heavily on context and cues, production is more difficult than comprehension, and learning occurs most rapidly with interaction and task-based instructional scenarios.

Model of Second-Language Acquisition

Researchers have found that second-language students progress through predictable stages as they advance from their first classroom encounters with a language to full proficiency. Recognizing which stage students are in will help ESOL teachers design appropriate learning activities.

1. **Silent period** (also called the preproduction stage): The learner knows around 500 words but is uncomfortable speaking. Teachers should allow the student to build receptive skills while gaining confidence.
2. **Private speech** (early production stage): The learner creates one- and two-word phrases using 1,000 words. Teachers should pose questions that allow abbreviated answers and scaffold their instruction.
3. **Lexical chunks** (speech emergence stage): The learner uses 3,000 words to form short phrases and sentences with frequent grammatical errors. Students are able to conduct short conversations with peers and read beginning stories.
4. **Formulaic speech** (intermediate language proficiency): The learner uses 6,000 words to make complex sentences, state opinions, and share thoughts. Learners can study content subjects in English. Teachers may shift the instructional focus to writing.
5. **Experimental or simplified speech** (advanced language proficiency stage): The learner approaches fluency and can make generalizations about grammar and semantics. The learner may exit the ESOL program but continue to receive assistance with writing and in the content areas.

Silent Period of Second-Language Development

The term "silent period" refers to a common first stage in language acquisition, during which a student speaks little while he or she gains confidence and consolidates comprehension of the spoken language. Experts agree that students at this stage should not be forced to speak. Teachers might elicit "yes" or "no" answers or head nods and shakes. They can also ask students at this stage to draw pictures that demonstrate their understanding or draw connections between pre-printed images. If a student is hesitating to speak due to a lack of confidence, the teacher can interact first with him or her in a one-on-one, protected environment, and generally strive to create a low-risk classroom environment.

Language Transfer

Language transfer is the influence of a native language (L1) on a learner's ability to learn a new language (L2). This influence can have either positive or negative effects—for example, the existence of cognates can help a learner understand L2, whereas the existence of false cognates can exert a negative influence. The term "**language interference**" is often used synonymously with "language transfer" but is also used to refer specifically to cases of negative influence.

Linguists often use **contrastive analysis**, or the comparison of two languages to identify similarities and differences, in order to determine whether language transfer is likely, and in which forms. In general, the more similar two languages are, the greater the likelihood of positive transfer.

Positive transfers often raise the confidence and spur the interest of language learners. Teachers can lessen the impact of negative transfers by becoming familiar with those most likely to arise from a given L1 and then explicitly teaching methods of overcoming those transfers.

Comprehension-Based Approaches to Second-Language Learning

Comprehension-based learning focuses on building students' **receptive skills** (listening and reading) before they are asked to produce the language (through speech or writing). Proponents argue that **listening comprehension** is the most fundamental linguistic skill and serves as a useful basis for the others. Listening is also viewed as the least stressful language skill and thus the one most likely to engage and encourage early learners. Students should not be forced to speak until they are ready, and an early silent period in which students listen to meaningful speech is expected. Stephen Krashen and Tracy Terrell's natural way methodology is a leading example of a comprehension-based approach to second-language learning.

Communicative Approaches to Second-Language Learning

Communicative approaches to second-language learning focus on providing students genuine, meaningful, experience-based interactions in the target language. Teachers spend little time talking about the target language or teaching grammar and instead focus on facilitating use of the **target-language**. Students often work in pairs or groups, role-playing or negotiating the transfer of information that one student has and another lacks. Unlike comprehension-based approaches, reading, writing, speaking, and listening are integrated from the beginning. Constructivist theories emphasize that learners don't acquire knowledge but construct it through their own experiences. Constructivists therefore seek to engage language students in as many reality-based participatory scenarios as possible.

As defined, communicative approaches are the most commonly used approaches in the modern classroom.

Grammar-Translation and Audio-Lingual Methods

The grammar-translation method relies on explanations in the students' native language of the grammatical structures of the target language. Students are challenged to read difficult texts in the target language and to translate sentences from L2 to L1. This model is based on the way Latin was traditionally taught: with a focus on verb declensions. Modern approaches focus on

communication rather than explicit knowledge of grammatical structures and favor sustained use of L2.

The **audio-lingual method** relies heavily on repetition and drills, with language skills built systematically from simple to complex structures. The focus is on accurate pronunciation and the minimization of errors. Oral exercises are designed to control the vocabulary and grammar structures in use rather than to reflect real-world communication. This method dominated in the US immediately after World War II but has since been replaced by methods that encourage dialogue in realistic settings and trust that learners will overcome most of their early errors in later stages of speech development.

Silent Way, Suggestopedia, and Total Physical Response

In silent way classrooms, teacher speech is minimized: after initially modeling an expression, the teacher uses a series of props, such as Cuisenaire rods (rods of different lengths and colors that can model both vocabulary and syntax), to help the students learn basic structures.

Suggestopedia relies on music and rhythm to reinforce language patterns. Students are given scripts of L2 to read aloud with games and music. Later in the lesson, they might elaborate on the script with their own inventions or compare the L2 script to an L1 translation before moving on to another script.

The **total physical response method** begins with the teacher giving elementary commands in L2 (e.g., "stand up!"). As students progress, the commands become more complex. Eventually, the students begin to give one another commands. This technique is still used in ESOL instruction today but is one of many teaching techniques rather than an exclusive approach to learning.

Michael Long's Interaction Hypothesis

Michael Long's interaction hypothesis is similar to Stephen Krashen's input hypothesis in emphasizing the importance of **comprehensible input**—language just beyond an ELL's mastery level—for language learning. Long, however, adds an emphasis on conversational interaction, suggesting that advances in language learning will occur most readily when conversation partners have to negotiate meaning to be understood—by paraphrasing, restating, asking for clarification, using context clues, etc. Proponents of the hypothesis often add the qualification that it helps if the conversation participants are of equal status or social position (peer conversations, for example, rather than student-teacher conversations) so that the conversational queries and negotiations can occur freely. Critics have pointed out that conversational clarifications are not always successful, particularly when conducted by non-proficient language speakers.

Cognitive Strategies in Second-Language Acquisition

Students use a variety of strategies in learning a second language, including cognitive strategies, social strategies, and communication strategies. **Cognitive strategies** are those that students employ to understand a task at hand and include such activities as memorizing, categorizing, summarizing, generalizing, deducing, and using inductive reasoning. Research has shown that students who use a variety of cognitive strategies are more successful in learning a second language.

The term "**metacognitive strategies**" refers to strategies that students use to improve their own learning process. Planning, self-monitoring, prioritizing, and setting goals are all examples of metacognitive strategies. The use of metacognitive strategies is highly correlated with language student success. Thus, an ESOL teacher should monitor and encourage the use of these strategies.

Robert De Keyser's Skill Acquisition Theory

The skill acquisition theory posits that individuals learn skills by gradually transforming **declarative knowledge** into **procedural knowledge** through meaningful use and practice. In this model, students learn declarative knowledge about a language through classroom instruction or observation—for example, they might be taught a specific grammatical form. They then begin to use it, ideally through contextualized practice. Repeated practice leads to automaticity marked by fluency and the absence of errors. The theory thus emphasizes that full competency requires processing of information by two representational systems of the mind—the declarative and the procedural—which reinforce one another in language learning. The distinction between declarative and procedural knowledge mirrors in some ways the distinction between learning and acquiring knowledge—the goal within De Keyser's framework is to move an ELL student toward further degrees of automaticity.

Contrastive Analysis

Contrastive analysis is the study of the similarities and differences between languages. Teachers can use the results of **contrastive analysis** to anticipate language transfer issues likely to be present in their student populations. One of the most common examples is the use in Spanish and French of the verb "to have" in many contexts in which English uses "to be"—for example, a translation of the English phrase "I am hungry" becomes "I have hunger" in Spanish and French. In many languages, including Arabic, adjectives typically follow nouns, whereas in English they usually precede them, resulting in many Arabic-speaking ELLs saying things like "She is a woman smart." Haitian Creole verbs do not change to indicate either tense or person, which might lead to a Creole-speaking ELL overusing a single present-tense form like "The bus leave at 2:25." As a final example, Russian speakers use the present tense to convey ongoing actions that in English require the present progressive—thus, rather than saying, "I am reading right now," a Russian-speaking ELL might say "I read right now."

Jim Cummins' Common Underlying Proficiency Hypothesis

The **common underlying proficiency** (CUP) hypothesis states that a bilingual or emerging bilingual individual will draw on a **common pool** of cognitive and linguistic abilities to speak either language. Thus, his or her abilities and knowledge in L1 are available for and will facilitate L2 learning. Cummins' idea is often called the **dual iceberg model** because he used this image to illustrate his idea that two apparently distinct peaks of visible ice (L1 and L2) are actually connected below the surface in a vast, single iceberg (the CUP).

The CUP stands in contrast to the **separate underlying proficiency (SUP)**, which theorizes that each language a person uses is processed and stored separately in the brain, and thus there is no positive transfer between the two. Proponents of SUP often argue that ELLs should be enrolled in full English immersion programs because their use and development of L1 will only distract from and slow their English acquisition. The preponderance of the evidence, however, supports CUP, as it has frequently been demonstrated that the frequent use of L1 by students in bilingual programs does not slow their acquisition of English.

Rebecca Oxford's Strategy Inventory for Language Learning

Oxford developed a six-category classification of strategies students employ when learning a language:

- **Memory strategies**—techniques used to remember and retrieve information. Acronyms, formulaic expressions, and forming connections with prior knowledge all count as mnemonic strategies.

- **Cognitive strategies**—strategies, such as analyzing or drawing conclusions, that allow students to manipulate the target language.
- **Compensation strategies**—strategies used when students lack vocabulary in L2. Code-switching, or the insertion of L1 into L2 utterances, is an example.
- **Metacognitive strategies**—strategies used by students to improve their own learning habits. Self-monitoring is one example; planning is another.
- **Affective strategies**—strategies students use to control their own emotions. Both appeals for assistance and requests for clarification might be examples of affective strategies, as students seek reassurance or reinforcement of what they already know.
- **Social strategies**—strategies students use to employ language in social settings. Role-playing is one example. Requests for clarification could be another, as students often ask for clarification as a way of continuing a conversation.

The strategy inventory for language learning (**SILL**) examination, developed by Rebecca Oxford, is designed to identify the learning strategies used by foreign language students. The first version was developed for English speakers learning foreign languages, and a second version (v7.0) was created for students learning English as a foreign language. The SILL examination is used both for research purposes and to give individual learners insight into their own learning profiles.

Oxford's model is perhaps the most influential of several that have emerged from a research focus on language learning strategies. The latter concept grew out of an earlier (1970s) focus on the characteristics of a good language learner. This line of research aims at identifying the strategies used by successful language learners and promoting their widespread use. The cognitive academic language learning approach is another popular model based on the idea of language learning strategies. Oxford, in turn, updated her thinking with the **strategic self-regulation model (S^{2}R) of language learning**.

CALLA and CALP

The **cognitive academic language learning approach (CALLA)**, developed in the 1980s by Anna Chamot and J. Michael O'Malley, is designed to help ELLs with limited English proficiency transition to mainstream content classrooms, usually in secondary school. CALLA emphasizes **cognitive and metacognitive approaches** to learning by explicitly teaching learning strategies and encouraging students to both plan and evaluate their undertakings in order to refine their use of these skills. Chamot and O'Malley developed a taxonomy of learning strategies based on three broad categories: metacognitive strategies, cognitive strategies, and social/affective strategies.

Cognitive academic language proficiency (CALP) shares with CALLA a focus on helping ELLs who are likely already proficient in social English (basic interpersonal communication skills, or BICS, in Jim Cummins' terms) gain proficiency in academic English, in what is often a daunting environment of an English-only mainstream classroom.

Interdependence between Social and Academic English

Related to Cummins' idea of underlying proficiency is the idea that social language skills and academic language skills are interdependent on one another. His **interdependence hypothesis** assumes that students who are learning academic English are standing on a foundation made up of social skills, cultural knowledge, and thinking patterns. These foundations, though informal, provide scaffolding for a student to build up to formalized thought patterns. When applied, this theory should encourage teachers to use students more naturalized interactions and not shy away from them in an academic setting. Put another way, a teacher may be able to use functional interaction to build its way to formal interaction in academics.

Stages of Second-Language Development

WIDA ELD Proficiency Levels

World-Class Instructional Design and Assessment (WIDA) is a group that developed proficiency standards for language learners of multiple languages, originally developed at the University of Wisconsin-Madison. The purpose of these standards is to give teachers an idea of what to expect from English learners (or learners of another language) at different levels of proficiency, as they make their way to fluency. The WIDA standards are broken down across the four domains of listening, speaking, reading, and writing and span across six levels: entering, emerging, developing, bridging, and reaching. The standards are worded in a way that describes what an ELL at each level should be able to do successfully. A teacher can make use of these standards to help ensure that goals and expectations are set appropriately for students at or slightly above their current proficiency levels.

WIDA ELD Standard Example

The following is a chart that represents some example standards for students in the language domains of speaking and writing, but at each proficiency level. The WIDA standards are grouped by age and across a variety of subjects, but this should give you an idea of how they progress in one group of students.

	Speaking and Writing
Level 1: Entering	• Words, phrases, or chunks of language • Single words used to represent ideas
Level 2: Emerging	• Phrases or short sentences • Emerging expression of ideas
Level 3: Developing	• Short and some expanded sentences with emerging complexity • Expanded expression of one idea or emerging expression of multiple related ideas across content areas
Level 4: Expanding	• Short, expanded, and some complex sentences • Organized expression of ideas with emerging cohesion characteristic of particular content areas
Level 5: Bridging	• Multiple, complex sentences • Organized, cohesive, and coherent expression of ideas characteristic of particular content areas
Level 6: Reaching	English language learners will use a range of grade-appropriate language for a variety of academic purposes and audiences. Agility in academic language use is reflected in oral fluency and automaticity in response, flexibility in adjusting to different registers and skillfulness in interpersonal interaction. English language learners' strategic competence in academic language use facilitates their ability to relate information and ideas with precision and sophistication for each content area.

Physical, Cognitive, and Educational Factors Influencing Acquisition

Lois Meyer's Four Barriers

Meyer identified four **loads**—or challenges requiring effort to overcome—facing ELLs in the classroom. The first is **cognitive load**—the number of unfamiliar or unpracticed concepts presented in a lesson. The second is **culture load**—the untaught, assumed cultural references embedded in a lesson which may present impediments to an ELL. The third is **language load**—the degree to which the lesson language is unfamiliar and stretches a student beyond the range of comprehensible input. Meyer's fourth category is **learning load**—the extent to which the classroom learning activity is unfamiliar or stressful to the ELL. (For example, if the ELL is asked to debate an issue with a classmate but has no prior experience with debating and is uncomfortable with the interpersonal dynamic, the activity would present a high learning load.)

Meyer's work reminds ESOL teachers of the multiplicity of factors that need to be planned or controlled in order to create an optimal classroom learning environment.

Student's Linguistic Background

A student's **relative proficiency in their native language** (L1) is a factor in L2 language development. Students proficient in L1 already possess the perceptual ability to distinguish sounds, words, and syntactical patterns. They will likely also possess certain useful cognitive skills, such as the ability to compare, generalize, and predict. In addition, there may be specific similarities between L1 and L2 that allow for positive transfer.

The **common underlying proficiency model** is based on these ideas—that the various skills and concepts developed during L1 acquisition are available for subsequent learning. The model hypothesized that all language learning draws upon a common core of cognitive-linguistic knowledge rather than knowledge segregated in the brain by language. This model has largely been confirmed by subsequent research.

Age and L2 Acquisition

The **critical period hypothesis (CPH)** argues that, due to brain development, there is an optimal age for learning a language (roughly from age two to puberty) and that a person's ability to learn languages declines over time.

While the CPH strikes many as intuitively true, subsequent research has rendered the issue more complex. There is no doubt that children and adults learn languages differently. Adults have cognitive and experiential advantages and usually make more rapid progress in syntax and grammar than do children. Children tend to enjoy more exposure to the target language. In addition, they appear to have advantages in affect and motivation. For example, the fact that adults are conscious of the learning process and are aware of the difficulty of learning languages often reduces their motivation to learn. As implicit, intuitive learners, children are less likely to be discouraged by the difficulties of learning. Further, adults tend to be more self-conscious about making mistakes, a distinct disadvantage when learning a language.

A fair conclusion might be that, while adults have more disadvantages in learning languages, these can be overcome. The one exception appears to be accent: research does sustain the claim that children acquire a native accent more often than adults.

Disability Misdiagnoses

The **Individuals with Disabilities Education Act (IDEA)** of 1975 established the right of students with disabilities to receive appropriate education tailored to their individual needs. The legislation qualifies students for what is called **special education assistance** if they do not reach age-level benchmarks in several language and mathematical competencies, including oral expression, written expression, listening comprehension, reading comprehension, and reading skill. However, IDEA specifies that these deficiencies cannot arise from **environmental variables**, including limited English proficiency or cultural differences. As many researchers have pointed out, however, many of the characteristics ELLs manifest during the normal L2 learning process resemble those of native speakers with disabilities, leading to frequent misdiagnoses.

School districts in the United States are required to have a process in place to evaluate children with potential disabilities. Student assessments are made by a team of professionals. If the assessment team, in conjunction with the child's parents, determines that a child needs special education services, the team creates an **individualized education program (IEP)** that specifies, among other things, the program accommodations, testing modifications, and counseling the child will receive.

> **Review Video: Development of the Individuals with Disabilities Education Act**
> Visit mometrix.com/academy and enter code: 100350

Individuals with Disabilities Education Act

The Individuals with Disabilities Education Act (IDEA) obligates schools to provide **special education and supportive services** to students with certain **disabilities**. The law covers 13 conditions. The most commonly encountered conditions include attention deficit hyperactivity disorder (ADHD), which is subsumed under:

- Other health impairment
- Specific learning disorders (including dyslexia, dysgraphia, dyscalculia, auditory processing disorder, and nonverbal learning disability)

The other categories covered by IDEA are:

- Autism
- Emotional conditions (such as anxiety and depression)
- Speech or language impairment (such as stuttering)
- Deafness
- Hearing impairments (other than deafness)
- Deaf-blindness
- Visual impairment
- Traumatic brain injury
- Orthopedic impairment
- Intellectual disability (such as Down syndrome)
- Multiple disabilities

> **Review Video: Medical Conditions in Education**
> Visit mometrix.com/academy and enter code: 531058
>
> **Review Video: Disorders that Impair Reading and Writing**
> Visit mometrix.com/academy and enter code: 306758

Learning Disability Characteristics

The responsibility to diagnose **learning disabilities** rests with trained professionals. However, ESOL teachers should have a basic understanding of how the manifestations of learning disabilities and **L2 learning complications** differ. The most important insight is that learning disabilities very rarely manifest in just one language, and so a teacher who witnesses the problematic performance in L2 can observe how that student interacts with colleagues in L1 or potentially ask his or her parents about L1 production at home. Another general indicator of a learning disability is a language deficit that doesn't improve over time or after targeted intervention. A third is a language deficit that comes and goes—in most instances of normal L2 acquisition, once a deficit is overcome, a student will make fewer and fewer repeated errors over time. Another sign of a potential learning disability is a domain-specific deficiency—if an L2 learner performs as expected in writing exercises, for example, but lags in speech production, a disability is likely.

Review Video: Understanding Learning Disability Needs of Students
Visit mometrix.com/academy and enter code: 662775

Lack of Formal School Experience

Students who lack prior formal education are likely to need additional support in the context of an ESOL program. Students who have had their schooling interrupted by war or political upheaval (such as refugees) may suffer from trauma in addition to experiencing gaps in their education. Students who have never attended school are likely to completely lack **literacy skills**, putting them far behind their peers. They will also lack basic **learning and study skills**, which many students and teachers take for granted after a certain age. While students without educational experience are often highly motivated to attend school, they also have high drop-out rates, due in part to the demotivation they experience from lagging behind their age group in educational attainment. Even when such learners make dramatic progress, they often underestimate their achievement.

Affective Factors Influencing Acquisition

Instrumental or Integrative and Intrinsic or Extrinsic Motivation

According to Robert Gardner's original classification, students are **instrumentally motivated** if they are learning English to achieve a specific goal, such as acquiring a job or getting into college. By contrast, they possess **integrative motivation** if they have a positive view of their future L2 community and wish to fully join it. According to Gardner, integrative motivation is more reliable and durable.

Psychologists often distinguish between **extrinsic motivation**, which is a focus on rewards or punishments; and **intrinsic motivation**, which exists when an individual wants to do something for the sake of it without concern for reward and punishment. Research shows that intrinsic motivation is more reliable, as extrinsic motivation tends to be temporary and inflationary and often shifts a learner's focus from the lesson to the reward itself.

People differ in the nature, sources, and degrees of motivation, and so it is valid to speak of motivation as a trait. However, human motivation is also heavily context- and situation-dependent, and thus motivation is also a state that can and does change.

Benjamin Bloom and the Affective Domain

Benjamin Bloom differentiated between three learning domains—the **cognitive** (thinking), **sensory** (doing), and **affective** (feeling)—and developed a **taxonomy of concepts** for each domain. His taxonomy of cognitive learning skills and associated action verbs (explain, describe, evaluate, etc.) has been widely influential. His taxonomy of the affective domain is also of interest.

Bloom identified five **processes that lead to student growth** in affective response and understanding. The first process, in order from simple to complex, is **receiving**—a passive condition that is necessary for learning but which does not by itself add value. The second process is **responding**, in which a student is attentive to learning and responds with positive emotion. Bloom's third process is **valuing**, in which a student develops preferences and commitments. In the fourth process, **organization**, a student develops a value system, combining elements to create a logical relational framework. In the final, **characterizing** phase, the student internalizes what he or she has learned and acts in principled ways according to this knowledge.

Bloom's concept serves as a reminder that education concerns more than just cognitive development and that the experiences and valuations that students encounter early in life have a lasting impact on their affective outlook.

Zoltan Dornyei's L2 Motivational Self System

Zoltan Dornyei built on the broader theory of the ideal self in proposing that L2 students draw upon three different sources of motivation. The first is the **ideal L2 self**—the image the learner has of the person he or she would like to become through the process of language learning. The second source of motivation is the **ought-to L2 self**, which is an image driven by a sense of obligation, often one imposed by others' expectations. Finally, the **L2 learning experience** captures situational motivations, the types that arise daily in the classroom. Dornyei argues that teachers should find ways to appeal to a student's ideal L2 self in order to ensure persistent and consistent motivation.

Dornyei argues that teachers must attend to motivation in different ways. First, they must create the basic motivating conditions in the classroom. Second, they must generate initial, individualized motivation. Third, they must maintain and protect that motivation. And finally, because positive self-assessment is necessary for sustained motivation, teachers must encourage students to self-monitor.

Teacher Expectations Contribute to Success

Research has demonstrated the importance of **teacher expectations** in student performance. The core finding is that teacher expectations are, to a degree, **self-fulfilling**—high expectations lead to better results. Other prescriptions are also well established: teachers should not create differential expectations based on demographic factors, they should form groups composed of all levels of language proficiency rather than marginalize low performers, they should call on low-proficiency students as often as high-proficiency ones, and they should foster a culture in which errors are seen as a normal part of the learning process.

ESOL teachers should also use their knowledge of language development and communicative competence to shape their **error-correction strategies**. Certain types of errors are natural at a given stage of language learning and will likely disappear without explicit correction; teachers can thus afford to let these pass. As a general rule, corrections involving vocabulary are easier for students to learn than corrections of grammar. And finally, teachers should focus on correcting errors that impede communication. Experts agree that error correction is less important to student success than allowing abundant opportunities for language practice and authentic communication.

Self-Efficacy

Self-efficacy is the perception people have about their competence. **Self-esteem** is a broader concept—it refers to a person's overall sense of self-approval or self-disapproval.

Attribution theory, first applied to the academic domain by the psychologist Bernard Weiner, uses the concept of self-efficacy to analyze what students believe is the cause of their success or failure on an academic task. Research shows that students tend to attribute academic outcomes to one of four general causes: ability, effort, perceived difficulty, or luck. Students with low self-efficacy tend to attribute academic outcomes to causes outside of themselves (such as difficulty and luck) and are less likely to respond constructively to academic setbacks. Students with a high sense of self-efficacy, in contrast, tend to attribute outcomes to internal causes and are likely to respond to setbacks by working harder.

Educational psychologists studying the effects of **praise** on performance have demonstrated that students perform better, at least in the long run, if they are praised for their efforts or for a specific academic result rather than for their intrinsic ability. This finding reinforces the idea that students perform best when they focus on what they can control and when they believe they can influence the outcome.

Self-Esteem

Self-esteem is an attitude of approval or disapproval toward oneself. The psychologist Jonathon Brown has created a **typology of self-esteem** that is widely used in ESOL contexts. This typology differentiates between **general** or **global self-esteem**, which is a person's broad sense of self-worth; **situational self-esteem**, which is specific to a certain domain, such as athletics, social skills, or foreign language aptitude; and **task self-esteem**, which arises in the context of performing specific tasks or activities. Research suggests that, once formed by late childhood, global self-esteem changes little over a lifetime.

Self-esteem and academic success are linked in a chicken-or-egg type of cycle: high self-esteem is linked to better academic performance, and successful performance has been shown to be the most important factor in building situational self-esteem.

Learning a foreign language poses particular challenges to self-esteem. One reason is that students often feel the gap between what they can express in L2 and what they think or feel. In other words, they feel a large gap between their genuine self and the self they can communicate.

Anxiety

Anxiety is defined as an abnormal sense of apprehension, often accompanied by physiological signs of stress. As with many features of personality, anxiety can be thought of as both a trait, something which people experience in different degrees as a background feature of their personality, and as a state, in response to a particular event or experience.

Educational psychologists often differentiate between **three types of anxiety** experienced by the second-language learner: anxiety over one's ability to communicate in L2, anxiety that peers will view one's L2 communication negatively, and anxiety about evaluations and grades. Understanding the source of a student's anxiety will help the ESOL teacher mitigate the anxiety's harmful effects.

In general, anxiety is **debilitative**—that is, it is something that detracts or distracts a student from learning. Research has shown, however, that anxiety can also be useful or **facilitative to the learning task**. Anxiety may lead to greater focus, greater effort, or a sense of competitiveness that can drive a student to mastery.

Inhibition

Inhibition is defined as the inner impediment to free expression or action. It is usually viewed negatively and is often a defense mechanism erected by individuals with low self-esteem. It is important to note, however, that the absence of inhibition can be pathological, as in the case of many mental illnesses.

Inhibition is a critical concept in language learning because of the importance of **performance** to language learning. Scholars agree that one's willingness to communicate—to seek out opportunities to communicate in L2—is a key factor in L2 learning success. Successful language learning also requires a measure of risk-taking—the willingness to make mistakes, often public ones, in learning a language.

Given the importance of production for language learning, good ESOL teachers find ways to **reduce student inhibition**. Teachers should keep the classroom affective filter low; develop a classroom group identity conducive to risk-taking; allow inhibited students to proceed stepwise toward production, recognizing the necessity of a silent period; and ensure that inhibited students experience early success and ratification.

Language Ego

The psychologist Alexander Guiora asserted that individuals learning or using a second language experience widescale changes in their perceived identity, caused by what he referred to as the **language ego**. According to this theory, a person's original identity is closely tied to their L1 competency and mastery and is challenged or disrupted by an attempt to learn an L2. Guiora used this concept to explain why children acquire second languages more readily than adults—as their egos are less full-formed and less rigid, they suffer less from the feelings of incompetence or social embarrassment inevitable in the language learning process.

Subsequent theorists introduced the notion of **thick and thin language ego boundaries**, suggesting that students with thick boundaries feel fewer inhibitions in language learning and are more comfortable with the performance activities necessary for full linguistic competence.

Affective Filter

The concept of affective filter refers to the emotional response an ELL has to a language-learning environment. An ELL's emotional state can either hinder his or her learning (in which case he or she is described as having a **high affective filter**) or promote learning (a **low affective filter**). Factors that could contribute to a high affective filter include overcorrection of errors, fear of speech performance in front of peers, or test anxiety. Teachers can lower student affective filters by being cognizant of personality differences and language development differences, ensuring that peers are supportive, communicating that errors are expected and considered to be routine, and limiting the number and significance of summative tests.

Cultural Factors Influencing Acquisition

Acculturation Patterns

Acculturation is the adaptation of one person or group to the culture of another, often in the context of immigration. The term implies one-way adaptation of a minority group to the culture of a majority group. If the adaptation is complete and the minority comes to resemble the majority, it is termed "**assimilation**." If a minority community resists acculturation, we speak of **preservation** of their distinct culture. The term "**transculturation**" refers to the rare phenomenon of two equally dominant cultures mixing and each adopting elements of the other.

Linguist John Schumann's acculturation model argues that a person's **success in an L2** is directly related to his or her **acculturation into the L2 culture**. If a language learner joins the dominant-language culture, they will necessarily have more L2 language experiences, resulting in greater L2 competency. Schumann theorized that a number of factors could limit or even prevent an immigrant learner's acculturation, including his or her perceptions of the L2 language community, whether he or she lived in a cultural enclave or was geographically integrated, and whether the L1 and L2 languages were linguistically similar.

Social Distance

Social distance, and the related psychological distance, refers to the degree to which individuals accept those that they perceive to be different from them—whether due to differences in race, age, gender, religion, economic class, linguistic ability, or any other category of identity important to an individual or group. In a strong form, **social distance** is a form of prejudice—an unfavorable image formed without basis—but it can be present in a weak form even where there isn't animus, as individuals in new social settings tend to gravitate toward people they perceive as being like themselves.

Teachers can reduce the social distance by encouraging or requiring students to interact with one another, by reinforcing the concept of cultural relativism, and by staging interactions that demonstrate the positive contributions of student differences.

Elective Bilingualism vs. Circumstantial Bilingualism

The linguist Guadalupe Valdés draws a distinction between individuals who choose to study a second language (**elective bilingualism**), often for reasons of personal gain, and those who are forced to learn a second language (**circumstantial bilingualism**), as in the case of children immigrating to an L2 country.

Elective learners of a language, Valdés argued, usually learn the second language in an **artificial environment**, such as a classroom, rather than through immersion. Although they may eventually reach proficiency, their native language will usually remain dominant. Circumstantial learners, by contrast, do not learn a language because of an individual choice but as a result of **new circumstances** and in order to survive or succeed. They are likely to achieve greater mastery of L2 over time, and L1 and L2 are likely to assume complementary roles in their lives, with either dominant in a given situation.

The distinction between elective and circumstantial learners is likely to be most relevant in a class of **adult students**. Other conceptual categories may be more important when teaching children, such as their age when they immigrated or whether they will remain resident in the US or return to another country.

Family Expectations

One of the mainstays of education research is that students are more likely to succeed if their parents hold them to **high academic expectations**. These expectations may manifest themselves in parental reinforcement and encouragement, parental involvement in school meetings and functions, or parental engagement with their child's homework. All three of these areas are potentially problematic in the case of ELLs. Setting aside the issue that cultures value education differently, especially for girls, families that seek to preserve their home cultures may inadvertently or purposefully limit a child's motivation to master L2—research clearly shows that language proficiency is affected by the degree of acculturation. More importantly, parents of ESOL students may not involve themselves in school functions or even attend meetings with teachers, either because of different cultural understandings or because of their own limited English ability. Parents with limited English may not be able to help their children with their homework. And finally, research has revealed that a vicious cycle may develop in relationships in which a child's English proficiency far outstrips that of a parent—in these cases, the differential language abilities may lead to estrangement, conflict, and even withdrawal of parental support for language learning.

Political and Institutional Factors

The **educational policies** instituted at the federal, state, and local level influence the ways in which ESOL programs are structured and administered in schools. Within the bounds of those laws, however, schools vary in their **initiatives** and **institutional approaches** to their ESOL communities.

One way in which schools may differ is the degree to which their ESOL students are **integrated** into the broader student community. Schools that celebrate diversity and promote the integration of different language communities achieve better language outcomes. Similarly, schools that **recognize and showcase minority languages and cultures** achieve greater buy-in from ESOL students—if the value of their own cultures is recognized, they are more likely to embrace a new culture. Finally, school engagement with minority cultures should not stop with the students—successful schools also engage with the **community**, inviting parents and community organizations to participate in school activities and sponsor events that showcase minority cultures.

Impact of Poverty

The effects of poverty on student performance are numerous and well documented: low-income students often lag behind their peers in cognitive abilities, experience emotional deficits (and thus fail to exhibit a full and appropriate range of emotional reactions), and experience ongoing stress, which substantially reduces their ability to learn. English language learners are disproportionately poor—by some estimates, more than 50% of ELLs come from low-income families—and thus ESOL teachers need to understand how **poverty** influences learning and how to recognize students who may be at risk of failing academically or dropping out.

Many states or school districts have specific lists of **at-risk behaviors**, such as erratic attendance, behavioral issues, apathy, negative interaction with peers, and sudden changes in behavior. The at-risk concept is controversial because many believe it is applied wrongly to entire groups of students as a form of stereotyping rather than used constructively to identify students in need of additional support.

Chapter Quiz

Ready to see how well you retained what you just read? Scan the QR code to go directly to the chapter quiz interface for this study guide. If you're using a computer, simply visit the online resources page at **mometrix.com/resources719/csetenglandev** and click the Chapter Quizzes link.

Applied Linguistics

Phonology

Phonetics vs. Phonology

Phonetics is the study of speech sounds in isolation, and phonology is the study of how speech sounds function in a context—in a syllable, a word, a sentence, or a language as a whole. The speech sounds that each discipline studies are called **phonemes**. English, for example, consists of approximately 44 unique phonemes, arising from the 26 letters of the alphabet used singly or in combination. A competent English speaker can distinguish between these phonemes. Substituting one for another will result in a change in meaning—for example, substituting /m/ for /b/ in the word "ball" results in "mall."

Phonetics considers how individual speech sounds are produced and perceived and might ask which sounds are present in a given language. **Phonology**, by contrast, would study the ways in which those sounds are used to create larger units of meaning. **Phonological rules** are the ways in which sounds change depending on where they occur and how they are used in speech. For example, the deletion rule states that an unstressed vowel is often deleted in rapid speech, as when the /o/ in "police" is dropped and the word is pronounced as /pleas/.

Review Video: Phonics (Encoding and Decoding)
Visit mometrix.com/academy and enter code: 821361

Phonemes, Graphemes, and Letters

A phoneme is the smallest unit of sound in a language that makes a difference in meaning.

Phonemes can be written in two different ways. Linguists commonly represent phonemes by using the **International Phonetic Alphabet**, which assigns a different symbol to each sound commonly found in languages around the world. A second way to represent a phoneme is by using **graphemes**, which are individual letters or groups of letters that depict how a sound is written in a given language. For example, in English, the sound /t/ is written either with a single "t" (as in "tall") or with two "t's" (as in the word "better,"). Thus, English has two graphemes, "t" and "tt," that correspond to the phoneme /t/. Linguists have a special term, digraph, to refer to any two-letter grapheme, such as "tt" or "ch."

Phonetic alphabets and graphemes are necessary because written alphabets do not by themselves provide language learners with knowledge of how to pronounce a given word. Many letters have more than one pronunciation, and often are silent. In other words, spelling is not a reliable guide to pronunciation.

How Phonemes Can Be Classified

Syllables typically have two components, an onset and a rime. The **onset** is the phoneme, or sound, that occurs at the beginning of the syllable. In English, only consonants can be onsets. If a syllable begins with a vowel sound, the syllable has no onset. The **rime** is the vowel and any consonants that follow the onset. Thus, every syllable has a rime, but not necessarily an onset. For example, the one-syllable word "and" has no onset, only a rime. In the word "bat," by contrast, the /b/ is the onset, and the /at/ is the rime.

A second way to classify phonemes is by their **order** in a word. The first phoneme in a word is called the **beginning phoneme**, the last phoneme is called the **end phoneme**, and any phonemes in the middle are called **medial phonemes**. Teachers often promote phonetic awareness in beginning readers using this classification. For example, the teacher might teach the word "bet" by highlighting the beginning /b/, the ending /t/, and the medial /e/.

Irregularities in English Spelling

Students of any language benefit if that language has **predictable rules** of grammar, spelling, or pronunciation. Learning is made even easier if the student experiences **positive transfer**—that is, if features of their native language are similar to those in English, and thus reinforce the learning process.

The fact that the 26 letters of the English alphabet combine to form approximately 44 distinct phonemes will complicate the learning process for ELLs, as there is no one-to-one correspondence between spelling and pronunciation. For example, the sound /k/ can be written in many different ways in English, as in "cat," "kite," and "tack."

Other features of English violate a regular one-to-one correspondence of letters to sounds. **Digraphs**, for example, are combinations of two or more letters to produce a unique phoneme—such as the /ch/ sound in English. **Diphthongs** are combinations of two or more vowels in a single syllable, often resulting in an unpredictable sound—for example, the word "chair" is usually pronounced with an /ur/ sound that is not evident from its spelling. **Consonant clusters** occur when two or more consonants combine to form a single sound, as with the /wr/ sound in "wreck." These features render English more difficult for the ELL.

The International Phonetic Alphabet (IPA)

No alphabet has a one-to-one correspondence between letters and sounds. In English, for example, 26 letters generate approximately 44 distinct phonemes. Nor do any two languages rely on the same system of sounds, even when they share an alphabet.

The **International Phonetic Alphabet (IPA)**, which was created in 1888 and revised repeatedly since, provides a standard system of symbols for all of the phonemes used in human languages. The existence of the IPA allows linguists to refer to sounds independently to how they are represented in a specific language.

The IPA uses many symbols derived from the Latin alphabet, but it includes symbols from other sources, such as the Greek alphabet and even the Icelandic alphabet.

By convention, when linguists want to refer to a phoneme, they place a symbol within slashes or brackets ("/a/" or "[a]") in order to distinguish it from a letter that might have different sounds in different languages or multiple sounds in a single language.

Linguists Sound Framework

Linguists who study the physiology of sound production have classified the phonemes according to how they are **produced**. Each phoneme is articulated in a unique way. Consonant and vowel sounds have different classification systems.

Consonants are classified according to three criteria:

- The **location** in the vocal tract where they are produced (the descriptive terms used are bilabial, labiodental, interdental, alveolar, alveopalatal, velar, and glottal);

- The **manner** in which they are produced (stops, nasals, fricatives, affricates, approximants, and glides); and
- The **voicing**, which refers to whether they are voiced or unvoiced. For example, the [b] sound is described as a "voiced, bilabial stop," and the [f] sound is described as a "voiceless, labiodental fricative.".

All **vowels** are voiced, and so the classification of vowels occurs along two dimensions, both of which refer to the position and movement of the tongue during utterance: (1) high, mid, or low; and (2) front, central, and back. Thus, the short vowel [u], as in the word "boot," is produced high and in the back of the mouth.

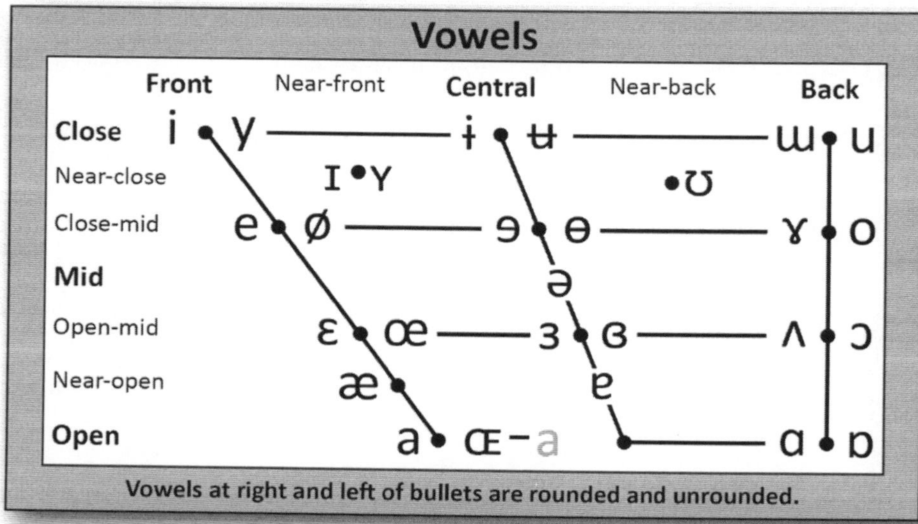

Vowels at right and left of bullets are rounded and unrounded.

Improving Pronunciation Skills

Perhaps the best way to help ELLs monitor their **pronunciation skills** is by using audio recordings in which ELLs repeat a word or phrase after a native speaker and then replay the recording. It may be helpful as well to provide students with surveys or question prompts that encourage them to reflect on which aspects of their pronunciation they need to improve on. Class activities like singing and choral reading are low-stress ways to focus on pronunciation. Above all, students have to be exposed to **modeled speech** at an appropriate level of phonetic complexity and given opportunities to practice in an environment in which they can focus on pronunciation rather than syntax or the complexities of social discourse.

Pitch, Tone, and Stress

Spoken language relies on differences in sound to create differences in meaning. The primary source of these sound differences is phonemes.

Differences in sound can affect meaning at a level above that of individual phonemes, however, by operating on syllables, words, or even sentences. Linguists refer to these as **prosodic features of language**. The two main prosodic features are **pitch** (which in turn is divided into *tone* and *intonation*) and **stress**.

- **Pitch**, while technically a difference in the frequency of the vibration of the vocal cords, is recognized by listeners as a continuum between low and high.

- Many languages use pitch to distinguish between words, in which case it is referred to as **tone**. Cantonese, for example, is a tonal language. If the pitch rises or falls over the course of a sentence, it is referred to as **intonation**. In English, intonation is often used to distinguish a statement from a question.
- **Stress** refers to a difference in force applied to an element of speech, usually a syllable. Multi-syllabic words in English have a standard pattern of stress. With some words, changing the pattern of stress may lead to a change of meaning, as between "con-VERT" and "CON-vert."

Segmentals vs. Suprasegmentals

A segmental is a discrete, identifiable speech segment that contributes sound in a sequential pattern. Examples include phonemes, syllables, diphthongs, and blends. **Suprasegmentals** occur when phonetic properties are spread over a broader range of speech segments, as occurs with pitch (tone or intonation) or stress. Suprasegmental properties are thus not *inherent* in the individual speech segments, but rather *supervene* on them, constituting an additional communicative tool. The term "prosodies" is often used as a synonym for "suprasegmentals." ELL students must master prosody in order to achieve full linguistic competency, as misplaced stress or tone can readily cause communicative failure.

Phonetic Interference

Language interference occurs when features of a speaker's native language affects his or her ability to learn a second language. **Phonetic interference** refers specifically to issues that arise when trying to learn the sound system of a new language. In general terms, phonetic interference occurs when a language learner attempts to speak the foreign language using familiar sounds from their own native tongue. For example, Spanish has far fewer phonemes than English, including just one sound associated with the letter "i," the sound English speakers learn as the short "i" sound. Spanish-speaking ELLs, then, will tend to pronounce all "i's" in English as long e's, a common example of phonetic interference.

One way to reduce phonetic interference is to introduce a word in **speech** before introducing it in **writing**, thus reducing the likelihood that a student will pronounce it according to native language rules. A second tactic is to devote large blocks of early instruction to the repetition of unfamiliar sounds.

Examples of the International Phonetic Alphabet

ʧ	**"ch" sound, as in "<u>ch</u>ore".**
ə	"uh" sound, as in "camp<u>u</u>s," or "l<u>o</u>ve". This symbol is called the "schwa" and represents a common English sound.
ʤ	"j" sound, as in "<u>j</u>elly".
ʃ	"sh" sound, as in "<u>sh</u>oe".
θ	"th" sound, as in "<u>th</u>ink".
ð	"th" sound, as in "<u>th</u>e".

Orthography and Writing Conventions

Need for Explicit Instruction about Orthography Writing Conventions

Orthography and writing conventions refer to the writing system and conventions surrounding how a language is written. This includes punctuation, capitalization, and methods of writing. As with other features of languages, conventions of writing can vary dramatically between languages.

Here are some brief examples of how writing conventions can vary from language to language:

- English only capitalizes proper nouns and words at the beginning of sentences, whereas German capitalizes every noun.
- Spanish and Vietnamese, as well as various other languages use accent marks to modify the typical pronunciation of letters.
- Spanish uses question marks and explanation marks at the beginning and end of sentences.
- Some languages, such as Hebrew and Japanese are written from right to left instead of left to right.
- Many languages, such as Hindi, Korean, Mandarin, Arabic, and Russian use different orthographic scripts.

The result of these differences means that students who are learning English may need specific instruction on alphabetics or other writing conventions that other students will have learned in early childhood.

Morphology

Morpheme vs. Phoneme

A morpheme is the smallest meaningful unit in a language. A morpheme functions as a **linguistic sign**—that is, it refers to something in reality. A **phoneme**, by contrast, is a unit of sound that can be put together with other sounds to form words.

All words are morphemes or combinations of more than one morpheme, but not all morphemes function as stand-alone words. A **free, or independent, morpheme** can occur by itself; a **bound morpheme** can only occur in combination with one or more additional morphemes. Prefixes and affixes are the most common types of bound morphemes—although they do have meaning and function to alter the meaning of the free morphemes to which they are joined, they cannot stand on their own in English usage.

Order of Morpheme Acquisition in English

Research suggests that students acquire English morphemes in a consistent order, regardless of their native language or the instructional context. The following are the **stages of morpheme acquisition**:

- **Stage 1:** The learner produces minimal "telegraphic" sentences with few words and little or no inflection (e.g., "Dog run").
- **Stage 2:** Present progressive "-ing" (e.g., eating), prepositions "in, on," and the plural "-s" (e.g., dogs).
- **Stage 3:** Irregular past tense verbs (e.g., He went out), possessive "'s" (e.g., John's book), and the copula form of "to be" when used as a linking verb (e.g., She is sad).
- **Stage 4:** Articles (a, the), the regular past tense "-ed" (e.g., walked), and third-person singular "-s" (e.g., She runs).

- **Stage 5:** The auxiliary form of "to be" used with present participles (e.g., He is eating), including both contracted and uncontracted forms (e.g., He's eating, He is eating).

Teachers should take these stages into consideration as they decide in which order to introduce these forms. Further, teachers may opt not to explicitly correct errors that this model will predict students to master at a later date, and instead focus on correcting errors that correspond to a student's present stage of acquisition.

Word Analysis

Word analysis is performed by breaking a complex word into its **constituent morphemes** in order to help students understand an unfamiliar word. Word analysis relies on the fact that many English words are composed of separate, frequently-used morphemes with identifiable meanings. For example, teaching students the meaning of the prefixes "re-" (again) and "un-" (not), or the Greek roots "auto-" (self) or "chrono" (time) allows them to understand a wide range of words composed of these elements. Another morphological regularity that students can exploit when analyzing unfamiliar words is the fact that English adverbs are often formed by adding the suffix "-ly" to adjectives. Thus, a student who knew the adjective "easy" could deduce that "easily" was an adverb by using word analysis.

Affix vs. Root

An affix, or **bound morpheme**, is a morpheme that cannot occur independently, but must be joined to another morpheme. A **root** (also called a base, or a free morpheme), by contrast, can stand alone.

One way to classify affixes is by where they are joined to the root morpheme: if they occur before the root, they are called **prefixes**; if they occur after the root, they are called **suffixes**; and if they occur in the middle of the root, they are called **infixes**. Infixes are rare in English but common in many other languages.

A second way to classify affixes is by how they change the meaning of the base to which they are joined. **Inflectional affixes** may change the number, gender, case, or tense of the root, but they do not change its basic lexical meaning, nor its grammatical form. An example is the addition of "-s" to "student": the word becomes plural but remains a noun. A **derivational affix**, by contrast, may change the meaning of the base word and/or its grammatical form. For example, the addition of "un-" to "happy" changes its meaning, and the addition of "-ish" to "child" changes a noun into an adjective.

Compound Words

Compound words are words created by combining two separate words. The resulting word often has a meaning that is difficult to predict from the meaning of the combined words. Many languages, including English, make generous use of **compound words**, while they are virtually non-existent in other languages.

While the meaning of many compound words adheres closely to the meaning of its separate parts—for example, the logic of "crosswalk" is easy to understand—others have either figurative meanings ("brainstorm") or meanings derived from older forms of English ("cobweb"), and thus may be difficult for ELLs to understand.

However, many compound words make delightful combinations and thus may appeal to ELLs: "bookworm," for example, or "skyscraper." Learning these words may also stimulate ELLs to propose compound words of their own, thereby providing them with an early experience of creativity in English use.

Cognates

Cognates are words that have a common origin, and retain similarities in meaning, spelling, or pronunciation. **Cognates** exist within a single language (in English, the words "biology" and "biography" share a common origin in the Latin root "bio," meaning "life") and between two languages that share a common origin. For example, the Spanish words "biologia" and "biografia" are cognates to their English counterparts, reflecting the common origins of Spanish and English.

The existence of cognates makes learning a new language easier, especially for beginning learners in need of comprehension early on. However, not all words that appear similar between languages actually have similar origins and meanings. Linguists refer to these as **false cognates**, and they make second-language learning harder rather than easier. For example, when English speakers encounter the Spanish word "embarazada," they often assume it means "embarrassed," but in fact, the two words are false cognates: "embarazada" means "pregnant."

English Etymology

Etymology is the study of the origin of words. Many English words have **Greek or Latin roots and affixes**. Learning those roots and affixes gives ELLs the ability to recognize the basic meaning of multiple English words and provides them with the means of deciphering the meaning of unfamiliar words by breaking them into their component pieces, which may be familiar. For example, knowing that the Greek root "micro" means "small" makes the following words accessible to an ELL: microsecond, microbiology, and microbrew.

Many English words are also formed from common Greek or Latin prefixes. Examples of common prefixes include "pre-," meaning "before"; and "semi-," meaning "half." Common suffixes include "-er," meaning "more"; and "-est," meaning "most." Knowing the meanings of these affixes will allow an ELL to decipher the meaning of many unfamiliar words.

The term "**derivation**" refers to the formation of new words by adding a derivational affix to a root. (Derivational affixes are affixes that typically change the meaning or word class of the root.) For example, the word "thankful," an adjective, can be derived by adding "-ful" to the root "thank," a verb.

Cognates vs. Loanwords

A loanword is a word adopted from a foreign language without translation, though it may be modified in small ways to fit the adopting language. **Cognates** are words in separate languages that have common origins. Cognates lead to similarities between languages by *descent*, whereas loan words lead to similarities by *borrowing*.

The existence of cognates is of great help to English language earners (ELLs) who speak closely-related languages. ELLs can often use the existence of known cognates to deduce the meaning of other words and even entire sentences. They are occasionally misled, however, by **false cognates**—words in two languages that appear similar but in fact have different origins and meanings.

Different languages loaned words to English at different times in history, depending on forces of exploration, colonization, and war. The leading **sources of English loan words** are German; Danish; French; Greek; Latin; and, following the colonization of America, Spanish and Native American.

Morphological Interference

Morphological interference occurs when a student's ability to learn a second language is influenced by the morphology of their native language. Languages differ significantly in how words are formed and what type of information can be conveyed in a single word (as opposed to being conveyed in a second word or conveyed simply by context). For example, English nouns typically have single and plural forms ("one goose," "two geese"), and verbs typically change with tense ("I eat," "I ate"). By contrast, nouns in Mandarin Chinese do not change with number, and verbs do not change with tense; this additional information is provided by context. Even closely-related languages exhibit significant differences. English speakers, for example, are accustomed to verbs that have the same form in the first-person singular, first-person plural, and third-person plural, but a different form in the third-person singular ("I talk," "we talk," and "they talk" contrast with "he talks"). Spanish, however, utilizes a different verb form in each of these cases. Having a sense of the variations possible in language can help an ESOL teacher understand the cause of a student's English errors.

Semantics

Semantics is the study of the meaning of words, phrases, and sentences. The **denotation** of a word is its most literal definition, the one listed in a dictionary. The **connotation** of a word is the associations and emotions that a word evokes, either because of personal experience or shared cultural understandings. Connotations may change over time, and even if they are relatively stable, they will likely be difficult for a non-native speaker to understand. For example, "slender" and "skinny" have the same denotations, but for most native English speakers, the former has a positive connotation, while the latter has a negative connotation.

Literal and Figurative Language

Literal language is language that means exactly what it says—the meaning of a literal sentence can be understood simply by understanding its component words. **Figurative language** conveys a meaning different from the literal meaning of its component words. **Metaphors** compare, or equate, two unlike things without using the words "like" or "as"—for example, "love is war," or "this problem is a real bear." **Similes** do the same, but use "like" or "as"—for example, "my throat is as dry as a bone."

An **idiom** is a figurative expression that has gained widespread usage in a language community. Unlike a metaphor or simile, it doesn't necessarily make a comparison. Many idioms carried a literal meaning when they were first coined, but that meaning has since been forgotten or rendered obsolete. For example, the idiom "Don't beat around the bush," which is now used to exhort someone to speak clearly and directly, originally described the practice whereby a group of hunters would beat bushes with sticks in order to flush out their prey. Idioms are particularly difficult for non-native students to learn because they can't be understood simply through a study of their denotation.

Homonym

Homonyms are words that are spelled alike or sound alike but have different meanings and origins. If two words are spelled alike, they are called **homographs** ("graph" in Greek means "to write"). If the two words sound alike, they are called **homophones** ("phone" in Greek means "sound"). Examples of homographs include "entrance" (as a noun, it means "a door"; as a verb, it means "to captivate.") Examples of homophones include "bear" (an animal) and "bare" (as a verb, it means "to uncover.") ESOL students should be shown the written form to help distinguish homophones, and the spoken form to help distinguish homographs.

Two words may share both spelling and pronunciation but differ in meaning and, critically, in origin. (If they don't differ in origin, then they are not two different words, but simply one word with two meanings.) These words are referred to simply as homonyms. An example is "saw," which is both a cutting tool the past tense of "to see."

Language Ambiguities

Language ambiguities arise when ELLs are confronted with a word that has multiple meanings (homograph) or multiple pronunciations (heteronyms) and they must rely on **context** to determine the actual usage.

For example, if presented with the sentence "Jack will lead the tour," an ELL could use his or her awareness of the basic English sentence structure subject-verb-object to realize that "lead" in this example (a homograph) is a verb and not a noun. Similarly, if presented with the sentence "Please don't tear the paper," an ELL can deduce from knowledge of syntax that "tear" is a verb rather than the heteronym "tear," a noun referring to moisture in the eye.

Deciphering language ambiguities is an example of the broader use of **context clues** to decipher the meaning of unknown words or phrases. ELLs can often use their knowledge of sentence structure to deduce at least what part of speech an unknown word might be. For example, an awareness that the verb "to give" is often followed by both a direct and an indirect object, and that the former is usually an object and the latter a person, will provide an ELL with clues about an unfamiliar word.

Syntax

Parts of English Speech

- **Noun**—a word that names a person, place, idea, or thing. Nouns are often combined with determiners to form the subject of a sentence. They are often replaced by pronouns.
- **Verb**—a word that expresses an action or state of being. Verbs are typically the core of the predicate of a sentence. In English, verbs change to agree with the subject and reflect tense, voice, mood, and aspect.
- **Pronoun**—a word that replaces a noun or noun phrase (its antecedent) that was previously used or understood.
- **Adjective**—a word that modifies a noun, typically by describing the quantity, quality, or by distinguishing one noun from another.
- **Adverb**—a word that modifies a verb, adjective, or adverb and often shows degree, manner, place, or time.
- **Preposition**—a word (such as "in," "to," "on," "with") that is usually combined with a noun or pronoun to establish a relationship between that noun and another part of the sentence. The relationships include things such as location or time.
- **Interjection**—a word or phrase used to express emotion or surprise.
- **Conjunction**—a word that links sentences, clauses, phrases, or words. Examples include "and," "or" and "but."

Review Video: Determiners in Grammar
Visit mometrix.com/academy and enter code: 385229

Noun

A noun is a word that names a person, place, thing, quality, or action. **Common nouns** refer to types or classes of things that have more than one member—for example, "president" or "state." They are not capitalized unless they begin a sentence. Proper nouns refer to specific people or things—for example, "President Lincoln," or "Florida." They are capitalized wherever they occur in a sentence.

Countable nouns refer to things that can be counted. They have separate singular and plural forms (one egg, two eggs), and in the singular form can be preceded by "a" or "an." Uncountable nouns, often referred to as mass nouns, cannot be counted (milk, rice). They do not have plural forms and cannot be used with "a" and "an."

Concrete nouns refer to things that can be perceived by the senses. Abstract nouns refer to things that cannot be perceived by the senses—for example, ideas, concepts, or beliefs. Whether a noun is concrete or abstract makes no difference in how it is used.

Review Video: Nouns
Visit mometrix.com/academy and enter code: 344028

Conjunction

A conjunction is a word that connects other words, phrases, clauses, or sentences. **Conjunctions** are one of the eight parts of speech, along with nouns, verbs, pronouns, adjectives, adverbs, prepositions, and interjections.

Coordinating conjunctions link together words or phrases that have the same grammatical function. For example: "I like to bike, *and* I like to run." There are seven coordinating conjunctions: for, and, not, but, or, yet, and so—these can be recalled using the acronym FANBOYS.

Correlative conjunctions appear in pairs and also join words or phrases with the same function. Examples of correlative conjunctions include "either... or," "both... and," and "no sooner... than." For example: "I am going to the game, *whether or not* you come with me.".

Subordinating conjunctions join unequal parts of a sentence. Specifically, they link adverbial clauses—a type of dependent clause that serves as an adverb—to an independent clause. There are many subordinate clauses, but some of the most common are "when," "because," "before," and "if." In the example "I will go to sleep *when* you come home," the conjunction "when" joins the independent clause "I will go to sleep" with the dependent clause "you come home."

Pronoun and Antecedent

A pronoun is a word that takes the place of a noun (or noun phrase), which is referred to as the pronoun's *antecedent*. There are three types of pronouns. **Personal pronouns** refer to a specific person (or persons) or an object. They include many of the most common words in English: I, me, you, he, she, etc. **Possessive pronouns** indicate ownership: my/mine, your/yours, its, their, etc. **Indefinite pronouns** refer to nonspecific persons or things: anybody, everything, no one, someone, etc.

Even native English speakers make frequent errors when using personal pronouns. These pronouns have two forms: the **subjective form**, to be used when the pronoun serves as a subject or complements a subject; and the **objective form**, to be used when the pronoun serves as an object. The subjective personal pronouns are I, you, he/she/it, we, you and they. The corresponding objective pronouns are me, you, him/her/it, us, you, and them.

Syntax vs. Grammar

Syntax is the way in which words are combined in a language to create phrases, clauses, and sentences. The word is often used synonymously with "**grammar**." However, "grammar" has a prescriptive sense that is often missing from "syntax"—the former describes the way words should be combined in order to be considered correct, whereas the latter describes the ways in which they are combined in reality to achieve effective communication. In common usage, "grammar" is a broader term than "syntax," referring not only to syntax, but also to phonology, semantics, and even punctuation.

The most common **syntactic form** of an English sentence is subject-verb-object, as in the sentence "The dog bit the man." While this may seem too obvious to a native English speaker to be noteworthy, it is important to understand for a few reasons. First, many languages are constructed differently—for example, the basic order in Japanese is subject-object-verb. Second, the order is altered in English when the passive voice is used. For example, "The man was bitten by the dog" yields the syntactic form object-verb-subject.

Transformational or Generative Grammar

Transformational grammar (or generative grammar) is an approach to syntax, developed by Noam Chomsky, that hypothesizes that the surface structure of any language can be explained as a transformation of an innate (or universal, or deep) structure of language which humans all share in common. The term "generative" refers to the idea that language learners learn to form (or generate) sentences by transforming the deep structures present in brains at birth. For example, Chomsky argued that declarative and interrogative sentences share a single deep structure, and linguists have established a set of rules by which the former can be transformed into the latter.

Subsequent proponents of generative grammar introduced the term "**principles**" to name the rules of the hypothesized universal grammar and the term "**parameters**" to name the constraints that any actual language places on the set of universal rules. For example, a parameter of English grammar is that, in a verb phrase, the verb must precede its object complements, as in "ate the cake.".

Subject and Predicate, Noun and Verb

Beginning students are often taught that English sentences need, at a minimum, a noun and a verb. In fact, many sentences contain nothing more than a **noun** and **verb**—for example, "John is running." However, this description of the *simplest* of English sentences does not describe the *entirety* of English sentences, most of which contain other parts of speech in addition to a noun and a verb. In contrast, the more formal terms subject and predicate are exhaustive: they refer to all the possible elements of an English sentence.

A **subject** is what or whom a sentence is talking about, and a **predicate** tells something about that subject. Everything in a sentence is either part of the subject or part of the predicate. Simple nouns or pronouns often serve as the subject of a sentence, but the role can also be filled by more complex structures. Some sentences have implied subjects, as in command: "Be quiet!" In addition to the verb, the predicate often includes an object (direct and/or indirect) and various compliments.

Review Video: Complete Predicate
Visit mometrix.com/academy and enter code: 293942

Tense

In grammar, **tense** refers to the location of events in time. In English, tense is expressed by changing the form of verbs. While linguists recognize only two tenses in English (past and present) and classify the other variations in verbs as changes of aspect or mood, non-specialists commonly recognize twelve different tenses, which we can order in a 3 x 4 chart:

	Simple	Progressive	Perfect	Perfect Progressive
Present	I walk	I am walking	I have walked	I have been walking
Past	I walked	I was walking	I had walked	I had been walking
Future	I will walk	I will be walking	I will have walked	I will have been walking

The progressive forms are also referred to as continuous forms, as they are used to describe actions or states that are ongoing at a certain point in time. These are fashioned by combining a form of the verb "to be" and "-ing." The perfect tenses are fashioned by combining a form of the verb "to have" and the past participle of the main verb. The perfect progressive tenses are built using features of both the progressive and perfect tenses.

Subject-Verb Agreement

The basic rule of subject-verb agreement is that a singular subject requires a singular verb, and a plural subject requires a plural verb.

One exception is in the **simple past**, in which a stand-alone main verb (one without an auxiliary verb) doesn't change when the noun changes: "The man gave me a box," and "The men gave me a box," use the same verb form. Many helping verbs, however, do function according to the rule in the simple past.

A second problem arises with **compound subjects**—two or more subjects joined by "and," "or," or "nor." If two subjects are joined by "and," they should be treated as a plural subject taking a plural verb. If they are joined by "or" or "nor," however, the subject nearest the verb should agree with the verb: "Neither the dog nor the cats like liver.".

A third common error arises when the subject of a sentence is separated from the verb by an **intervening phrase** that contains a noun. Correct usage requires that the verb agrees with the subject, not the nearby noun. Thus: "The students who pass the test receive a prize."

Classifying Verbs

A **transitive verb** requires an object in order to constitute a complete thought, whereas an **intransitive verb** does not. "Throw" is an example of a transitive verb: it is incorrect to simply say "I threw" without adding an object. "Jump," however, is intransitive: "I jumped," is an acceptable sentence. Some verbs are both transitive and intransitive, depending on context.

Linking verbs do not indicate action, but instead connect the subject to a word or phrase that describes the subject. The verb "to be" is the most common linking verb.

Verbs that are conjugated to agree with a subject are called **finite verbs**. The three main types of non-finite verbs are infinitives, gerunds, and participles. An **infinitive** is a verb with the word "to" in front of it: to eat, to read, etc. A **gerund** is an "-ing" verb functioning as a noun—as in the example "I like swimming." A **participle** is a word formed from a verb but used either as an adjective, adverb, noun, or as part of a compound verb. For example, the past participle "gone" forms a compound noun in the phrase "has gone."

Independent Clause vs. Dependent Clause

A **clause** is a group of words with a subject and a predicate. A **sentence** goes one step further: it is a group of words with a subject and predicate that expresses a complete thought. For example, "When I saw him," is a clause, but it is not a complete sentence.

An **independent clause** is a clause that can stand alone as a sentence but can also be joined with other clauses to make other sentences. A **dependent clause**, by contrast, cannot stand alone as a sentence, but must be combined with another clause or clauses to form a sentence.

A **simple sentence** is a single independent clause—in other words, a complete thought consisting of a subject and predicate. A **compound sentence** consists of two or more independent clauses, often joined by a conjunction, such as "and" or "or." A **complex sentence** consists of an independent clause and a dependent clause joined by a subordinating conjunction such as "when" or "because." A **complex-compound sentence** is one with two or more independent clauses joined to one or more dependent clauses.

Appositive

An appositive is a noun, noun phrase, or noun clause that serves to explain or identify another noun nearby in the sentence. In the sentence "Your brother Skip called me," "Skip" is an **appositive** identifying the noun phrase "your brother." "Skip" and "your brother" can be described as being in *apposition*. In the sentence "Carla—the only teacher to attend the training session—was well-prepared for the exercises," "the only teacher to attend the training session" is an appositive that provides information about the noun "Carla."

In general, appositives that are essential to the meaning of the sentence are not set off by punctuation marks, whereas those that are not are set off by commas, dashes, or parentheses. Knowing this usage pattern would allow an ELL to recognize, for example, that the author of the sentence "Your brother Skip called me" recognizes that the person he or she is writing to has more than one brother, and thus signaled that the appositive "Skip" was critical to the meaning of the sentence by declining to set it off by commas.

Classifying Sentences

Sentences can be classified in various ways—for example, the categories "compound sentences" and "complex sentences" classify sentences according to their *syntax*. Another common way to classify sentences is by their *purpose*, or what they are meant to achieve in a communicative setting. In this context, experts usually identify four different kinds of sentences. **Declarative sentences** make a statement: "Jodie is a tall woman." **Interrogative sentences** pose a question: "Is your mom home?" **Imperative sentences** give a command: "Please come here." And **exclamatory sentences** express strong feelings: "I can't wait for tomorrow!".

Review Video: Intro to Sentence Types
Visit mometrix.com/academy and enter code: 953367

Phrasal Verb

A phrasal verb is an idiomatic combination of a verb with another word, usually a preposition or adverbs. Examples include "blow up," "break down," "chip in," "get away with," and "add up." These verbs pose unique difficulties for ELLs because the word combinations are idiomatic and yet fixed. Further, many **phrasal verbs** can be split when used in a sentence—for example, when referring to a column of numbers, we can ask "Can you *add* them *up*?", interposing the word "them" in the phrasal verb.

ELLs are likely to find three aspects of phrasal verbs challenging: their idiomatic meanings, their seemingly arbitrary choice of preposition or adverb to couple with the verb, and the contexts in which they can and cannot be split.

Tag Question

A tag question is a declarative statement turned into a question by the addition of an interrogative fragment, as in the example "Portland is the capital of Maine, isn't it?" **Tag questions** are often rhetorical—the speaker does not seek an answer—and they are also used to communicate a desired answer to the listener. Many languages utilize tag questions ("n'est ce pas" in French and "da" in Russian are two frequent examples), but those in English tend to be complex and varied, thus posing production if not reception challenges for ELLs.

Predicate Nominative and Predicate Adjective

A predicate nominative is a noun or noun phrase (thus making it nominative) that follows a linking verb (and thus is in the predicate of a sentence) and renames the subject. For example, in the sentence "John's favorite book is *War and Peace*," "War and Peace" is a **predicate nominative**.

A **predicate adjective** is a word or words that follows a linking verb and modifies the subject of a sentence. In the sentence "The dog is brown," "brown" is a predicate adjective. Predicate adjectives are distinguished from ordinary or attributive adjectives, which typically precede the noun that they modify. Instead, a predicate adjective follows the noun and is paired with a linking verb.

Gerunds vs. Present Participles

Gerunds and present participles are both formed using the "-ing" form of a verb, and both are often parts of a broader phrase. **Gerunds**, however, function as *nouns*, while **present participles** function either as progressing verbs (their most familiar use) or as *adjectives*. In the sentence "Hiking to the top of Mount Kilimanjaro is hard work," the word "hiking" is a gerund: it is a noun, the subject of the verb "is." In the sentence "Hiking to the top of Mount Kilimanjaro, John fell and sprained his ankle," "hiking" is a participle that initiates an adjectival phrase modifying the noun "John."

Modal Verb

A modal phrase is an auxiliary verb that adds shades of meaning to the main verb of a sentence by adding an opinion, attitude, or feeling. The most common **modal verbs** in English are "would, will, can, could, may, and must."

Modals present several challenges to ELLs. First, student L1s may not have corresponding forms: Spanish, for example, has no word for "will" or "would." Second, modals often have several unrelated meanings—"may," for example, can convey both possibility ("I may come") or permission ("May I go?"). Third, modals are irregular in their conjugation—for example, the verbs listed above do not add an "-s" in the third-person present. Finally, when a modal is combined with another verb, the second verb is not used in its infinitive form, as is generally the case when a sentence contains two verbs. Thus, native speakers say "I can go," not "I can to go," but would use the infinitive form "to go" in most instances, as in "I want to go."

Pragmatics

Pragmatics is the study of how meaning is affected by context—or, stated differently, how people may use shared understandings and implications to reach understandings that are not entailed by the literal meaning of their words. An **implication** is a conclusion that can be drawn even though it isn't stated.

We rely on **shared understandings** in order to carry out conversations. For example, if a person tells me that she has two daughters, I assume that she has *only* two, although logically, her statement is consistent with her having five. When I ask someone "Could you pass the salad?" we rely on the implied understanding that I want the salad, not a yes or no answer. Even the length or nature of our casual exchanges with strangers are driven by shared understandings: when the cashier in the supermarket asks how we are doing, we both know that he or she isn't asking for a detailed reply.

These examples help illustrate the broader point that communication always takes place in a context that creates implicit meaning in addition to the explicit meaning represented by the words themselves.

Paul Grice's Cooperative Principle

The philosopher Paul Grice's work focuses on how pragmatics function in language—that is, on how we rely on shared assumptions, background knowledge, and implied meanings to communicate more or more clearly than our stated words would seem to allow. Grice's **cooperative principle** can be paraphrased to state that, when we engage in conversation, we assume that our interlocutor will cooperate in achieving understanding by speaking truthfully, logically, and concisely. Grice emphasized that what we *mean* is often *implied* by what we *say* and that a competent member of our language community will grasp the implications of our speech.

We successfully communicate implied meanings, Grice argues, when we obey four maxims of conversation. The **maxim of quality** states that we speak the truth. The **maxim of quantity** states that we provide as much information or detail as is necessary to fulfill our conversational purpose. The **maxim of relevance** states that we will stay on topic. The **maxim of manner** suggests that we will avoid ambiguity, use language our interlocutor can understand, and organize our speech in a logical way. Grice argues that these assumptions allow us to communicate many implied meanings without resorting to explicit explanations.

Register, Eye Contact, Physical Proximity, and Gestures

Pragmatic features of communication are the non-linguistic factors that influence what and how effectively we communicate in a given language community. These features are particularly important to ELLs because the conventions of their adopted language community might differ from those of their native language community.

Register refers to the formality of language. By convention, English speakers will speak more formally in a professional setting than when talking to a close friend; ELLs may need instruction and practice to master these conventions. Students from different cultures may also have a different understanding of the significance of **eye contact** during the conversation: whereas in the United States, direct eye contact signals transparency, in many cultures it is seen as an aggressive assertion of status. Similarly, ELLs may have a different sense of appropriate **personal space** when conversing than their typical American interlocutor, which can interfere with effective communication. The use of **gestures** in communication also varies widely by culture, as well as by context within a culture, and ELLs will have to learn or acquire the conventions of the language community in order to communicate effectively.

Locution, Illocution, and Perlocution

The philosopher John L. Austin launched what came to be known as **speech act theory** in the 1970s by distinguishing between **locution** (what a person says), **illocution** (what a person means), and **perlocution** (the effect the person's utterance has). The classic example is the utterance at the dinner table of the locution "Is there any salt?" which has the illocutionary meaning of "Please pass the salt" and the perlocutionary effect of the salt being passed.

A **pragmatic failure** occurs when a person fails to understand what is *meant* even though he or she correctly understood what was *said*. For example, a teacher might call the fact that a student is late to class by asking him or her "What time is it?" A pragmatic failure would occur if the student took the question at face-value and failed to understand it as a reprimand.

Distinct Features of Sheltered English Immersion

Sheltered English Instruction (SEI)

In a **sheltered instruction program** (also called sheltered English instruction), intermediate English language learners are taught the full curriculum in English and are given appropriate support to further their content learning. SEI programs explicitly target **content knowledge** and only address English development indirectly by creating highly contextualized learning environments in which students can practice their English skills. Schools with large, homogenous ELL populations may have separate SEI content classes—sheltered 8th grade life science, for example—or a teacher may simply implement sheltering teaching techniques in a classroom of mixed native English speakers and ELLs.

SEI teachers deliver the same content as ordinary content instructors but attempt to communicate that content in ways that don't depend on **student English proficiency**. Thus, they often simplify, use demonstrations and realia, and allow students to use L1 resources to supplement their learning.

States and school districts use different variations of SEI. The most widely used include the Sheltered Instruction Observation Protocol (SIOP), the Specially Designed Academic Instruction in English (SDAIE) model, Guided Language Acquisition Design (GLAD), Quality Teaching for English Learners (QTEL), and the Cognitive Academic Language Learning Approach (CALLA).

Differences Between ESL and SEI

	English as a Second Language	**Sheltered English Immersion**
Main Focus	ESL focuses on English as a primary subject.	SEI focuses on teaching a content area, but with modified English to support student acquisition.
Language Use	ESL may use multiple languages to support learning.	SEI uses only English, but may modify the difficulty of language use.
Primary Goal	English learning over time.	Rapid English learning while keeping up with on-level academic subject knowledge.

Classroom Style	ESL classes can be separate classes or integrated classes with scaffolded supports.	SEI typically has a self-contained immersion classroom.
Duration	ESL classes can be long-term or short-term, depending on the students' needs	SEI intends to be a short-term program, with the intention of transitioning out after one to two years.

Sheltered Instruction Observation Protocol (SIOP)

The Sheltered Instruction Observation Protocol (SIOP) was originally developed in the early 1990s as a 30-item **survey** to evaluate the effectiveness of a teacher's planning, implementation, and assessment of sheltered English instruction. The survey has been demonstrated to be valid and reliable and is still widely used to evaluate sheltered English programs, even those that do not follow SIOP as an **instructional model**.

The originators followed up on the success of SIOP as a survey tool by elaborating a full-scale approach to lesson planning and delivery, intended to give content instructors a systematic approach to teaching English language learners. SIOP divides the instructional process into **eight components**: lesson preparation, building background, comprehensible input, strategies, interaction, practice and application, lesson delivery, and review and assessment.

Content-Based Instruction

Content-based instruction (**CBI**) teaches language indirectly by teaching **content in the target language**. CBI is an **umbrella term** that subsumes all teaching methods—such as sheltered instruction—that teach language and content simultaneously. In general, proponents of CBI argue that students can best learn languages indirectly, by focusing on (and being motivated by) interesting subject matter content. Some CBI programs carefully structure the subject matter content so that it systematically treats sequential features of the target language, while others are more immersive in the sense that they rely more heavily on the student's ability to infer meaning from a context-rich learning environment.

Discourse

Coherent Texts or Conversations

Discourse may be defined as a coherent sequence of written or spoken sentences. Linguists study the way in which competent language users connect individual sentences in order to create coherent wholes. Linguists may focus on small-scale (word- or phrase-based) connectors called **cohesive devices** or on broader, logical relations between sentences. For example, a sentence might **add information** to the broader text, perhaps through the use of a phrase like "In addition…" A sentence might illustrate the **effect** of a previous cause, using, for example, "Consequently…" Sentences might also **clarify** previous sentences (e.g., "That is to say…"), provide a **summary** (e.g., "In conclusion…"), establish a **logical or temporal order** (e.g., "First… second…"), furnish an **example** (e.g., "For example…"), or **qualify** or **contrast** a previous point (e.g., "However…"). Each of these ways of relating one sentence to another contributes to the overall **coherence** of a text or conversation.

Coherence vs. Cohesion

Coherence and cohesion are terms used in discourse analysis to describe written texts. A text is **cohesive** if its individual sentences are linked in ways that bring them together into a single whole.

A text is **coherent** if its ideas, or content, belong together. Although it doesn't incorporate the entirety of the concepts, cohesion can be thought of as an achievement of grammar or rhetoric, whereas coherence demands that the text corresponds to logic or reality.

Linguists have identified five cohesive devices that establish links among sentences.

- **Reference** occurs when a word in one sentence refers to a word in another, such as a pronoun to its antecedent.
- **Conjunction** occurs when a sentence begins with a word or phrase, such as "however" or "alternatively," that ties it to the previous sentence.
- **Substitution** occurs when a specific word is replaced with a general word in a subsequent sentence—for example, first writing "I doubt he will study," and then "But if he does..."
- Writers may also intentionally leave out parts of a phrase previously used, a technique called **ellipses.**
- Finally, writers may employ lexical cohesion by replacing a word with an appropriate **descriptor**, as when "Edison" is replaced with "the inventor."

Connected Speech

"Connected speech" refers to the way in which the pronunciation of a word can be changed by the words around it. **Catenation** is the joining of the last consonant sound of one word with the beginning vowel sound of the next, as when "an apple" sounds like "a napple." **Elision** occurs when a sound is left out of a word—often a sound in a consonant cluster, as when "sandwich" is pronounced "sanwich." **Assimilation** is the blending of two sounds to create a new sound, as when "don't you" sounds like "doan chu" when spoken rapidly. **Intrusion** is the insertion of an unwritten sound into a phrase, as when "do it" is pronounced "dewit."

Connected speech presents obvious listening comprehension challenges for ELLs. In addition, ELLs who rely heavily on reading to learn English (as with grammar-translation methods still in use abroad) may not use any connected speech when speaking, and thus sound unnaturally formal or stilted.

Language Forms and Functions

Social Language vs. Academic Language

Social language is language used in everyday communication. **Academic language** is used in the classroom and workplace and on standardized assessments. Most students are exposed to social language earlier and more completely than they are exposed to academic language and become more proficient in social language as a consequence.

Social language often doesn't follow grammatical conventions—in casual settings, people often speak in phrases rather than complete sentences, use slang, repeat themselves, and use narrative strategies that favor expediency rather than economy or logic. In an academic setting, by contrast, people are expected to use full sentences linked by grammatical transitions. Academic language typically requires a specialized or higher-level vocabulary, and variety is expected instead of repetition.

It isn't uncommon for ESOL students to be fluent in social language while struggling to achieve even minimal competence in academic language. The students' perceived mastery of the more common social language may lessen their motivation to improve their academic language performance.

Use vs. Usage

The linguist Henry Widdowson drew a distinction between **language usage**—knowing how to construct words and sentences in accordance with formal rules—and **language use**—knowing how to use language in order to achieve an objective. Widdowson used these terms to draw a sharp distinction between **linguistic competence** and **communicative competence** and argued that the latter takes more time for second-language learners to achieve. Extending the same distinction, Widdowson argued that sentences have *significance* in isolation but *value* in the context of a communicative act. Widdowson's ideas influenced the **communicative approaches** to language learning, with their emphasis on authentic speech acts and the importance of pragmatic dimensions of communication.

Different Social Functions of Language

The primary purpose of language is to allow people to communicate with and understand one another. Linguists often distinguish between academic language and social language—the latter being the everyday language we use in informal settings—and classify various types of social language based on their function. For example, the linguist Geoffrey Leech identified five different functions of social language. First, language is **informational**: we use it to convey information, and in this form, we value its accuracy and relevance. Second, language may be **expressive**, as when we use it to convey feelings or attitudes. Third, language may be **directive**—we may use it to convey orders or exert influence. Fourth, language may be **aesthetic**, as when it is used creatively or artistically. Fifth, language may be **phatic**—that is, it may be used simply to sustain a social relationship, such as when we engage in small talk with a stranger.

Other linguists have classified social language in other ways—for example, many add a category of apologetic language. The importance of all this research is that it draws attention to the various functions of everyday language.

Various Functions of Language

Language has a number of functions. The most obvious is to **communicate facts, thoughts, or opinions** to others. Linguists describe this function as referential in that the language we use refers to something that exists in our minds. We also use language to **express emotions**—often involuntarily, as when we cry out in alarm. Language has a social function beyond the expression of thought—as when we engage in ritualistic pleasantries with a neighbor as a way of cementing a social bond. We use language to **record information** for future use, usually in written form. We also use language to **influence reality**—what the philosopher J. L. Austin called "perlocutionary acts," as when we christen a ship with the invocation "I hereby christen..." We also use language to **facilitate thought and memory**, as when we talk to ourselves to overcome a mental block. Finally, we use language to **express our personal or collective identity**, as when we join a cheer at a sports stadium.

Basic Interpersonal Communication Skills (BICS) and Cognitive Academic Language Proficiency (CALP)

The terms "BICS" and "CALP," coined by the educational psychologist Jim Cummins, correspond to the broader concepts of social and academic language. Social language, or **BICS**, is the language used in everyday life; while academic language, or **CALP**, is the language used in formal academic settings.

Cummins highlighted the importance of treating the two types of language as **separate systems**. An ESOL student will typically become proficient in BICS in as little as six months, while proficiency in CALP may take seven to 10 years. Furthermore, many English language learners never achieve full facility in CALP, whereas failure to acquire BICS is rare. Cummins warned educators not to make the mistake of assuming that a student proficient in BICS is also proficient in CALP—rather, it is natural for students to master the two competencies at different rates.

Different Academic Functions of Language

Academic language is the language used in the classroom, the workplace, and on formal assessments. ESOL students also need to become proficient in **academic language** in order to express, or demonstrate, their knowledge in various content areas of interest.

Whereas **social or everyday language** is used to convey information, express feelings, or simply to cement social bonds, **academic language** is used to achieve other functions. One classification suggests that academic language is used to describe, define, explain, compare, contrast, make predictions, and persuade.

Most ESOL students achieve proficiency in social language long before they achieve academic language proficiency. An ESOL student is likely to be immersed in social language early in his or her language experience but will need academic language to be expressly modeled, scaffolded, and reinforced through targeted practice.

Basil Bernstein's Theory of Language Codes

A language code is the way language is used by a particular social group, in part as an expression of social identity. In the 1970s, the linguist Basil Bernstein suggested that language could be described as consisting of either elaborated code or restricted code. Individuals use an **elaborated code** when they communicate with strangers or people who do not share a common experience. In these instances, they speak explicitly, at length, and with minimal colloquial or expressive language. When in the company of friends or members of a shared community, by contrast, people use a **restricted code**, which relies on implied meanings and references, thereby communicating a lot with few words. Only individuals with shared background knowledge and experiences can understand restricted code, whereas any listener can understand an elaborated utterance. Bernstein argued that restricted codes are used primarily in narrow, unchanging social contexts where shared values can be assumed, whereas elaborated codes are used for broader, unpredictable interactions. He also associated the use of restricted codes with the working class.

Communicative Competence

Communicative competence, a concept developed by the linguist Dell Hymes, refers to a language learner's ability to communicate effectively in various social settings. In order to succeed in communication, we need to know not only how to speak (or write) but what to say to whom and under which circumstances.

Later, Michael Canale and Merrill Swain identified four components of communicative competence. **Linguistic competence** refers to proficiency in grammar, vocabulary, and orthography. **Sociolinguistic competence** is the understanding of how to vary language use depending on the context or audience. **Discourse competence** is the knowledge of how to produce cohesive and coherent written or oral texts. **Strategic competence** is the ability to avoid or repair communication breakdowns—for example, by paraphrasing or using gestures to overcome the lack of useful vocabulary.

The concept of communicative competence focuses attention on the fact that there is more to communicative success than mastery of syntax or acquisition of vocabulary. Effective ESOL teachers implicitly or explicitly teach all of the component competencies.

Spoken vs. Written Language

Spoken and written language differ greatly in both form and purpose. The grammar of spoken language is generally less rigid, to the extent that many linguists believe that phrases are the fundamental units of speech, unlike the full sentences used in formal writing. **Spoken language** tends to include many repetitions, ellipses, and self-corrections and relies more heavily on slang and first-person pronouns than writing. Successful oral communication depends on paralanguage features—the nonverbal aspects of conversation, such as tone, gesture, and facial expression.

Written communication, by contrast, is more planned, uses more formal (and often complex) grammatical structures, avoids repetition, and relies on orderly presentation and evidence in order to be persuasive. Whereas speech is reciprocal—that is, it can be adapted to the reactions and emotions of the audience—writing is non-negotiable, as it is usually a non-synchronous medium, and thus must be crafted to be comprehensive. The differences between these types of communication, like many things, are not absolute; there are definite exceptions to the levels of formality, planning, and structure. Additionally, there are types of communication that blur the distinction between spoken and written language like prepared speeches and texting.

English-language learners have far more exposure to spoken English than to written English due to common social use of language. Written language learning tends to lean toward academic English and may be more challenging for English language learners than social English usage. ELLs tend to write in the same way in which they speak—that is, in phrases rather than sentences. Similarly, the argumentative forms typically used in writing, with ideas presented in a logical sequence or with a thesis followed by evidence or examples, are not the same as those used in typical speech and need to be expressly taught. Teachers should be aware that the English learning needs of their students will likely vary between their use of spoken and written language.

Variations in Languages and Dialects

Sociolinguistics, Dialect, and Sociolect

Sociolinguistics is the study of the factors that lead to variation in language use, such as region, gender, class, ethnicity, age, occupation, or bilingual status. A **dialect** is a variation in one or more features of a language, such as spelling, pronunciation, or word choice. **Sociolect** refers to language variations shared by members of the same social class.

Sociolinguists also study how our language use varies depending on the **situation**—people have a tendency to adopt the dialect of those they are speaking to, especially after lengthy exposure. People often adopt shared language as a means of showing solidarity with one another, as in numerous examples of working-class English. Many studies have shown, however, that people often adopt an **aspirational dialect**—in other words, they adopt the language patterns of a social or economic class they hope to join. Research has also suggested that women use higher-status language on average than men, perhaps to compensate for their perceived lower status in society.

Dialect vs. Language

A dialect is a variation in a spoken language that nevertheless is intelligible to the larger language community. (If the variation is so large as to prevent mutual intelligibility, it is considered to be a separate language.)

Dialects naturally arise when a language is spread across a wide area. Often gradients emerge such that all of the members of a dialect community can understand the neighboring dialects, but the differences between the communities farthest apart are so great as to impede communication.

While the linguistic distinction between language and dialect is clear, the reality in use is complicated by political and cultural interests—Hindi and Urdu, for example, are treated as separate languages even though they are mutually intelligible, whereas Chinese is, in fact, a collection of mutually unintelligible dialects unified only by a written language and a national identity.

English language learners may bring varying dialects into the classroom, and teachers should be careful to appreciate legitimate variation rather than impose an arbitrary standard. Differences in dialect may also slow language comprehension and acquisition, though the overall effect is likely to be slight.

World English and World Englishes

The similar terms "World English" and "World Englishes" refer to different applications of the use of English internationally. **World English** describes English used as a means of communication across language barriers, especially those in business or other professional and educational fields. For instance, a Spanish-speaking individual might not be able to directly communicate with a Hindi-speaking individual, but due to the worldwide prevalence of English, they may be able to find a common path to communication by speaking in English instead of eithers' first language. The concept of communicating across language barriers using a third language as in this example is known as "**lingua franca,**" which means a common tongue.

World Englishes, on the other hand, refers to international variations of English as it is used and modified to suit the local populations. This is similar to the use of hybrid-languages, such as "Singlish" to denote a blend between English and the varied languages of Singapore (Mandarin, Malay, and Tamil) or "Spanglish," denoting a blend between English and Spanish. While World Englishes may have strong variance geographically, they remain distinct from hybridized languages. Scholars of World Englishes map its spread along the lines of colonial influence, through commercial and scientific hubs, among the world's educated and economic elite, and increasingly through the instruments of modern technology, such as the Internet or cell phone platforms.

Diglossia

Diglossia is the use of two different languages (or two forms of one language) by a single speech community. One form is usually distinguishable as a high form, which is taught in school, used in formal situations, is associated with prestige, and has a written form. The low form, by contrast, is acquired rather than taught, is used in informal settings, is often considered to signal low status, and often lacks a written form. Individuals who speak both forms typically engage in code-switching, alternating between the two languages to fit the context.

Classic diglossia describes the situation in which a community speaks two forms of a single language. Extended diglossia occurs when the community alternates between two separate languages depending on context.

Accentedness

Accentedness refers to how a language learner's pronunciation differs from that of a native speaker. **Accentedness** is a major factor in determining both the comprehensibility of speech, or how difficult it is to understand; and the intelligibility of speech, or whether it is, in fact, understood.

These definitions have led scholars to suggest that, given limited instructional time, English language teachers should prioritize improving the elements of accentedness that have the most effect on **comprehensibility and intelligibility**—in other words, not all irregular pronunciations are equal. Linguists have developed the concept of functional load to measure how important the proper pronunciation of a phoneme is for the production of intelligible speech. One pragmatic conclusion is that teachers should focus on correcting pronunciation errors that carry high functional loads and spend less or no time correcting those with low loads. Some educators argue that a student's accentedness should only be of concern if it affects intelligibility. Comprehensibility, while desirable, is not a priority when instruction time is limited.

Safe and Collaborative Learning Environment

Safe and Collaborative Environments

Teachers have an obligation to ensure that the learning environment is a safe place for a student to learn, as well as for parents to get involved in. Learning environments need to be physically safe, including meeting the physical needs of a student, such as having food, water, and a restroom), emotionally and socially safe, and safe to think and express ideas. Without having a safe learning environment, students may exhibit a variety of behaviors such as skipping class, not participating, lashing out at the teacher or other students, or just performing poorly because they are not able to focus. A safe environment is also one that allows for collaboration between students, other school staff members, and family members. Students should not have to experience enmity between a school culture and a home culture and should feel free to bring information from school to their parents. This may be particularly important in the ESL setting, as cultures and communication can place additional burdens on the relationship between home and school.

Respecting an ELL's Home Language

Learning a second language can be an intimidating experience in any circumstance, but it is even more daunting for students who are adapting to life in a new country or attempting to gain social acceptance from their peers. ELLs often feel stressed and are wary of making errors, which can impede the learning process. Teachers should create a positive environment that recognizes student competence in their native language. Teachers should also ensure that all languages are treated equally and that one native language doesn't have priority over another. This is particularly important during group work, when cliques of like-language students might exclude others. Teachers should enforce rules about when students are allowed to speak in their native language. Teachers can also organize activities that invite translation of home languages or presentations by students of elements of their home cultures. Finally, teachers should attempt to involve parents in their students' lessons to create continuities between home and classroom experiences.

Collaboration with Other Professionals

Safe and supportive ESL environments also means that teachers and staff members need to be on board with **collaborating** with other **professionals**. English language learners enjoy participating in extracurriculars just as much as native English speakers and should not be inhibited from participating in them. ELLs also frequently have need for **specialty classes or services** such as after-school tutoring, counseling, or other services. ESOL specialists may need to coordinate with content-area teachers to help develop supplementary or modified materials to help students make sufficient progress in class. If teachers are resistant to collaboration then the students will ultimately receive neglectful instruction on materials that they need more help with. If teachers encounter strive between staff members where it affects instructional quality, the school administration should be notified to help improve the culture and find a solution.

Chapter Quiz

Ready to see how well you retained what you just read? Scan the QR code to go directly to the chapter quiz interface for this study guide. If you're using a computer, simply visit the online resources page at **mometrix.com/resources719/csetenglandev** and click the Chapter Quizzes link.

Cultural Foundations

Nature and Influence of Culture

External and Internal Culture

Culture is an integrated pattern of knowledge, belief, and behavior, held by a particular human group, that is learned and transmitted through generations. The term is broad, but culture can be thought of as consisting of what people (a) do, (b) believe or know, and (c) make and use.

Another way to think about culture is to differentiate between external and internal culture. **External culture** (often called material culture) refers to the objects and physical space people use to express their shared culture. Elements of external culture include architecture, clothing, food, technology, the arts, and language. **Internal culture** (often called non-material culture) refers to the shared patterns of thought and social behavior that exist as collective beliefs and customs. Elements of internal culture include values, family structures, social roles, beliefs and expectations, and worldview. External cultural markers are easier to recognize, but with the exception of language, the elements of internal culture have a greater influence on how students learn.

Deep and Surface Culture

Culture can be loosely divided into deep and surface culture. **Surface culture** refers to cultural artifacts or tangible aspects of culture that can be seen and interacted with. Examples include food, clothing, art, religion, and even language. **Deep culture** refers to elements of culture that are more subjective and harder to see, including beliefs, thought processes, and core values. An example of this might be how a specific culture internally perceives family or elders. Outsiders to a culture may be able to easily see elements of surface culture, or even emulate them, but elements of deep culture are usually invisible and hard to interact with.

The Sapir-Whorf Hypothesis

The Sapir-Whorf hypothesis, which combines the work of the linguistic anthropologists Edward Sapir (1884–1939) and Benjamin Whorf (1897–1941), is the assertion that **language** has a strong, constraining influence on **thought**. Thus, they argued that speakers of different languages have different **worldviews**. In other words, language doesn't only reflect reality, but influences our perception of reality.

For example, research shows that a person is *more likely* to understand an idea or concept that they can name in their language with a single word, but that the lack of a word does not *prevent* conceptualization of an idea. The *strong form* of the Sapir-Whorf hypothesis is now commonly referred to as **linguistic determinism**, meaning that a person's language determines or sets hard limits a person's ability to think about concepts. Modern linguists largely reject linguistic determinism as the conceptualization of an idea is still possible through adoption of new terms, loan words, or through circumlocution. Language is also recognized as being in a constant state of adaptation to keep up with culture and technology, such as the adoption of new terms and the retirement of outdated phrases.

The Sapir-Whorf hypothesis is an example of a theory that posits that thought is dependent on language. The common-sense view holds the opposite: people have thoughts and put them into words when they wish to communicate. The consensus view is that both mental processes occur.

HOFSTEDE'S CULTURAL DIMENSIONS THEORY

Geert Hofstede's cultural dimensions theory is a useful tool for understanding cultural differences. In the late 1960s and early 1970s, Hofstede conducted a multinational survey of national values, and concluded that key differences could be explained along six dimensions.

- **Individualism versus collectivism** is whether people think primarily in terms of "I" or "we."
- **Uncertainty avoidance index** is the degree to which people are uncomfortable with uncertainty and ambiguity.
- **Power distance index** is the extent to which people expect hierarchy versus equality.
- **Long-term versus short-term orientation** includes a measure of whether people are pragmatic toward change or prefer to preserve cultural values.
- **Indulgence versus restraint** refers to whether a culture promotes leisure and self-gratification.
- **Masculinity versus femininity**, in Hofstede's theory, refers to masculinity as a preference for assertive behavior, achievement, and material success and to femininity as a preference for modesty, cooperation, and caring for others.

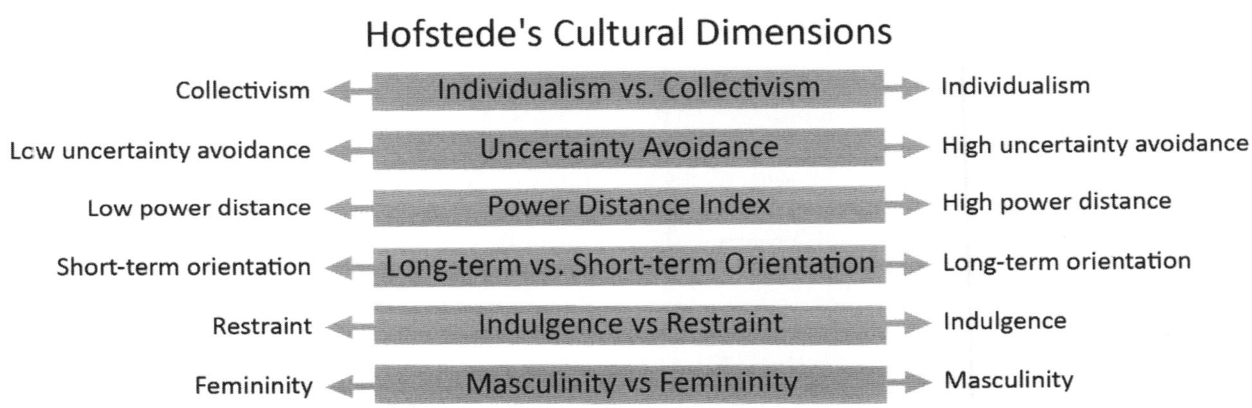

A teacher might use Hofstede's dimension of power distance index, for example, to understand a student's degree of comfort or formality in interacting with his or her teacher. Students with a sharp sense of hierarchy might be unlikely to speak to the teacher unless spoken to or offer an opinion different than the teacher's.

INDIVIDUALIST VS. COLLECTIVIST CULTURES

The distinction between individualist and collectivist cultures is the element of Geert Hofstede's cultural dimensions theory that has had the most influence on educational psychology. **Individualistic cultures** are those that value individual achievement and development above those of group success or cohesion. Individualistic cultures (like mainstream American culture) value freedom and individual initiative and tend to ascribe success and failure to individual traits such as motivation or intelligence. Individualist cultures encourage students to stand out from the group, and students who do not are often viewed as mediocre and underachieving. **Collectivist cultures**, on the other hand, value group harmony and social acceptance, and may see standing out as a cause for concern or stress. In a collectivist culture, education is less the means to individual achievement and fulfillment and instead a means to social acceptance and fulfilling an expected role.

Teachers need to be aware of these differences in order to understand **student motivation** and also to understand the impact of classroom activities that emphasize **individual performance** or bestow **individual praise**. It may be particularly hard for teachers raised in an individualistic culture to understand that, for some students, public individual praise may be distinctly unwanted and a source of shame.

SPEECH ACT

A speech act is an utterance aimed at achieving something (rather than describing something), such as requesting, promising, complaining, or apologizing. The form **speech acts** take in a given language and culture are often highly standardized and routinized. For example, a native English speaker will recognize the question "Do you have a dollar?" as a request, but it may appear as a simple and out-of-context question to a non-native speaker.

Speech acts perform a pragmatic function that cannot be understood by means of literal semantic analysis. The existence of language features such as speech acts makes it imperative that a language learner also develops **cultural competence** in order to become a full and effective member of the L2 culture.

DIFFERENTIATING BETWEEN AUTHORIZED AND UNAUTHORIZED IMMIGRANTS

Contrary to popular opinion, a majority of school-age ELLs were born in the United States. Approximately 75% have **legal status**. Of the 25% who do not, the majority entered the United States legally, usually with a nonimmigrant or visitor visa, and then failed to leave.

The centerpiece of US immigration policy is **family reunification**. The majority of immigrants qualify to come to the US by virtue of having a close family member who is a US citizen or permanent resident. **Refugees** from war, discrimination, or natural disasters are another significant class of immigrants. Fewer immigrants qualify by virtue of having high job skills in short supply or by investing money in job-creating businesses in the US. Finally, the United States administers a **diversity lottery program** through which a limited number of high school-educated people from underrepresented countries qualify to immigrate each year.

Since the 1982 Supreme Court case *Plyler v. Doe*, school districts cannot exclude students on the basis of **immigration status**. However, unauthorized immigrants are often afraid to enroll their students in school, or to engage with school officials, out of fear of being reported to immigration authorities.

PUSH AND PULL FACTORS

Everett Lee coined the terms "push factors" and "pull factors" in a 1962 book in order to classify people's motives for **migrating** (moving from one area to another) or **immigrating** (migrating from one country to another). **Push factors** are the unattractive features of a home country that compel people to leave. The most common push factors are a lack of economic opportunities, war, natural disaster, and repression or discrimination. **Pull factors** are attractive features of the destination country. The most common pull factors are economic opportunity, the prospect of reuniting with family members, and social and political freedom.

SECONDARY MIGRATION AND TRANSNATIONAL MIGRATION

Secondary migration is the entry of people into the US from a location other than their country of birth. There are two primary types of **secondary migrants** to the US: refugees who flee their home countries to neighboring countries and from there arrange legal entry into the US, and individuals who first immigrate to countries with more lenient immigration policies, such as Canada, and then stage economic or family-based immigration to the US. The term is also used to describe the movement of refugees within the US from their original point of resettlement to locations they find more attractive. ELLs who experience secondary migration are more likely to have experienced interrupted or uneven schooling, including potential instruction in a non-English foreign language.

The term "**transnational migration**" refers to the practice of immigrants to the US maintaining close ties to their country of origin. Common expressions of these ties include regular home visits (students may spend their summers in their countries of origin), sending money or remittances to family members abroad, or making plans to return to the home country for retirement or after achieving citizenship. Transnational migration is often seen as a challenge to assimilation, but ESOL teachers can cultivate students' ongoing ties to their home countries as an educational resource.

Generation 1.5

The term "generation 1.5" refers to individuals who immigrated to the United States in their late childhood or early teen years, and thus are neither first generation (adult immigrants) nor second generation (born in the US). They are likely to have substantial remaining ties to their home countries and, unlike younger siblings born in the US, may lack citizenship and thus be vulnerable to deportation. As late arrivals to the US school system, they may resist being labeled ELLs and thus avoid integration into standard ELL programs. While many will have a basic proficiency in social English, they may lag in the acquisition of **academic language**—a deficiency they might be unwilling to address if they are out of step with their peers who immigrated earlier in life or were born in the US. At the same time, as relatively mature ELLs, they are likely to have a very good grasp of the **social and pragmatic** aspects of communication, and to infer meaning readily from context.

Acculturation, Assimilation, Accommodation, and Biculturalism

In the context of cultural contact, **acculturation** is the adaptation of a person or group to another culture, often in the context of immigration. The terms "**assimilation**" and "**accommodation**" refer to how complete that adaptation is: assimilation occurs when the individual adapts fully to the new culture and largely abandons the cultural markers of his or her first culture; whereas accommodation occurs when an individual accepts certain elements of the new culture, especially those necessary for public life in school or at work, but retains many elements of the first culture, particularly when at home and with family. **Biculturalism** occurs when a person functions fully and simultaneously in both cultures, balancing each without a drive to either assimilate or exclude the new culture.

Accommodation and assimilation are defined and used differently in discussions of language development, derived largely from the work of Jean Piaget.

Cultural Universals, Cultural Generalities, and Cultural Particulars

Cultural universals are aspects of culture that are shared by all human societies. The comparative ethnologist George Murdock created a list of more than 70 **cultural universals** in 1945—for example, fire-making, incest taboos, and inheritance rules. Cultural generalities are cultural features that occur in many cultures, but not all. Nuclear families are an example. Cultural particulars are cultural traits that are unique to a single culture - specific recipes or celebrations are examples. Anthropologists distinguish between **cultural traits** that arise independently from those that are spread through contact, or **cultural diffusion**. Cultural traits are generally viewed as *adaptive*—as furthering the survival and success of the social group—but *nonadaptive* traits exist as well, including many modes of production that are harmful to the environment in the medium or long-term. The forces of globalization have rapidly increased the rate of cultural diffusion and, in many instances, the extinction of narrowly held cultural particulars.

CULTURE SHOCK

The term "culture shock" refers to the feelings of confusion or alienation a person may experience when first living, studying, or working in a new culture. In broad terms, a person experiences **culture shock** when he or she is taken out of a cultural context that provided them with reinforcement and a sense of control and is inserted into another that they don't fully understand or feel competent in.

Adler's model proposes that individuals progress through various stages of culture shock. In the first, which Adler calls *contact*, but is often referred to as the honeymoon stage, the individual feels excitement and tends to focus on similarities between the home and new cultures. In stage two, *disintegration*, the individual focuses on differences and may feel alienated. In stage three, *reintegration*, the individual rejects the new culture. As the individual becomes more competent in the new culture, he or she will experience *autonomy*, the fourth stage, and relax the previous defensiveness. In the final stage, *independence*, the individual feels comfortable in the new setting and is able to offer generalizations and perspectives on the process of cultural adaptation.

ADJUSTMENT OF NEWCOMERS

Individuals adapt to a new culture in different ways, at different rates, and to differing degrees. Research suggests that the most important factor leading to rapid and large-scale adjustment is **language proficiency**. A second factor is **personality type**—outgoing individuals who are comfortable interacting with others tend to adjust quickly. **Cultural intelligence** also plays a role: if an individual is conscious of cultural differences (perhaps due to prior travel), he or she is more likely to recognize differences for what they are and develop appropriate strategies in response. Individuals with strong **social and family support networks** tend to adjust better and more rapidly, though if the home-culture network is dominant, it may lead to an incomplete adjustment. An individual's **emotional intelligence** also plays a role—knowing the cause of one's emotions and how to regulate emotional responses is important. Finally, the **response of the host community**—in the classroom or the larger community—is important: whether diversity is tolerated or even championed will make a difference to the adjustment process.

CULTURAL CONGRUENCE

In the educational context, **cultural congruence** exists when classroom experiences and instruction reinforce, or are at least consistent with, student home cultures. A culturally congruent classroom acts as a bridge between a student's first and learned cultures. Proponents argue that students learn best in **culturally congruent classrooms**—in part by eliminating the perceived choice that students in minority cultures make between learning and maintaining a loyalty to their own cultural traditions. In order to promote cultural congruence, teachers can incorporate content from student cultures or adapt their teaching techniques to reflect student learning preferences or customary patterns of interaction.

CULTURAL PLURALISM

Cultural pluralism occurs when several distinct cultural groups and traditions coexist in a single society without an impetus toward assimilation to the majority culture. A commitment to **cultural pluralism** implies that cultural and linguistic differences are not a problem to be overcome, but rather a resource to be utilized in the education process. Historically, and in line with broader societal views, teachers tended to minimize cultural differences and work toward rapid assimilation of immigrants, in part by fostering a new and single-group identity. While rapid assimilation still exists as the perceived ideal in the minds of many Americans—and for many immigrants as well—many curriculums now emphasize the celebration of cultural differences and the promotion of bilingualism as a language goal.

PREJUDICE, STEREOTYPING, AND ETHNOCENTRISM

Prejudice is a negative opinion formed about an individual or group without basis or sufficient knowledge. **Ethnocentrism** is the belief that one's own culture is superior to others. It is contrasted with cultural relativism—the recognition that every culture has value and may serve needs and interests different from those of one's own culture. To **stereotype** is to hold a simplified and overgeneralized view of a group, often with a critical or prejudiced view.

Teachers should find non-confrontational ways to address and discuss expressions of **cultural bias** when they occur. Teachers should emphasize the difference between recognizing legitimate cultural differences and stereotyping. Teachers often shy away from discussions of cultural bias in multicultural classrooms out of fear of offending students or initiating disagreements. Training, such as that offered by the National Association for Multicultural Education, can help teachers overcome these fears and facilitate useful discussions.

IMPLICIT BIAS

Implicit bias occurs when unconscious stereotypes or opinions influence our behavior, often in direct contradiction to our consciously held beliefs. Psychological research demonstrates that we all hold **implicit biases**. The vast majority of human cognitive and emotional processing occurs unconsciously, and the mind's tendency to generalize and simplify is a necessary cognitive adaptation to a complex world. Thus, biases should not be seen as a personal fault.

Teachers can become aware of their implicit biases through **diagnostic tools** such as the implicit association test. In order to overcome these biases, teachers should be self-reflective, reviewing their actions and interventions at the end of the day to assess their evenness. Research shows that decisions made hurriedly, under stress, or with incomplete information are more likely to be biased—thus, when possible, teachers should slow their reactive decision-making. The best way to overcome bias is to get to know students as individuals rather than simply as members of a group. Implicit biases are heuristic devices our minds employ in the absence of information.

SHAPING TEACHER PERCEPTIONS OF STUDENTS

Fundamental attribution error is the tendency to attribute the negative behavior of others to a personality flaw, while attributing one's own negative behavior (or the behavior of people like ourselves) to situational, environmental factors. **Confirmation bias** is the tendency to make quick first impressions about a person or situation, overvalue subsequent information that confirms that judgment, and undervalue subsequent information that discounts it. **In-group bias** is the tendency to attribute positive motivations and personality characteristics to people like ourselves and not to people we perceive as different.

Teachers can minimize the effect of these implicit biases by avoiding early judgments about student abilities or motivation, by charitably seeking situational explanations for poor performance or behavior, and by getting to know students and their life circumstances.

Diversity within the ELL Population

DIVERSITY WITHIN THE ELL POPULATION

Even among the population of English language learners, there is a great diversity. ELLs can be people with different cultural and ethnic backgrounds, have different educational backgrounds, or even have different experiences with encountering and learning English. The individual factors involved for each student paint a picture of what types of unique support a student might need and what types of rich experiences they can bring to a diverse classroom.

- **Newcomers** - students who have only recently begun to learn English and are learning from scratch.
- **Long-Term English Language Learners** – students who have been learning English for an extended period of time, but who still do not have mastery or sufficient fluency in the language to discontinue ESOL services.
- **Refugees** – people who have been forced to flee from their homes due to adverse circumstances such as natural disasters and war.
- **Immigrants** – people who have permanently moved to a new country. Immigrants may or may not be in the country with documentation or legal status.
- **Migrants** – people who frequently move from place to place, usually experiencing disruption from frequent life changes.
- **English Language Learners with Disabilities** – students who are ELLs who also have a disability. These students may require some combination of special education services in addition to language supports.
- **Students with Interrupted Formal Education (SIFE)** – students who have had their formal education interrupted. These students may have gaps in understanding or may have strong social skills, but weak academic skills, especially in reading and writing.
- **Students with Limited Formal Education** – students who have not spent much time in an academic setting. These students commonly struggle to understand academic expectations and often need remediation in areas such as reading and writing.
- **English Language Learners with Trauma** – students who have trauma may have experienced war, abuse, or other forms of loss and may have problems that distract or motivate them differently than other students. Students with trauma frequently have physical, emotional, and behavioral issues.

Supporting a Class with Students from Different Language Backgrounds

Students in a single class or school may come from a variety of language backgrounds. For instance, a single class could have students from Mexico, Japan, and Russia, representing three completely unrelated languages with completely different linguistic needs. While challenging, a teacher should try to understand the characteristics of the students' languages that differ from English to anticipate areas that a student is likely to struggle in. Languages may have different syntax, use different preposition combinations, and may be missing whole features that other languages use. Features of language may either facilitate or hinder learning another language, often in predictable ways.

Here are a few examples of how some features compare across languages:

Topic	English	Comparative Language
Gendered vs Ungendered Articles	English uses neutral articles: a, an, and the	**Spanish** uses gendered articles that must agree with the noun: El, la, los, and las
Gendered vs Ungendered Articles	English uses neutral articles: a, an, and the	**German** uses both gendered and articles that must be memorized.

Orthography	English uses the Latin script and is semi-phonetic, but uses multiple sounds per letter.	**Korean** has its own script that has a roughly one-to-one letter-sound correspondence. Each unit of letters makes up a syllable.
Plural Marker	English indicates whether a noun is singular or plural by adding -s or -es to the end of a word.	**Chinese** (Mandarin) does not have a singular or plural marker at all.

Shared Teacher Responsibility for Teaching and Supporting English Language Learners

Shared Responsibility Among All Staff and Faculty

As part of a multi-cultural school, all educators on a campus share the responsibility of caring for, producing, and supporting English language learners. Some teachers may have classes with ELLs only, but these are by-far the minority. Most teachers will encounter ELLs at some point in their career, whether it be a student who is highly proficient at English or one who is just starting to learn the language. Administrators and support staff likewise have a duty to be aware of students with particular needs to help prevent abuse or exploitation and to promote communication among those who need assistance. Most commonly, this shared responsibility is led by a designated ESOL leader who helps other teachers plan instruction that is going to support the student inside the classroom. This may mean providing professional development and insight, as well as help modifying or supplementing the content with extra vocabulary instruction or visual aids to make content more accessible.

Maintaining High Expectations

Educators have long recognized that **teacher expectations** are one of the key factors that contribute to the academic achievement gap that exists between minority and low-income groups on the one hand, and white and privileged students on the other. In a broad sense, students tend to do as well as teachers expect them to. Research shows that teachers are often unaware that they exhibit these biases—making it critical that teachers of diverse students consciously model **high expectations**. ESOL teachers should ensure that they view and treat student backgrounds as an asset rather than an obstacle, that they maintain a clear distinction between student language proficiency and cognitive ability, and that they recognize that student progress may start slowly but accelerate once the student achieves a threshold level of proficiency and acculturation.

School Policies for Identifying and Supporting English Language Learners

Schools have a responsibility for providing an appropriate education for all students, including providing any services necessary to adequately support students who need accommodations to access the material. To that end, schools are required to gather enough information to identify ELLs who need services. The identification process can include self-reporting from families, home language surveys, or language proficiency assessments to determine a student's level of need. Schools use the results of these assessments to place students appropriately.

Whereas students may receive more targeted instruction from an ESL-specific classroom, students have a right to be in the **least restrictive environment** (LRE). Schools have a duty to provide as much help to students as possible in a general education classroom and not pull them away from the general population of students. While providing students with the appropriate level of intervention, the school must also continue to assess the student's proficiency to ensure their needs do not increase over time. The desired effect is that students may eventually be able to remove all language supports and perform well independently. Even if a student eventually is tapered off of supports, the school still has an obligation to periodically check in and ensure the student isn't experiencing problems from premature integration.

Different Cultural Approaches to Teaching

Approaches to Teaching Across Cultures

Different cultures may tendencies toward specific teaching styles. Cultures are often considered to be more or less individualistic or collectivistic, meaning they may place different emphases on individual or group preferences. Similarly, they may have higher or lower views of institutions, authority figures, and peers. Some of the spectra that are considered include:

Inductive vs. Deductive Teaching and Reasoning

Inductive reasoning refers to working from specific examples up to general principals. It may also be called bottom-up thinking. A teacher using inductive reasoning to provide instruction might give examples of concepts first and expect students to infer conclusions. For instance, a teacher might ask a student to write out characteristics of a variety of birds and infer conclusions about identifying a bird.

Deductive reasoning refers to working from a premise which is then tested against various examples. This method is often called top-down thinking. A teacher using deductive reasoning might provide the premise that all birds have feathers. The students then might have to deduce whether or not an animal is a bird by testing the premise.

English language learners may be more or less receptive to one of these approaches to reasoning and both may be employed in teaching new linguistic concepts.

Cooperation vs. Competition

Students from different backgrounds may view working with other students in different ways. Some cultures and students may view education as highly competitive and individualistic, preferring to be the best in school and not be willing to help other students improve in their own academics. Likewise, other students may be very interested in working with others to have a general culture of collaboration and learning. This can vary between cultures and may be particularly tied to family dynamics. At the same time, this may change over time during a student's academic career. As they approach more competitive academics, such as high school and college, students may start to perceive academics in a more competitive light and be less willing to cooperate with other students.

Competitive students face some vulnerability, especially as ELLs. Students who are highly competitive are often at risk of having painful motivational consequences if they do not do particularly well in a class. As a teacher, it is important to respect a student's motivations, but should still help students to strive a healthy balance between academic cooperation and competition.

Multicultural School Environments

Promoting Multicultural Perspectives

Teachers can promote **multicultural awareness** in the classroom in many ways. One is by explicitly teaching students about prejudice, stereotypes, and ethnocentrism. A second is to establish and enforce clear classroom policies regarding tolerance and cultural sensitivity. Building on this, teachers might ask students to reflect on their own behavior and identify an occasion when they might have acted based on an unwarranted stereotype.

Teachers can also structure the curriculum around **multicultural themes or events**, drawing examples and information from the students' home cultures. They can also adopt **multicultural resources** for use in the classroom, such as books, films, or works of art. Teachers might encourage students to consider minority viewpoints when discussing topics in history or current events. And finally, teachers should encourage students to draw connections between classroom lessons and their experiences in, and knowledge of, their home countries.

James Banks

In a 1989 article, the educator James Banks identified four different **levels of commitment** that schools take toward multicultural education. At the first level, the *contributions approach*, schools simply add a few references to minority or female contributions to the existing curriculum. This is often called, derisively, the holidays and heroes approach to multiculturalism. Banks calls the second level of engagement the *additive approach*. At this level, teachers incorporate numerous multicultural themes and concepts into the curriculum, but do so in a superficial way, teaching the issues from a traditional perspective—i.e., from the perspective of the dominant majority. Schools using the third level, the *transformative approach*, incorporate first-person minority perspectives on key issues and use teaching methods to investigate key issues from those points of view. Banks calls the fourth approach *decision-making or social action*. Schools that adopt this model encourage students to use what they learn about societal inequities to become agents of social change.

Review Video: Multiculturalism/Celebrating All Cultures
Visit mometrix.com/academy and enter code: 708545

Multicultural Education and Paolo Freire

The term "multicultural education" generally refers to the practice of adapting the curriculum and classroom environment to reflect or incorporate the viewpoints of multiple, minority, or non-dominant student groups. **Critical pedagogy** is a type of social action that calls upon teachers in multicultural classrooms to be agents of change in addressing societal and institutional inequalities. In this view, teachers should strive not for equality, or treating everyone the same or being color blind; but instead strive for equity, an outcome that can only be achieved by providing additional help to students disadvantaged by multiple factors outside of the classroom.

Paolo Friere, an educator best-known for his work *The Pedagogy of the Oppressed*, focused on the potential of education to **transform**: education, and in particular literacy, is an instrument of power, and traditionally has served as a means (or one of them) of disadvantaging the poor. Teachers must not only work to empower disadvantaged minorities, but also help these students develop a critical approach to understanding their own treatment by society.

Review Video: Equality vs Equity
Visit mometrix.com/academy and enter code: 685648

Linguistic Imperialism

The term "linguistic imperialism," popularized in a 1992 book by Michael Phillipson, refers to the spread and domination of one language over others, often in association with acts of power or violence. The classic example of **linguistic imperialism** is the spread of European languages in association with colonial rule, but proponents of the concept argue that it is still ongoing, with the adoption of English increasingly necessary to function in a global economy or to understand a reality shaped by an English-dominated media and Internet. In its radical form, proponents use a biological analogy to argue that the spread of English causes the extinction of local languages. Others point out that the widespread use of English does cause resentments at times, and spurs movements to revitalize waning languages. The concept might be most useful, however, as a reminder of the extent to which learning a second language—often, but not always, English—is necessary for individuals seeking to participate in a globalized world, even if only via the Internet.

Deterring and Addressing Cultural Conflict

Teachers can best deter cultural conflict in the classroom by openly discussing and celebrating cultural differences. Teachers should also ensure that students from different cultures interact frequently in group settings—first with explicit roles and clearly-defined procedural rules, and then, once students are comfortable with one another, with fewer teacher supports. When misunderstandings occur, teachers might lead open discussions (at a level of generality that won't call attention to a specific conflict) that reveal different cultural interpretations and expectations of common events. A teacher's ability to **mediate cross-cultural conflicts** will depend in part on how well they understand the competing cultures, and it may be necessary and wise to talk to each party to the conflict separately in order to fully understand their interpretation of the conflict. Assuming that two students from different cultures are acting in good faith, a mediated solution might take some version of the form "s/he didn't intend it the way you perceived it."

Family Structures of English Language Learners

English language learners can come from a variety of family backgrounds. These backgrounds shape how a student thinks and acts and plays a huge role in their childhood development and attitudes. Teachers should be aware of the variety of family structures represented in his or her classroom and recognize strengths and setbacks that can come along with each.

- **Nuclear or traditional family** – Consisting of two parents and their children living in a single household.
- **Extended family** – Consists of grandparents, aunts, uncles, and cousins who are involved in the family dynamics.
- **Single-parent family** – Consists of one parent raising a child or children, often due to adverse circumstances such as divorce, separation, or death.
- **Blended or step family** – Consists of a family with a parent who has remarried, providing a child with a step-parent and potentially with new half siblings or step-siblings added to the dynamic.
- **Adoptive family** – Consists of a family with one or more adopted children. These can commonly have language dynamics if the adopted child has a different language than the adoptive parents.
- **Separated family** – Consists of a family structure in which a member is separated either permanently or temporarily, often for work or migration reasons. One good example of this is a family in which the father is in active duty in the military.

- **Communal family** – Consists of a family structure made up of chosen community members, friends, church members, and mentors who stand in when a person has no biological family to connect to. This is especially common when a person relocates to a new location and essentially assembles a family-like structure from his or her social circumstances.
- **Transnational families** – Consist of families that are split into two or more countries, often coming with generational and linguistic divides.

Role of Families in Student Learning and Development

Family Involvement and Student Success

Decades of research has demonstrated the strong correlation between **family involvement** and **student success**. ELLs are disproportionately at risk for academic failure and, thus, in need of support. Therefore, securing ELL parental involvement is particularly important and difficult to achieve, given language differences and cultural differences that may discourage parents from actively involving themselves in their children's education.

In order to overcome these obstacles, teachers should get to know each student's **cultural background** and **family circumstances** relevant to building a relationship between home and school. Teachers should introduce themselves to parents and guardians and invite them to group meetings and one-on-one conferences. Teachers should establish multiple means of communication (email, phone calls, office hours) and, where feasible, translate messages into frequent L1s. Parents should be encouraged to volunteer in the classroom or chaperone field trips. Teachers should establish certain periods when parents can visit and observe the classroom. ESOL teachers with relatively homogenous student populations might sponsor information sessions during which translators are available, either to discuss concerns specific to the ESOL classroom or to provide general school-related advice and information to interested parents.

Overcoming Parental Communication Challenges

While the **parents and guardians** of students are one of the most important audiences to target with school outreach and communication strategies, they are also one of the most difficult to reach because of multiple factors. Language barriers are the most obvious, but ELL parents and guardians may also come from cultures that discourage parental involvement in schooling. ELL families are also disproportionately low-income, and parents may work long hours or multiple jobs, preventing them from attending scheduled school events.

ESOL teachers should develop proactive and multipronged **outreach strategies** to overcome these obstacles. Teachers should distribute information through multiple channels, such as emails, blogs, and newsletters sent home with students. Teachers should strive to make their students' daily activities and responsibilities visible to parents in some way.

Teachers should signal their availability and strive to be approachable. They might perform home visits if allowed. Teachers should schedule regular (monthly) meetings as well as repeatedly invite parents to attend one-on-one conferences. Teachers may consider communicating with parents through student homework folders. In all of these engagements, teachers should provide translations and interpretations when possible and strive to use simple, clear language.

Chapter Quiz

Ready to see how well you retained what you just read? Scan the QR code to go directly to the chapter quiz interface for this study guide. If you're using a computer, simply visit the online resources page at **mometrix.com/resources719/csetenglandev** and click the Chapter Quizzes link.

Foundations of English Learner Education

History and Law Surrounding English Language Programs

Bilingual Education Before the 1960s

Scholars customarily speak of the **American approach to bilingual education** as one of neglectful tolerance from independence until approximately 1960. While the federal government provided no educational support to non-English speakers, individual schools with high immigrant populations often did on an *ad hoc* basis. In most schools, however, **English language learners** were given no instructional support and were expected to assimilate rapidly. While ELLs dropped out of school at higher rates than native English speakers, few attempts were made to determine why or offer remedies.

Several factors turned American opinion against bilingual education, beginning in the 1880s when an influx of non-English speaking immigrants raised worries that America might lose its identity—of which English was an important component. These concerns were exacerbated by the American experience in the two World Wars and the insecurities caused by the Great Depression. Restrictions were placed on immigration during this period, an English language requirement was added to the naturalization process, and bilingual education programs were scaled back in districts where they had previously existed.

Bilingual Approach and ESOL Approach

Bilingual instructional programs begin instruction primarily or entirely in the student's **native language** and then transition to greater use of **English** over time. Most bilingual programs phase out classroom use of the native language over time, but some continue instruction in both languages, targeting full biliteracy as a goal.

ESOL instructional programs, in contrast, provide **English-only** classroom instruction, with possible occasional use of a student's L1 in support. ESOL programs include those that focus solely on developing English proficiency and those that focus on teaching ELLs academic content in ways that reinforce English language learning.

Research points to many benefits of bilingual instruction—perhaps most clearly, a student's literacy skills in L1 facilitate literacy in L2. However, a bilingual approach is often not feasible, as it requires a fairly homogenous L1 population (in the United States, this leads overwhelmingly to Spanish-English bilingual programs), a sufficient pool of bilingual teachers, and a legal framework that allows for non-English instruction.

Transitional Bilingual Education (TBE)

Transitional bilingual education (TBE) programs are one of the three main bilingual **language instruction educational programs (LIEP)** in use in the United States. Students typically enter a TBE program as soon as they start school and initially receive all or most of their instruction in L1. The goal of a TBE is an early **transition to the mainstream curriculum**, and this typically happens after 2–3 years (another name for a TBE is an *early-exit program*). TBE programs do not target L1 proficiency as a goal, and seldom explicitly teach L1 literacy. Instead, L1 is used as a transition to L2. Students in TBE programs often experience difficulty transitioning to the mainstream curriculum, requiring additional support during their first years after exiting the TBE.

Developmental Bilingual Education (DBE)

Developmental bilingual education (DBE) programs are one of the three main bilingual **language instruction educational programs (LIEP)** in use in the United States. Like transitional bilingual education (TBE) programs, DBE programs (also called *maintenance* and *late-exit programs*) begin with instruction in L1 as soon as students enter school, and gradually transition to instruction in English. Unlike in TBE programs, however, students never transition fully to English—DBE programs aim to develop **biliteracy** and to maintain a student's proficiency in L1 throughout the program—which typically lasts through 6th or perhaps 8th grade. Students in a typical DBE program might begin with 90% of their instruction in L1, and in their last year receive a 50/50 L1-L2 mix. DBE programs often evolve as an option in an already-established TBE program. DBE programs differ in how students learn in the two languages—L1 and L2 might be used in alternate periods, on alternate days, in alternate semesters, or to teach different subjects.

Dual Immersion

Dual immersion (**DI**) or **two-way immersion (TWI)** programs are one of the three main bilingual **language instruction educational programs (LIEP)** in use in the United States. The defining feature of DI programs is that all students (both ELLs and English speakers) are taught in both languages, with the goal of **full bilingualism** for the entire school population. Some DI programs balance the two instructional languages equally, beginning with the earliest grades, but it is more common for DI students to begin with a higher proportion (80/20 or 90/10) of instruction in the non-English language, and transition gradually to equality. Even a 50/50 instructional balance, however, doesn't lead to equal language proficiency—research has demonstrated that native English speakers do not obtain the same level of L2 proficiency as non-native speakers obtain in English. This difference can be attributed both to motivation (learning English is more of a necessity than is learning a foreign language) and to the fact that the surrounding world provides far more opportunities to practice English than a foreign language. In addition to the language benefit, DI programs are credited with promoting biculturalism and tolerance.

Newcomer Programs

Newcomer programs are a type of **language instruction educational program (LIEP)** developed specifically for immigrants who enter the United States between grades 6 and 12 and have experienced either **interrupted schooling or no schooling** in their home countries. These students often lack the basic literacy skills necessary to function in standard ESL classes, and almost invariably lack the academic English skills necessary to join their peers in content classrooms. School districts often create specific programs for these students, often off-site (thus the frequent term "newcomer centers"). A typical newcomer program provides separate, all-day instruction for a year, and may include after-school programs to help students and their families acculturate.

Heritage Language Programs

A heritage language is a language spoken in a student's home, or by his or her ancestors, which the student has a strong desire to learn or retain. In the United States, the term is used most often to refer to Native American languages, though not exclusively so: the term may refer to the home language of recent immigrants as well. The teaching of **heritage languages** became a public issue when Arizona passed **Proposition 203** in 2000, limiting ESOL instruction to full immersion to last no longer than a year. The proposition was seen as threatening Native American language programs in schools on or near reservations. While Arizona addressed the issue in part by issuing waivers allowing for dual-language instruction, many heritage language communities have resorted to after-school and weekend instructional programs. Many colleges offer heritage language programs, including in Spanish for individuals whose Spanish proficiency may have eroded after transitioning in school to an English-only curriculum.

Structured English Immersion (SEI)

Structured English immersion (SEI) is an ESOL instruction model designed to transition ELLs to mainstream classrooms quickly (usually after one year) by emphasizing **English-language instruction** and deferring **academic content instruction** until students transition to mainstream classrooms. Students in SEI classrooms are typically grouped by proficiency. SEI teachers do not simply teach *in* English but teach the *rules and forms* of English—proponents argue that explicit teaching of grammar facilitates the eventual transition of ELLs from intermediate to full fluency. SEI was one of two language models prescribed by California's Proposition 227 in 1997 (since repealed) and is the language model required under Arizona's Proposition 203. Critics argue that one year is not enough time to achieve the proficiency to succeed in academic subjects; further, SEI's focus on explicitly teaching challenging grammatical forms at a relatively early stage of instruction is controversial.

Types of Support

As an alternative to either a bilingual program or an English-immersion program, many districts place English language learners in **mainstream classes** and then use pull-out or push-in methods to provide them with additional English-language assistance.

In a **pull-out model**, language specialists pull ELL students out of the classrooms for short, individual or group English language instruction. Lessons are often tailored to reinforce what the ELL is learning in the content classroom. Critics argue that ELLs pulled out of class may suffer social stigma; further, it is disruptive.

In the **push-in model**, the language specialist joins the mainstream classroom in one of several ways. The language specialist and the classroom teacher may co-teach, coordinating and dividing the curriculum. Alternately, they might divide the classroom into ELLs and native speakers during some portion of the day and teach simultaneous lessons at different degrees of English proficiency. More commonly, the language specialist can work with individuals or small groups in succession and serve as a ready resource for ELL students in need of assistance.

Civil Rights Act of 1965

Title VI of the Civil Rights Act of 1965 prohibits **discrimination** on the basis of race, color, or national origin in any program that receives funding from the federal government. In May of 1970, the Department of Education wrote a memo to school districts with high concentrations of Spanish-language students, warning them that a number of common educational practices denied these students their rights to an equal education, and thus constituted discriminatory policy in violation of the Civil Rights Act. Specifically, the memo stated that (a) when a lack of English ability excludes students from effective participation, districts must take steps to rectify the language deficiency; (b) districts must not misclassify ELL students as having special needs; and (c) ESOL programs must be designed to achieve proficiency rather than simply lead to academic dead ends.

The **May 25 Memorandum**, as it came to be known, helped define access to appropriate language education as a civil right, and it identified several broad areas in need of reform. However, as a cabinet-level memorandum, it did not have the status of law. The principles within it, however, were endorsed as law by the Supreme Court in the 1971 case *Lau v. Nichols*.

Bilingual Education Act of 1968

The Bilingual Education Act of 1968 is a descriptive name given to **Title VII of the Elementary and Secondary Education Act (ESEA)** originally passed in 1965. ESEA was a cornerstone of President Lyndon B. Johnson's War on Poverty, reflecting Johnson's view of the importance of education in overcoming poverty. ESEA redefined the federal government's role in education, providing for dramatic increases in federal funding, as well as standards for equal access, educational achievement, and accountability. ESEA has been periodically reauthorized ever since its enactment. The 2001 reauthorization is called the **No Child Left Behind Act (NCLB)**, and the 2015 reauthorization is termed the **Every Student Succeeds Act (ESSA)**.

The Bilingual Education Act provided federal funding for districts to develop bilingual programs but provided no guidelines on what those programs should look like. The Act did not require that schools adopt ESOL programs, but it encouraged and funded district-led innovations and did much to elevate ELL rights as a concern separate from that of racial discrimination.

Lau v. Nichols

The *Lau v. Nichols* suit was brought by Chinese students in San Francisco, who argued that the fact that their classes were taught in English rather than Chinese violated their rights under the Equal Protection Clause of the Fourteenth Amendment.

In its unanimous decision in favor of the plaintiff, the Supreme Court ruled that schools receiving federal funding must provide **English-language instruction** to students who lack English proficiency. The Court based its decision on the Civil Rights Act of 1965 (rather than the Fourteenth Amendment), finding that the lack of appropriate language education represented a failure to grant **equal access to educational opportunities**. The Court's decision meant that schools could no longer allow students to succeed or fail in an English-only curriculum but had to actively help students overcome language deficiencies.

The **Lau Remedies** are guidelines issued by the Department of Education to help districts develop language policies in accordance with *Lau v. Nichols*. The Remedies stipulate that districts should develop the means to identify and evaluate ELLs, provide them with appropriate instruction, and evaluate their readiness to exit the ESOL program.

No Child Left Behind (NCLB)

The No Child Left Behind Act (NCLB) was based on the premise that setting and holding schools and students accountable to high standards would promote academic excellence. The act mandated that all schools receiving Title 1 funding adopt **annual standardized tests**. Schools that failed to demonstrate adequate yearly progress on test results were required to create improvement plans and faced escalating penalties if they failed to improve.

The NCLB established, for the first time, **accountability and funding provisions for ELL programs** (under Title 3) separate from those allocated for the entire spectrum of socio-economically disadvantaged students (under Title 1). This separate attention raised the profile of ELL education issues. It also obliged states to monitor ELL academic performance more closely, and most developed uniform metrics for doing so. The NCLB required that states track three **annual measurable achievement objectives (AMAO)**—two that measured ELL English proficiency, and a third that measured ELL progress toward *content* standards. The third element proved problematic—few states managed to provide full accommodations for ESOL students taking content exams. A large percentage of schools serving ESOL populations failed to meet these standards and, they often argued, failed to receive the resources or other federal assistance necessary for improvement.

Every Student Succeeds Act (ESSA)

In the broadest terms, the Every Student Succeeds Act (ESSA) represented a devolution of authority from the federal government to the states. While ESSA retains the No Child Left Behind Act's (NCLB) basic framework of standardized testing and school accountability, ESSA grants states more discretion in how to **measure school success** (for example, states may include measures of progress in addition to measures of attainment) and how to address low-performing schools.

ESSA incorporates a measure of **ELL progress**—the rate at which students achieve English proficiency – into the overall Title 1 measure of school effectiveness, raising the potential that states and schools will make English-language education a stronger priority. (Critics worry that, by contrast, the relatively small population of ELLs will be lost, for funding purposes, in the larger Title 1 population.) ESSA also requires states to develop uniform **standards** for identifying, placing, and exiting students from ESOL programs (previously, districts and schools could develop separate standards). ESSA also allows the **content test results** of ESOL students in their first two years of schooling to be exempted from a school's reported results, reducing what were perceived to be unrealistic pressures under NCLB to realize early ELL success on academic content exams.

Castaneda v. Pickard

In 1978, Roy Castaneda, the father of two Mexican-American students, sued the school district of Raymondville, Texas, arguing that his children had unlawfully been placed in a classroom segregated by language ability, and further that the school district had failed to establish an adequate bilingual education program that would allow ELLs to re-enter the mainstream curriculum. Castaneda's case effectively challenged the courts to enforce *Lau v. Nichols*, which dictated that school districts take the necessary steps to allow ELL students to overcome their English language deficiencies.

In 1981, the Fifth US Court of Appeals issued what came to be called the **Castaneda Test** to assess whether district bilingual education programs were meeting the standards of the right to equal education concept in the Civil Rights Act of 1964 and the Equal Educational Opportunities Act of 1974. Specifically, bilingual programs (a) had to be based on sound theory and have a legitimate design, (b) had to be supported with appropriate resources and personnel, and (c) must be evaluated to determine if they are effective.

Plyler v. Doe

The Supreme Court ruled in *Plyler v. Doe* that children could not be denied education because of their **immigration status**. The case arose when the state of Texas passed a law that withheld funds to pay for the education of, and allowed districts to expel, students who lacked legal status. In 1982, the Supreme Court ruled that the Texas law violated the **Equal Protection Clause** of the Fourteenth Amendment. *Plyler v. Doe* only applies to K-12 education. Legal battles continue over the issues of whether college students without status can be denied in-state tuition benefits, and whether public schools can gather information about student legal status during the enrollment process for possible reporting to the immigration authorities.

Proposition 227 and Proposition 58

As the state with the largest number of English language learners, California's ESOL policies and innovations are important for teachers in any state to understand.

In 1998, California voters approved **Proposition 227**, which effectively **ended bilingual education programs** in public schools, requiring that ESOL students enroll in one-year English immersion programs and then transition to mainstream English content classrooms. Studies showed mixed results—while students achieved greater success on standardized tests following implementation, so did students who continued in bilingual programs, suggesting that other factors, such as teacher training or the accountability measures of No Child Left Behind, were driving the improvements.

In 2016, Californians passed **Proposition 58**, which repealed Proposition 227 and gave public school districts the right to decide the best way to teach ESOL students while retaining the responsibility to ensure that students achieve English proficiency. Given the apparent success of the Proposition 227 framework in raising student scores, its repeal is best seen as the result of a growing awareness of the value of **multilingualism** in an interconnected world.

LULAC v. State Board of Education

A **consent decree** is a mutually-binding agreement enforced by a court. In 1990, the **League of United Latin American Citizens (LULAC)** filed a suit claiming that Florida was failing to provide English language learners with equitable and comprehensible education under the existing framework of federal laws.

The case was settled in US District Court according to the terms of the consent decree. The consent decree—which covers issues such as identification and assessment, equal access to programming, teacher qualifications and training, monitoring, and outcome measures—now serves as the framework for Florida's ESOL programs. Within education circles, the agreement is simply known as the **Florida Consent Decree**.

Role of the ESOL Instructor to Support Other Staff Members

Supporting and Collaborating with Other Staff Members

Schools have variable setups for how they develop instruction for ELLs. Schools with larger ELL populations may have dedicated ESOL staff to help with coordination and modification of materials, whereas schools with less-developed ESOL programs may only have staff with supplemental ESOL training. Some schools may have integrated English instruction, while others may have sheltered English immersion (SEI) programs. In any of these cases, the ESOL staff should recognize that not all instructors have education or certifications in second language instruction and may need help modifying, supplementing, and scaffolding content. The ESOL instructor should make themselves known on a team and be both proactive and receptive to other team members to help look for areas that the school can be more prepared to help ELLs engage with content better.

Helping to Shape the School Culture

An ESOL professional may also be helpful in shaping the school culture to one that is multicultural, or supportive of students from a variety of backgrounds. In addition, it is easy for ethnocentric teachers or teachers who are unaware of the dynamics of second-language learning to have misconceptions about language and content learning ideas. The following are some concepts that the ESOL professional might try to promote to help develop the school culture.

- English language learners might speak less than other students, but that does not mean that they are not learning or actively engaged.

- English language learners should be encouraged to maintain their home languages and not try to just suddenly switch to English. The first language can also be helpful in facilitating crossover language learning.
- English language learners will not simply absorb a second language. Teachers need to provide explicit instruction to help facilitate language learning in all classrooms.
- English language learners have as much cognitive potential as native English students. Teachers need to learn to curb biases that might make them think that ELLs are less intelligent than other students. This will also help with reducing overrepresentation of ELLs in special education programs.
- English language learners can have strong social language skills, but still have weak academic skills.
- English language learners have parents that care and who should be brought into the loop and provided with resources that can help them communicate and participate.

Educational and Social Advocacy for ELLs

Changing Public Views of Bilingualism

Public debate on bilingualism in society and in schools can be simplified into two pools of thought: one worries that bilingualism **erodes national unity and identity**, and thus the growing numbers of non-native speakers in schools is a problem to be overcome; the other views bilingualism as a **resource to be cultivated**, arguing that a child's L1 helps him or her acquire English—and further, that globalization proves the importance of multilingualism. This debate is also often framed as one between the prioritization of *assimilation* versus *multiculturalism*.

The **Bilingual Education Act (BEA)** of 1968 (Title VII of the broader Elementary and Secondary Education Act, or ESEA) provided federal funding for bilingual education programs and recognized, at least implicitly, the value of students retaining their native languages and cultures. The **No Child Left Behind Act (NCLB)**, which replaced ESEA in 2002, struck all mention of bilingualism and implicitly repealed the BEA, renaming it the English Language Acquisition, Language Enforcement, and Academic Achievement Act. The NCLB's focus on standardized test results and short-term, transitional ESOL programs mirrored broader national trends promoting assimilation, including the adoption of Proposition 227 in California and Proposition 203 in Arizona. **ESSA**, while not explicitly promoting the benefits of bilingualism, grants greater policy latitude to the states—leading some to adopt bilingual education programs.

The English-Only Movement

The term "English-only movement" in a broad sense refers to efforts to establish English as the only official language in the United States (which currently has no official language) and prohibit the conduct of government business in other languages. Various initiatives to pass English-only legislation in Congress have failed—however, more than 20 states have ratified some form of English-only legislation.

English-only initiatives in education customarily take the form of prescribing English as the only language of instruction, eliminating bilingual education programs, and accelerating ESOL transition programs. Proponents of English-language programs often argue that both the nation and recent immigrants are served by rapid assimilation and that the latter are best served by rapid transitions to mainstream classrooms. This sentiment led to the passage of several propositions **banning bilingual education** in the late 1990s and early 2000s, notably in Arizona, California, and Massachusetts. The latter two states subsequently repealed their propositions due to both popular pressure and growing recognition that L1 proficiency and use does not delay L2 acquisition and may accelerate it. While research supports the efficacy of bilingual education, the broader cultural debate continues about what constitutes national identity and whether that identity is threatened by the use of non-English languages in school and society.

Overrepresentation in Special Education Programs

Research demonstrates that English language learners are referred to **special education programs** more often than their native English-speaking peers. The issue arises primarily because normal second-language development patterns can resemble emerging special education issues, especially to non-specialists. For example, if an ESOL student doesn't speak much or respond to questions, he or she might have a hearing impairment or processing deficit—or simply be in the silent period stage of language learning.

An accurate referral requires the ability to differentiate between the effects of a student's language ability, content knowledge, and cognitive abilities—a complex assessment that should only be made by a trained evaluator. The Department of Education recommends that, whenever feasible, disability assessments be done in the **student's native language** in order to avoid confounding disability and language issues.

Disparities in Teacher Qualifications and Retention

Nearly half of school funding in the United States comes from **local property taxes**, which leads to significant discrepancies in funding for schools located in wealthy and impoverished neighborhoods. While federal Title 1 funds and some state funds lessen that funding gap, it still exists, and in many states and school districts, it remains dramatic. Fewer funds result in fewer resources, larger classes, and lower teacher salaries—which deters more experienced and qualified teachers from taking these jobs. In turn, the less experienced teachers take these jobs due to their availability. Placing these under-equipped teachers in overcrowded classrooms contributes to **sub-par student performance** and **high teacher turnover**. A high percentage of ELLs live in low-income neighborhoods and thus experience these funding inequities.

Tracking

Tracking refers to the practice of placing students in separate academic tracks based on their academic or test performance at an early age. Tracking is closely related to **ability grouping**, the grouping of students with perceived similarities in academic ability to allow for efficient and targeted teaching. Critics of the practice argue that it is self-perpetuating—students in low-track courses receive instruction that is less cognitively-challenging and utilizes less academic language, all but ensuring that they will remain on that track. For example, ELLs enroll in high school college-preparatory classes at lower rates than their peers—and have lower rates of participation in post-secondary education as well.

The vast majority of high school students have access to at least some **advanced placement (AP) exams** due in part to federal funding of AP programs and teacher training, but the number of exams offered at a given school is directly correlated with socio-economic status, as is student participation in the AP program. AP classes, which are often writing-intensive and demand the use of academic English, are often seen as poor fits for ELLs.

Ability Groups

The separation of students into groups on the basis of their **perceived ability to understand a topic** is a long-standing teaching practice. It appeals to the parents of high-performing students who generally want their children to receive targeted, accelerated instruction; it often appeals to teachers as well, as it allows them to give specific instruction to different groups, avoiding unnecessary and redundant explanations. Research, however, suggests that the minimal advantages that ability grouping confers on high-performing students would better be gained by placing them in separate, gifted programs, while the negative effects of ability grouping on low-performing students are extensive and self-perpetuating—in other words, students who are placed in low-performing groups tend to fall further behind in their education. In-class ability grouping is thus looked upon with the same disfavor as its larger-scale counterpart, tracking.

UNDERREPRESENTATION IN GT PROGRAMS

ELLs remain underrepresented in GT programs, despite long-standing awareness of the deficits and of the fact that selection should be based on cognitive aptitudes independent of English language proficiency. Many explanations have been offered for the discrepancy, including (a) the challenge for teachers in recognizing giftedness through the filter of another language and culture, (b) a bias toward verbal aptitude in the definition and assessment of gifted students, (c) the lack of appropriate cognitive testing in students' native languages, (d) a lack of systematic communication between school ESOL and gifted programs, and (e) an unspoken sense that ELLs must become proficient in English before their cognitive skills can be recognized.

Though the US Department of Education offers **Jacob Javits grants** to help states identify and serve gifted ELLs, the bulk of funding and guidance for gifted programs comes from the individual states. As a consequence, states differ greatly in how they administer these programs and in the measures they take to identify gifted candidates among the ELL population.

RESTORATIVE JUSTICE

Research shows that (a) in recent decades, schools have made dramatically more use of **harsh disciplinary measures**, such as suspensions, even for non-violent student offenses; (b) these disciplinary measures disproportionately affect ELLs beginning at the secondary-school level; and (c) students subjected to disciplinary actions are far less likely to succeed academically. The high correlation between disciplinary action and student socioeconomic status suggests that the problem has complex and deep-seated societal roots. **Lack of student engagement at school** is one often-cited factor for the increase of discipline incidents. Within the ELL context, this can arise if ELL students are unable to successfully join the mainstream curriculum or are tracked in marginal and unchallenging courses.

Restorative justice refers to actions that schools can take to address disciplinary problems without suspending or expelling students. Restorative justice programs emphasize mediation of conflicts, the creation of support groups composed of peers and adults for students at risk, and the creation of disciplinary practices that keep students in school or at least engaged in academic activities.

ESOL ADVOCACY

ESOL teachers today are expected to not only be effective teachers, but also to serve as advocates for the interests of their ELL students. The importance of **ESOL teacher advocacy**—which has been codified as standard by bodies such as TESOL and NBPTS (National Board for Professional Teaching Standards)—stems from the idea that ELLs are often disadvantaged in the education system, and that ESOL teachers are uniquely positioned to *understand* what actions are necessary to improve ELL education and to act to *effect* change. Advocacy includes a wide range of activities, such as ensuring ELLs have fair access to school resources and programs, engaging the parents of ELLs to make sure they are aware of educational opportunities for their children, helping educate peers who may not have received training in delivering content instruction to ELLs, and correcting misperceptions at the school and in the community about ELL aptitude and education.

Types of Support Services for ELLs Both In and Out of the School Setting

Supports Services for ELLs in the School Setting

English language learners (ELLs) may require additional support services that help make the appropriate curriculum more accessible or inclusive. Some supports that are available in the school or class setting include

- **Sheltered English Instruction (SEI)** – Instruction at the appropriate level, but with simplified language, additional visual aids, or examples to help make the content accessible. The content is the same content that the student's peers are learning, but the comprehensibility is modified to overcome language-based difficulties.
- **ESL Pull-Out Classrooms** – Sometimes students need particular instruction in English outside of the content classrooms. These may be done in conjunction with integrated classrooms.
- **English for a Specific Purpose (ESP)** – Not typically used in the grade-school levels, these are English classes that focus mostly on vocabulary that can help a student communicate in a specific context, such as a job site that mostly needs to know the vocabulary for specific objects and tasks. Grammar and other linguistic features are usually put in lower priority to functional communication in ESP programs.
- **Bilingual Education Programs** – Programs in which students are placed in a classroom with other students and a teacher who share common language backgrounds. Classes in a bilingual education program may be taught in both languages as needed to accomplish curricular goals.

Supports for ELLs in the Classroom

- **Visuals and Multimedia Support** – Pictures, videos, or other visual instructions that can help support and reinforce concepts or instructions.
- **Scaffolding** – Additional supports to help bridge the student's background knowledge to current tasks.
- **Reference Materials** – Dictionaries, translation-dictionaries, and thesauruses that can help students comprehend terms that are confusing or new.
- **Modified Classroom Environment** – Alterations to the classroom, such as labels or instructions that ELLs may need to help learn or remember terminology. For instance, if a student was in a cooking class, labeling tools or drawers with cooking implements in either English or both languages may help a student pick up on unfamiliar vocabulary.
- **Peer work** – Students can be paired with other students to help expand vocabulary, make the classroom more welcoming, or help split up work.
- **Differentiated instruction** – Students can benefit from teaching the same information in a variety of ways, including reteaching the same concept with different words to ensure the concepts are accessible at different levels of language proficiency.
- **Additional Instruction or After-School Tutoring** – Many students may require more one-on-one time than a classroom can provide. After-school tutoring can provide additional practice or focused-time with a teacher.

Supports for ELLs out of the School Setting

Some supports are also available in the community or outside of the school context:

- **English Language Support Programs** – Summer language camps and church or community-based ESOL programs may be helpful to students and even families of students who want to learn English outside of the school
- **Multicultural Supports** – Schools and governmental bodies often provide translation or communication services to help with language barriers in the community. For any school meeting, most schools are obligated to provide a professional translator upon request.
- **Translated Materials** – Schools and governmental bodies usually have to provide informational material in multiple languages to support the community.
- **Technology-Based Resources** – Many tools are available to help learn and cross language barriers, including games, translation apps, and remote communication tools.
- **Counseling and Psychological Services** – Many ELLs and their families have needs for supports due to related hardships. The school and other community-based organizations often provide counseling and related services to help meet this type of need.

Environments that Support English Acquisition

Language-Rich Classroom

A language-rich classroom is one in which students are continuously exposed to the language in many different forms. The concept includes ways in which the **classroom** is constructed. For example, teachers may build word walls (in which relevant spelling words, commonly-used words, or target vocabulary words are displayed), display student writing or other examples of written work in multiple genres, or label objects with various names or descriptive terms. The concept also refers to **student access to reading material**, such as ensuring that students have access to the school library and that the classroom itself is stocked with level-appropriate books. The concept also includes **teaching activities**, including classroom reading in all of its forms (shared, guided, etc.), and questions and activities that call upon students to read outside of the classroom and report on how they have done so.

Visually-Supportive Environments

English language learners often benefit from having visual supports in addition to textual supports. In a classroom that sets out to visually support learners, texts are often reinforced with images, labels, symbols, and color coding to help reinforce ideas. Word walls are useful, especially when paired with pictures of the vocabulary being taught on. Picture dictionaries for the class can also be helpful when a student is still learning the meaning of new words. When made with binders or on a word wall, teachers can add and subtract words as the students need to keep them fresh and free from unnecessary reinforcements. Symbols and colors can be helpful and subtle reminders where a picture of a word or idea is too explicit. Finally, realia (or real-life objects) play a huge role in having learners interact with ideas in a tangle way, providing a great method of reinforcing vocabulary or concepts.

Environments that Support Meaningful and Authentic Communication

An ESL classroom should support **meaningful** and **authentic c**ommunication as opposed to inauthentic communication that is unnatural and uncommon in normal life. Communication that is motivated by actual use-cases is more natural and functional for students to learn, but it also allows for students to be more comfortable as they can speak about things that are happening in their own real lives. Ways to support meaningful or authentic communication in the classroom is to use more open-ended tasks, such as group work in which interaction is required, task-based activities or community research, in which students have to learn about something they find in the real world, or through more open-ended writing and speaking lessons. These types of tasks encourage the discovery of new and authentic language and effective practice using the new concepts they learn. Keep in mind that authentic tasks also tend to be easy to find visuals and **realia** to use, as authentic topics are usually tangible. Some examples of authentic and meaningful topics could include pets at home, food preparation in a kitchen environment, and current events such as weather, news, and music.

Classes that Have Reduced Affective Filters

Students often bring the stress of other classes, home life, and current events into the classroom, causing what is known as an **affective load**. If a student is focused on something outside of the class or even has underlying stress that is taking up some of their emotional and intellectual capacity, this will surely hinder their performance and openness in the classroom. An ESL classroom would do well to be a shelter from things that add to the students' affective loads or **affective filters**. Here are a few ways that a teacher can try to make a classroom that reduces stress upon entry and helps reduce affective loads for his or her students:

- Make the class culture about **growth** and fun, not just accuracy and grades. Students who are only worried about their mistakes are going to struggle more with their affective loads.
- Use primarily **positive reinforcement**, including rewards, kind words, and constructive feedback
- Make a **classroom community** in which students are encouraged to interact, build teamwork, and check in with each other to provide a safe space.
- Use ice-breakers to help transition the class from the outside into the safe space of the ESL classroom.
- Use assessments that are more **informal** and **formative** to keep classwork non-threatening. Some formal testing is always necessary, but maintaining a balance can keep students at a lower-operating stress threshold.
- Allow students to use **code-switching** to speak as naturally as they need to get to an answer. An overly formal classroom can prevent some students from speaking at all and can inhibit the learning process.
- Make classwork **predictable** and **routine**. Students can be thrown off and stressed by not knowing what to expect from their teachers on a given day. Routines can help set a natural and productive pace for every class.
- Center classwork on **student interests** to improve engagement. Especially in a language-centered class, activities that help students engage with the material naturally will be less stressful and more effective.

Instructional Planning and Objectives

ESOL Instructional Planning to Meet Standards

Teachers of English language learners (ELLs) need to balance both **language objectives** and **content objectives** when planning for instruction. In language-focused classes, this is simpler, as there are a narrower set of goals to meet, using language performance indicators showing the proficiency levels of students. Content-focused classrooms need to use the content standards as the primary objectives, but use language performance indicators to help teachers identify what types of content modifications and focal-points are necessary to help students meet both goals. For instance, a content objective might require students to learn about the plant life cycle. Students may not be familiar with lower-level vocabulary involved in the topic, so the teacher may need to isolate some vocabulary words to pre-teach alongside the objective. Similarly, the language objective might be to use sequence words correctly. The teacher can simultaneously teach about the order in which a plant develops while demonstrating sequence language (first, second, third, last, finally, etc.). Other factors, such as modifications, accommodations, and modeling need to be included in tasks to make the content more accessible to ELLs throughout an objective.

Task Complexity

Peter Skehan developed the concept of **task complexity** in the late 1990s as a framework for understanding the complexity of learning tasks in an L2 classroom. Skehan identified three factors that contribute to the complexity of a task: its **code complexity**, which is determined by language factors such as vocabulary and sentence complexity; its **cognitive complexity**, which is determined by the nature of cognitive processing required of the students and whether they are accustomed to that type of cognitive processing; and the amount of **communicative stress** involved in the task. Examples of communicative stress include time constraints or uncomfortable group dynamics. According to the theory, effective teachers will scale the scaffolding they provide to match the complexity of the task evaluated within this framework.

Task-Based Language Teaching

Task-based language teaching (**TBLT**) promotes student language learning through the accomplishment of **real-world tasks**—for example, ordering a pizza or buying a phone. Proponents argue that instruction organized this way teaches both the formal aspects of successful communication (linguistic competence) and the social aspects of communication. In some contexts, TBLT can resemble English for special purposes, in which advanced students are taught the vocabulary and rhetorical patterns particular to a given occupation or medium.

While teachers implementing TBLT might pre-teach key vocabulary needed to perform a task, the method emphasizes students' use of their whole repertoire of language skills, including the negotiation of meaning in situations where their formal knowledge of English is inadequate. Critics suggest that completion of a task is a poor measure of language improvement—once students reach a certain baseline competence, they can navigate a broad range of performative tasks, but may not be motivated or receive the instructional assistance to improve.

Creating Background Knowledge

Teaching is most effective when it builds upon what a student already knows in order to introduce something new. Accordingly, teachers learn techniques for **activating student prior knowledge**, using techniques such as brainstorming on know-want to know-learned (KWL) charts. However, ELLs may have little or no knowledge to activate about certain topics (for example, US history). In these situations, teachers may need to create background knowledge before launching the core of a lesson.

In order to **create background knowledge**, teachers might use techniques such as anticipation guides, visuals, or parallels to the students' first culture or history. Teachers may also focus on key vocabulary by using techniques such as concept maps or word walls. If the new lesson depends on students drawing connections with a previous lesson, the teacher may need to make that connection explicit; while native English speakers may pick up on cues that suggest the connection, ELLs may not.

21ST CENTURY LEARNING

The 21st Century Learning Initiative, launched in 1995, attempted to identify the most important skills students need to learn in order to succeed in the 21st century. The initiative's organizers strove to update the 20th century model of education, which was based on the three Rs (reading, writing, arithmetic) and the objective of providing students with content knowledge. The transformative effect of the internet suggested that the next generation would succeed not by simply *knowing* things but by knowing *how to do* things. After multiple revisions, the organizers defined the key 21st century skills as the **four Cs**: communication, critical thinking, collaboration, and creativity. These skills have been increasingly incorporated into state standards.

Teachers may need to pay specific attention to ensure that ELLs engage in the four Cs. When ELLs collaborate with native English speakers, they often get left out or left behind. In sheltered instruction content classrooms, ELLs may lack the English proficiency to easily express the higher order concepts required for critical thinking and may require specific prompts or scaffolding to engage effectively in communicative activities.

MODELING TASKS FOR ELLS

ESOL teachers should not rely entirely on verbal instructions when staging a classroom task or activity. Even if ELLs understand enough to begin the activity, they may lack critical procedural understanding or the contextual understanding necessary to learn from the activity. In setting up such activities, teachers should **demonstrate** the key steps using both actions and words. When possible, verbal instructions should be supplemented with **visual displays**, such as flow charts, which divide the activity or process into identifiable stages. Teachers can also supplement verbal instructions with written summaries, ideally set out in brief, stepwise format. Finally, teachers might choose to **chunk** the instructions or stages in a task, pausing the students repeatedly to check their work and understanding before providing a demonstration of the next step.

SCHEMA

A schema is the **background knowledge** someone has about a certain topic. The knowledge might be information, associations, remembered life experiences, or even emotional responses. Research has demonstrated that background knowledge is essential to reading comprehension, as written texts invariably rely on implied meanings and a reader's background knowledge. Only the simplest reading passages rely entirely on stated meaning.

Teachers can help **activate** student background knowledge by posing questions that help students relate the text to what they already know or that prompt them to involve their own experiences in their understandings of the text. Activating student background knowledge is important not only to enhance comprehension, it also raises student confidence by demonstrating that they have relevant experience and the tools to understand what they read, and it builds student enthusiasm for reading by connecting what they read to their broader lives.

COMPREHENSIVE READING PROGRAM

The US National Reading Panel issued an influential report in 2000 calling for literacy teachers to create a **balanced reading curriculum**, incorporating a range of activities and reading skills: phonemic awareness, phonics (relating sounds to their written representations), fluency, vocabulary development, and comprehension. The panel built on the core insight that students with advanced phonics knowledge were not necessarily skilled readers. Reading well is a multi-faceted skill that requires attention to context and the ways in which successful communications are structured.

A well-balanced reading program incorporates a **range of reading activities** to help students build literacy, from phonics activities to shared and guided reading, cloze activities, and teacher prompts that require students to draw connections between texts or search for implied meanings.

Purposeful Activities vs. Decontextualized Language

Meaningful and purposeful literacy activities are ones that engage the student in something beyond the text. For example, a text might engage the student with subject matter taught in a content classroom. Or the text might appeal to something of particular interest to a student, like a hobby or an aspect of their background or experience. A text might direct the student to accomplish something, as when they follow instructions or create a project based on a written description, or to negotiate something, as when they follow up a reading passage with a small-group or peer-to-peer discussion.

Decontextualized language is language that addresses a subject that is unfamiliar to a student, and which offers few context clues that a student can use to aid comprehension. Reading and understanding decontextualized language is important for academic language fluency, but it is less appropriate for early learners. On the other hand, at appropriate levels of development, students should be challenged by inquiries that invite generalizations and abstractions rather than engage only with concrete and immediate things.

The Language Experience Approach

The key feature of the language experience approach to literacy development is the creation of a **class-specific text** based on a **shared student experience** (a field trip, for example). Typically, the teacher writes the first draft of the text, using student sentences and contributions, which can then be read for practice. The class revisits the text over time, adding new vocabulary, new syntax, and expanding the text to relate to new educational experiences. The text serves as a basis for both reading and writing instruction.

Proponents of this method of literacy development point to the strong association between student lives and the classroom text of which they are, in essence, authors. The approach is not widely used, however, in part because of the near-universality of statewide or region-wide curricula planning, which leaves little room for a text that evolves in undefined directions.

Motivation to Read

A strong correlation exists between frequent reading, skilled reading, and academic success, and yet reading in the traditional sense—as a sustained engagement with a printed text—has declined significantly in the student population. Teachers can encourage student reading by strengthening their **intrinsic motivation**. One way to do this is to make sure that the books they read are relevant to student interests, to contemporary events, and to their different cultures. A second way is to engage in pre-reading activities that activate their background knowledge. A third is to allow students an element of ownership in the reading process, such as allowing them to choose which book to read, or when to read, or how they will be assessed on their reading. Choosing **level-appropriate books** is critical. Students forced to read books that are either too hard or too easy quickly lose interest. Students should be allowed and encouraged to discuss what they read with their peers. Not only does conversation aid comprehension, but it can also foster the sense that reading is worthwhile. Finally, teachers should make sure students are exposed to **reading role models**, whether they are parents, celebrities, or the teacher him or herself.

Kenneth Goodman

Goodman's 1967 research discounted the idea that students read by systematically processing and compiling sequential information. Rather, he argued, reading is a "psycholinguistic guessing game" in which students take rapid **surveys** of the written text and use it to make **predictions** on the basis of their background knowledge and assumptions of what is to come. Goodman argued that reading this way, with a constant interplay between thought and language, is actually more efficient and effective than reading with careful and systematic attention to the text. In his view, the better a student is at reading, the less of a text they actually need to read in order to understand it. Goodman argued that many of the typical errors of early readers are in fact the manifestations of logical guesses that get refined through reading experience.

Appropriate Reading Materials

Extensive research, as well as common sense, attests to the importance of quality, age-appropriate **reading material** for the success of a literacy program. While ESOL teachers often don't have a choice of which materials to use in their classes, whenever they do, they should select materials that:

- Stimulate student interest, in part by including content and themes that are part of student **background knowledge**.
- Provide the proper **conceptual load**, or the amount of new versus familiar structures and vocabulary.
- Furnish sufficient **contextual support** for the narrative.
- Do not contain any **culturally insensitive** references.
- Are an appropriate **length**.
- Represent a **diversity of genres**.
- Have a **clear textual layout** that enhances comprehension rather than impedes it.

Explicit vs. Implicit Instruction

Explicit instruction is when a teacher informs students of a specific lesson goal, provides an explanation of the important concepts, demonstrates their use, and then guides the students in practice. With **implicit instruction**, the teacher does not explicitly teach targeted concepts but instead relies on the students to learn them during the course of communication-based activities. In a rough sense, advocates of implicit instruction model language as something that is **acquired**, and advocates of explicit instruction see it as something that is **learned**. Modern research suggests that teachers need to use both strategies; however, a consensus has emerged that certain skills should be explicitly taught. In the reading domain, this includes the vocabulary and syntax of academic (as opposed to social) language and various comprehension strategies, such as how to infer meaning from a text or synthesize information from multiple texts. In the writing domain, the process of writing itself is thought to best be taught explicitly, proceeding from planning to drafting, evaluating, revising, and editing, with best practices for each. At earlier stages of literacy, phonics instruction is often approached explicitly, as well as those grammatical structures that are least transparent or held in common with the students' native languages.

Implicit vs. Explicit Strategies

Teachers should teach grammar both **implicitly** and **explicitly**, according to both the subject matter and student needs. In general, students whose L1 is grammatically very different from English will require more explicit instruction. Several aspects of English grammar are hard for even speakers of closely-related languages—for example, word order, prepositions, auxiliary verbs, and modal verbs—and thus should be taught explicitly.

The goal of language instruction is **effective communication**, and teachers who are tempted to explicitly correct a student error should first ask themselves whether the error prevented communication. There are many reasons not to explicitly correct a student's spoken errors. Doing so interrupts the conversational flow, possibly embarrasses the student or discourages them from speaking in the future, and may not even help—research shows that certain types of errors appear during the normal process of language development and then disappear without explicit correction. Teachers should be more liberal when correcting written work, both because the affective consequences are fewer and because students need more explicit instruction when learning academic language.

The Importance of Scaffolding

Scaffolding is a teacher's use of supports to help student understanding of concepts or mastery of skills. Well-chosen **literacy scaffolding techniques** allow students to engage with texts and writing projects just beyond their current proficiency levels, or in what Vygotsky referred to as their **zones of proximal development**.

Numerous scaffolding techniques exist to support both reading and writing instruction. For example, a teacher using the **directed listening and thinking activity (DLTA)** would pause a story frequently to ask students questions that led them to predict what might come next and then eventually prompt the students to formulate their own questions and predicted answers. **Shared reading** is a common scaffolding technique in which a teacher reads along with a class, modeling things like pronunciation and fluency. For writing, an example is an **interactive dialogue journal**, in which a teacher and student pass a journal back and forth, each writing in response to the others' comments and prompts. **Mapping**, in which students brainstorm about the words and concepts that relate to a central theme, is a useful scaffolding technique to use in the planning stages of a writing activity.

Gail Tompkins' Five-Level Scaffolding Model

In an influential 2011 textbook, *Literacy in the Early Grades*, Gail Tompkins outlined a **five-stage model of scaffolding** conceived for widespread use in the classroom. The stages are designed to be used either successively—as a teacher gradually reduces the amount of support provided as students become more independent—or selected for use based on a given task or classroom composition. In the **stage of greatest support**, a teacher models the skill or task. In the second, **shared stage**, the students contribute to the task, but the teacher still performs the act or records the product. In the third, **interactive stage**, the students and teacher share in both the conceptualizing and the creation of the product. In the fourth stage, **guided practice**, the students undertake the task, either alone or in groups, with the teacher providing assistance as needed. In the final stage, **independent work**, the students perform the entire activity without significant teacher assistance.

Integrating the Four Basic Language Skills

The main reason to teach reading, writing, speaking, and listening in conjunction is that they all **reinforce** each other. All contribute, in a unique way, to a student's overall language knowledge and ability. Further, there is a *pragmatic* reason to teach all four: in the wider world (beginning in content classrooms) the students will need to use all four skills, often simultaneously, in actual communication contexts.

The ESOL teacher who is tempted to privilege the teaching of oral skills over written skills should remember that second-language learning often follows a different **pattern** than first-language acquisition. With L1, oral competency almost invariably precedes written competency; however, the sequencing is far more variable with L2. In particular, students with strong L1 literacy may progress more rapidly in L2 reading than in L2 speaking, and their reading skills will support and stimulate their speaking progress.

Teachers should find ways to combine the skills in **mutually-reinforcing ways** when designing learning activities. For example, students could read a text, discuss it, and then write about it, explicitly incorporating ideas that they heard in conversations with their peers.

Appropriate Cultural Content

Research demonstrates that students learn to read and write more effectively when texts activate their **background knowledge**. ELLs are likely to have acquired a substantial portion of that knowledge in a different cultural context.

Using **culture-specific content** accelerates language learning in at least two ways. First, students tend to be more interested in texts that relate to their culture. Second, when students read a text for comprehension, they are essentially using what they *already* understand as a means to grasp what they *don't* understand. A text that incorporates familiar cultural references will provide them with more points of comprehension with which to leverage meaning from the unfamiliar text.

In selecting culturally-specific texts or calling upon students to speak about their culture, teachers should be aware that not all students are experts on their native cultures. Nor should a teacher assume that a student wants to speak about their native culture or even be identified by cultural origin.

Integrating English Language Learning

Perhaps the stereotypical image of English language instruction is that of a full-time, separate program that focuses on English proficiency, developing everyday vocabulary and scenarios to build social language skills. While this model of instruction exists, it is increasingly rare, due primarily to the recognition that students benefit most when **language and content** are taught at the same time. One reason is that if students are not taught content until they are proficient in English, they will be significantly behind their peers in content knowledge. Furthermore, content classrooms put language in context, allowing students to build mental networks of related terms and concepts. Content classrooms also give students a setting in which to *apply* the English they learn, making it much less likely they will forget it.

School districts and states differ in *how* they integrate English and content instruction for second-language learners. There are many different program models based on variations of **three fundamental approaches**: having ESOL-trained teachers incorporate content knowledge into their curriculums, having content-trained teachers incorporate English language instruction into their curriculums, and having ESOL and content instructors work in tandem, either through co-teaching or via a pull-out or push-in model.

Rhetorical Registers

Purpose, Audience, and Subject Matter

In the context of language, the term "**register**" refers to the degree of formality of speech or to the way members of a group speak to one another. For example, a group of doctors may speak to one another in a medical register. Scholars often speak of three distinct registers: **informal** (which students might use in casual conversation among themselves), **neutral** (which might govern most student/teacher interactions), and **formal** (which students might use in a presentation or when speaking to an unfamiliar adult). In transitioning from informal to neutral or formal conversational registers, students will need to learn to use complete sentences rather than rely on contextual meaning, eliminate slang and excessive discourse markers, and avoid hyperbole and repetition.

English language learners also need to learn the basic conventions of the various **academic disciplines**. For example, it may be appropriate to use figurative language when writing or speaking about the arts but not when discussing math or logic. Language use also varies with purpose: the conventions that apply to speech intended to persuade are different from those that apply to exposition.

Review Video: Writing Purpose and Audience
Visit mometrix.com/academy and enter code: 146627

Promoting Oral Language Development

Verbal vs. Oral Communication

The term "verbal communication" is usually contrasted with "nonverbal communication," and in this sense, it means communication that occurs via words. **Verbal communication** can include all four **major language skills**: speaking, listening, reading, and writing. The term "**oral communication**" narrows this set of skills to two: speaking and listening.

One way to think about oral communication is to consider the various aspects of spoken language—beyond word choice—that convey meaning in conversation. These **prosodic aspects of language** include pitch, stress, rhythm, length, and loudness.

A second way to think about oral communication is to focus on the goals of a conversation and the different skills required to achieve those goals. For example, in some contexts, ELLs must be able to identify the main point of an utterance while setting aside details or irrelevant information; in other contexts, they may need to focus on the details. Similarly, the skills needed to recount an event or conversation when speaking to a peer are very different from those needed to give an oral presentation. ESOL teachers need to understand the range of necessary skills and provide instruction and practice in each.

Demonstrating Listening Comprehension

In the early stages of language learning, students may only be able to signal understanding by nodding, smiling, or performing whatever action is being requested. Their responses will be based heavily on **nonverbal signals** and references to **illustrations** or **realia**. Next, students will develop the capacity to signal comprehension by choosing one of a set of options ("Where did John go? Home or to the store?") before developing the capacity to formulate **simple answers without scaffolds**. In later stages, students will be able to provide **full-sentence answers** to comprehension questions and eventually to provide **multi-sentence summaries** that reveal their comprehension of literal and implied meaning, central and supporting arguments, and connections to other texts and real-world experiences.

Discourse Markers

A discourse marker is a word or phrase used to organize speech, manage the flow of a conversation, or convey an emotional attitude. **Discourse markers** are often inessential to the literal semantic meaning of a sentence but can be critical in conveying the **attitude** of the speaker. Examples include "well," "um," "you know," "right," and "maybe." Research shows that even proficient ELLs use fewer discourse markers than native speakers and that early ELLs misunderstand their pragmatic use. Discourse markers are heavily bound to context and are thus difficult to teach in any systematic way. However, ESOL teachers may illustrate some common forms, such as how the expression "Yeah, right" can signal either agreement or skepticism, depending on stress and tone.

Framing a Listening Comprehension Activity

Students who listen to audio or watch video files at their **zone of proximal development** are unlikely to be able to answer questions about multiple levels of meaning—at least not without repeated listening or viewing. Teachers can help **facilitate student listening comprehension** by identifying in advance what they are listening for: the main idea, details in support of an argument, or the attitude of one or more interlocutors toward a proposed idea. Teachers can also prime students to listen for implied meanings or idiomatic expressions by providing suggestive clues: for example, "The narrator in this video uses an interesting expression that means 'to lose something forever'—let's see if we can find out what it is." Teachers might divide the class into groups, have each group listen for a different element of comprehension, and then combine the elements in a subsequent discussion. Teachers should be aware that students may understand almost nothing that they hear—either because they panic and lose focus when they can't understand or because they translate L2 into L1 and miss the overall meaning.

Frontloading, Chunking, and Debriefing

Teachers frontload or pre-teach when they teach specific vocabulary, rhetorical devices, sentence structures, or content that students will encounter in a subsequent lesson. **Frontloading** or **pre-teaching** is particularly useful in preparing students for listening comprehension activities to ensure that students don't disengage when they encounter unfamiliar words or forms.

Chunking is the practice of dividing a lesson or text into mentally digestible parts, often by stopping and inviting students to ask questions, draw connections to prior knowledge, or make predictions about what is to come. Teachers often chunk a reading comprehension exercise to ensure that students understand one section of the text before moving on to the next.

Debriefing is a type of lesson summary or wrap-up, usually used to revisit a key point or reinforce a specific learning goal and to assess how well students mastered the lesson.

Initiating and Negotiating Conversations

Enabling students to hold successful conversations is one of the most important outcomes of any ELL program. Students who speak flawless English will nevertheless fail to achieve their communication objectives if they do not learn the patterns and conventions of conversational discourse. In order to become proficient in oral communication, students must learn how to **initiate a conversation** with greetings and formalities, using a **register** appropriate to the setting. Students must also learn how to **reinforce** their interlocutor's utterances, either through nonverbal cues (nodding, smiling) or appropriate and well-timed interjections. For social purposes, students should learn how to **alternate** conversation, ensuring that all parties are equal participants. Students should develop a repertoire of **active listening** techniques and learn to extend a conversation with open, closed, and clarifying questions. These skills are particularly important when students have a specific conversational objective, such as achieving a consensus or securing specific information. Finally, students must learn the conventions of **closing a conversation**.

Retelling, Restating, and Summarizing

Real-world communication relies heavily on one person summarizing an idea, event, or encounter for the benefit of others. ELLs need to learn how to deliver concise and accurate **summaries** for purposes of work and school and how to accurately **paraphrase** conversations and **telescope** narrative events during social interactions.

Learning how to use **reported speech**—such as reporting Joe's words "I am sick" as "Joe said that he was sick"—is a relatively advanced language skill. Even early ELLs, however, can practice retelling events and experiences, and more advanced students can practice narrating them in different registers, as when talking to a teacher rather than a peer. One common technique to practice this skill is to have students interview one another and then report their findings to the class. Another is to have the students summarize a story or video using a targeted number of sentences—with the target set to help the students approximate the amount of detail they should provide.

Listening and Speaking as an Analog to Reading and Writing

Much of what is needed in the process of **speaking and listening** is **analogous**, or corresponds to, what is learned in the processes of **reading and writing**. Students who are listening need to find main ideas and structures of spoken speech, much in the same way that reading a short passage will require the student to recognize main ideas, supporting details, and organizational patterns. In the same way, students who are learning to speak need to use mood, tone, and organization to clearly meet a purpose and communicate effectively. Teachers who want to support these connected ideas should connect these four domains of language learning into class tasks. For example, a class might need to write a report on stories. A student can work on reading a story, analyzing how the author presents information, and then write a paper about his or her findings. In a subsequent class, the students can then come up and take turns presenting their findings to the class. While one student presents and practices speaking, the other students can practice listening and writing down main points. These tasks can be also be brief and frequent, rather than long term and high-stakes. By engaging the whole class in all four types of language tasks, they can reinforce the connections between the four modes of communication.

Cooperative Learning to Support Aural Language Skills

Cooperative learning simply means that students will learn by cooperating with one another. Students will be placed into groups of a size determined by the teacher. With such an approach, students work together to succeed in learning. Students may work together to learn a topic, complete an assignment, or compete with other groups.

Examples of cooperative learning include Think-Pair-Share and Jigsaw. **Think-Pair-Share** is a cooperative learning strategy that involves thinking about some given topic, sharing ideas, thoughts, or questions with a partner, and then sharing the partner discussion with the whole group. For example, in the mathematics classroom, a teacher may ask the class to think about the meaning of a proportional relationship. Each student would think for a set period of time, share ideas with a partner, and then each partner group would share their ideas regarding the meaning of proportionality. **Jigsaw** is another cooperative learning strategy that involves dividing among each group member reading material or ideas to be learned. Each student will then read his or her information, summarize it, and share the findings or ideas with the group. In a biology context, students might be required to think about animal characteristics that make birds, reptiles, amphibians, and mammals different from one another and write down their thoughts. Then they would be given information to read on characteristics of mammals. Students could then share what they learned about real-world mammals they have encountered with other students in a group.

Vocabulary Development

Encouraging Vocabulary Acquisition Through Reading and Writing Activities

If a new text contains unfamiliar vocabulary words that are central to the meaning and/or may be difficult to decode, a teacher may **preview** the words with the group. After introducing the topic of the text, the teacher may flip to the words, show students their spellings, and ask students to share what the words may mean based on prior knowledge and picture clues. Exposure to these words before reading will build readers' confidence and help them recognize and decode the words faster, maintaining fluency. Knowing the meanings in advance will also assist with comprehension.

When reading aloud to students, teachers may pause at new vocabulary words and model how to use context clues, prior knowledge, and picture support to decode and comprehend the new words. Students can be encouraged to use these strategies when reading independently.

Readers need repeated exposure to vocabulary words to develop automatic recognition and comprehension. Teachers may display classroom charts containing vocabulary words and their meanings, possibly using picture clues for young readers.

Students can also be encouraged to incorporate vocabulary words in their own writing. Word walls or charts containing the words can assist students with spelling and remembering the meanings of the words.

Helping Readers Explore the Meanings of Unknown Vocabulary Words

First, it is important for students to identify unknown vocabulary words when reading. Readers who are not monitoring their own comprehension may decode the words and continue reading, even if they do not understand their meanings. Teachers can model how to stop when they reach words they don't understand, even if they can decode them, and encourage students to do the same.

Next, readers need to determine which unknown words are central to the meanings of the text and worth exploring further. This is important because there may be many unknown words and, if readers stop extensively at each one, fluency and comprehension may be interrupted. Therefore, students can be encouraged to consider whether or not they can comprehend the sentences and overall meanings of the texts without devoting more energy to these particular unknown words.

If readers determine that the unknown words are central to the meaning of the text, they can be encouraged to use strategies such as using context clues, looking for known roots or affixes, or consulting dictionaries. Overall, readers should be encouraged to monitor their own reading and comprehension and determine when to apply known strategies.

Review Video: Acknowledging the Unknown When Reading
Visit mometrix.com/academy and enter code: 712339

Supporting Vocabulary Acquisition and Use Through Listening and Speaking

Young children begin their vocabulary development through listening well before they begin to read and write. Through listening to family members, caregivers, and others, children develop their meaning (oral) vocabularies. These are words that children understand when heard and eventually use in their own speech. These vocabularies can be developed by talking to the children frequently and for a variety of purposes, reading to them, exposing them to songs, rhymes, and poems, and many other language activities.

Children continue to build vocabulary through listening and speaking activities when they begin school. Teachers can read aloud to students often, varying the genres and purposes for listening. Engaging students in discussions about what was read aloud can give students a purpose for listening and opportunities to use text-related vocabulary in their own oral responses. Teachers can also incorporate key vocabulary words in class discussions.

Students should also have frequent opportunities to speak in the classroom. In addition to informal class discussions, students can present projects to classmates and explain their thinking during problem-solving. They should be encouraged to use content-specific vocabulary when appropriate.

Teaching Word Analysis Skills and Vocabulary to English Language Learners

Focusing on cognates is one way to help build word analysis skills and vocabulary for English language learners (ELLs). Cognates are words in different languages that share the same roots. For example, the English word *directions* and the Spanish word *direcciones* are cognates. ELLs can be encouraged to look for known parts of unfamiliar words. They can then use knowledge about the meanings in their native languages to determine the meanings of the English words. This strategy builds upon ELLs' prior knowledge. Explicitly teaching common roots and affixes can help ELLs quickly increase their vocabularies as well.

Scaffolding should also be provided when introducing ELLs to new words. This can be done using visuals that help demonstrate the meanings of the words. Real objects, pictures, and gestures can all be used. Graphic organizers can also be used to show how new words are related and how they connect to specific topics.

Teaching Word Analysis Skills to Struggling Readers

Struggling readers require consistent and explicit instruction, which often includes a combination of both whole-class instruction and targeted individual or small-group instruction daily. They also need frequent opportunities to manipulate words. Both building and breaking apart related words using letter tiles can help struggling readers develop understandings of patterns in the ways words are made.

Struggling readers can also benefit from explicit instruction on chunking words into component parts. Depending on the ages and prior knowledge of the students, this might include identifying syllable patterns, onsets and rimes, roots and affixes, or smaller sight words that are part of the larger words.

Struggling readers also need frequent opportunities to practice their word analysis skills using real texts. After explicit instruction on recognizing prefixes in words, for example, students can read texts that contain several prefixes. They can identify these words and their meanings. This will help them transfer their word analysis skills to realistic contexts. Scaffolding can be provided through anchor charts, graphic organizers, and teacher support during these independent reading experiences to provide reminders of known strategies.

Teaching Word Analysis Skills to Highly Proficient Readers

Proficient readers still have a need for differentiated reading instruction, even if they are meeting or exceeding grade-level expectations. They can benefit from developing the same word analysis skills as other readers, such as looking for known parts in unfamiliar vocabulary words, breaking words into components, and finding relationships between the meanings and spellings of different words. These strategies should be presented using materials and interactions that are both engaging and appropriately challenging for proficient readers. Use of texts that have some unfamiliar words will ensure that readers have opportunities to apply these strategies and continue to increase their vocabularies. Using assessments to determine reading levels or teaching readers to self-select appropriate texts can help ensure that the selected materials offer some challenges and learning opportunities for proficient readers.

Because proficient readers often devote less energy to decoding words than struggling readers, they are able to allocate more energy to reading comprehension, analysis, and reflection. Proficient readers can be asked to evaluate authors' word choices and discuss the effect that certain words have on the meaning or tone of the texts.

Understanding Graphophonics, Syntax, and Semantics

Reading strategies can be used and applied to different situations as needed. The types of text a student reads may differ greatly in terms of vocabulary, quality of context clues, picture support, and connections to the reader's prior knowledge. Therefore, the strategies that work to determine an unknown word in any one sentence or text may not work as well in another. These strategies are often unreliable. Instead, teachers should encourage readers to use phonics knowledge to decode unknown words. Proficient and skilled readers do not rely on cues when identifying an unknown word.

While these reading strategies are not recommended for instructional purposes, it is important to know the difference between strategies a reader may be using. Decoding words using graphophonic clues is a strategy where readers consider the letter-sound relationships in the word. Another strategy is to consider syntax, or how the word sounds in the sentence and fits into the overall sentence structure. A third strategy is to consider semantics, or the meaning of the text, to guess the unknown word. Basically, the reader is trying to determine if the unknown word looks right (graphophonics), sounds right (syntax), and makes sense (semantics).

When it comes to reading unknown words, it is best practice for students to use phonetic knowledge to decode words. Students who lack a basic understanding of phonics may rely on cues while reading unknown words. Thus, explicit and systematic phonics instruction is necessary in order to develop proficient readers.

Helping Students Use Context Clues

Teachers should explicitly introduce students to different types of context clues, including definition, antonym, synonym, and inference clues. Examples of sentences containing each type can be provided, and students can be asked to mark the clues, label each type, and explain the meanings of the unknown words. They can also be asked to find examples of each of these types of context clues in other texts. An anchor chart listing the different types of context clues and examples of each can also be posted in the classroom.

Students can also be given sets of words that are related in some way, such as pairs of synonyms or antonyms. They can be asked to write sentences that incorporate the word pairs, creating context clues for other readers. The students can then share their sentences with peers, asking them to identify the context clues and meanings of the unknown words.

Review Video: Reading Comprehension: Using Context Clues
Visit mometrix.com/academy and enter code: 613660

Importance of Knowing Latin and Greek Roots

Many English words are formed from Latin and Greek **roots**. Therefore, recognizing these roots and knowing their meanings can help readers with both decoding and comprehending.

When readers automatically recognize Latin and Greek roots, they will be able to quickly decode the main parts of words that contain them. If they automatically recognize the affixes as well, they will be able to break words into parts and decode them effortlessly. This will allow the readers to maintain speed and fluency while reading.

The roots also hold most of the meaning in words and form the bases of entire word families. Knowing the meanings of these roots will help readers quickly determine the meanings of many newly encountered words, especially if they also know the meanings of any attached affixes. For example, if readers know that the Latin root *port* means to carry, they will have clues about the meanings of the words *transport, transportation*, *import*, and *export* as well.

Helping Readers Identify Latin and Greek Roots in Unfamiliar Words

When teaching readers about Latin and Greek roots in English words, one strategy is to help them see the relationships between words in the same word families. This can be done by creating charts or other visual representations of word families and their meanings. For example, a root and its meaning can be written in the middle of a web, and words containing the root and their meanings can be written in circles branching off from the root.

Another strategy is to create three sets of cards, including prefixes, suffixes, and roots. Students can experiment with combining the sets of cards to try to form real words. When real words are created, students can explain their meanings. Students can also be given words containing prefixes, roots, and suffixes. They can be asked to break the words into their components and identify the meanings of each part.

Additionally, students can be encouraged to locate words containing Latin and Greek roots in the texts they read independently. They can use their knowledge of the roots to define the words.

Approaches to Vocabulary Learning

- A **definitional approach** to vocabulary learning is the most traditional. Students are either provided definitions of words or look them up in a dictionary, and they are drilled until they commit the meanings to memory.
- A **structural approach** to vocabulary learning emphasizes the morphological features of words—the roots, prefixes, and suffixes. Once students learn the recurring morphemes in English, they can deduce the meaning of a word in isolation without relying on its context.
- A **contextual approach** to vocabulary learning provides the students with multiple examples of a word used in realistic contexts, allowing them to infer the meaning without resorting to a dictionary or an explicit definition.
- A **categorical approach** to vocabulary learning groups words into categories based on a semantic similarity. For example, a student might be given a list of words associated with driving a car, such as "steering wheel," "to brake," "to accelerate," and "gear shift."
- A **mnemonic approach** to vocabulary learning builds associations between target words and mental images so that hearing a target word evokes the image, facilitating recall of the word's meaning.

Review Video: Types of Vocabulary Learning (Broad and Specific)
Visit mometrix.com/academy and enter code: 258753

Role of Non-Contextual Strategies in Vocabulary Development

Non-contextual strategies are used when new vocabulary is learned without seeing or hearing the words in context. For example, teachers may give students lists of new vocabulary words they have not yet encountered in texts. The teachers may ask students to define the words, use them in sentences, and memorize them. Quizzes may then be given in which students must match the words to their definitions or provide examples of the terms.

There are times teachers may use non-contextual vocabulary strategies, such as when students are learning content-specific words that are not often found naturally in texts. When studying parts of speech, for example, teachers may have students memorize the definitions of *noun*, *verb*, and *adjective*. These words are important for students' understanding of sentence structure, yet students are not likely to encounter these words written in texts with contextual clues. However, it is recommended that teachers do use contextual strategies whenever possible.

Students can be taught to use tools such as dictionaries to define unknown words when contextual clues are not available. They can be prompted to draw pictures to explain word meanings or use graphic organizers to show the relationships among words.

Role of Contextual Strategies in Vocabulary Development

Contextual strategies are used to determine the meanings of unknown vocabulary words when they are encountered in context. The ability to use these strategies to quickly determine word meanings is important for both reading fluency and comprehension. Because words can have multiple meanings, readers also need to use contextual strategies to determine which meaning makes sense in a given sentence.

Teachers can explicitly teach students about the different types of contextual clues often found in sentences. They can encourage students to highlight the words and phrases that provide clues about meanings of the vocabulary words.

Contextual clues often include synonyms or antonyms for the unknown vocabulary words. Therefore, when introducing new words, teachers can assist students with creating lists of synonyms and antonyms. Teachers can also ask students to solve analogies or determine which word does not belong when given a group of related words. These activities will help students recognize synonyms and antonyms and understand relationships among words when they are encountered in context.

Criteria for Selecting Vocabulary Words for Instruction

Vocabulary words can be divided into three tiers. Teachers should consider these tiers when determining which words to focus on during instruction.

- **Tier one words** are common words used in everyday speech. They are typically learned by the early grades through normal conversation. Explicit instruction on the meanings of these words is seldom needed.
- **Tier two words** are found in both fiction and nonfiction texts and are common enough that readers will likely encounter them in multiple texts. Tier two words carry a lot of meaning and can negatively affect comprehension if they are not understood by readers. When deciding which tier two words to focus on, teachers should consider how the words affect the overall meanings of the texts and their morphologies. They should consider if students will be able to form connections between these words and other words, helping them understand unfamiliar words encountered in the future.
- **Tier three words** are mostly found in nonfiction texts and are domain-specific. These words are important for understanding the texts and their domains. Because students are unlikely to have encountered these words before, explicit instruction is needed. This often includes pre-teaching the words and analyzing them in context.

Teaching Reading

Decoding

Decoding, an essential early reading skill, is the practice of sounding out written words. In order to succeed at **decoding**, students need to understand the basics of **phonics**—how sounds correlate with letters—as well as how to blend sounds and segment words into **discrete sounds**. Successful decoding reveals what the word is but not what it means, either in isolation or in context. However, ELLs who decode a word may discover that they already know the word through speech. For this reason, decoding is often referred to as **word identification**.

Research suggests that phonics is best taught explicitly—teachers systematically teach letter/sound correspondence and advance through progressively more complex words by grouping words with shared sounds. Alternatively, phonics may be taught implicitly—teachers present whole words and then break them into sounds, inviting students to identify common, known sound patterns.

Print Awareness

Print awareness refers to a student's recognition that the written symbols on a page represent letters and words and correspond to spoken language. The term also refers to the awareness that English text is read from left to right and pages are turned from right to left. **Print awareness** is an essential skill which students must grasp before they can learn how to read, spell, or practice handwriting.

Teachers can develop print awareness in early ELLs by modeling how a book is read, using a finger to trace the progression of reading from left to right and then wrapping around to the next line, showing how pictures are associated with parts of a story, explaining the role of title and author, and discussing how a book represents a complete narrative.

Reading Fluency

Fluency in reading is the ability to read a text accurately, rapidly, and with feeling. The most important thing a teacher can do to promote fluency is to read aloud often, taking care to read with expression—modeling how words are not read one by one with equal spacing, but in groups with uneven pauses.

Students can practice reading a line of text after listening to the teacher read it or read the text in unison with the teacher—either one student at a time (**duet reading**) or the entire class (**choral reading**). Research suggests that **reading aloud** is more helpful to developing fluency than reading silently and that students can profit from reading the same passages repeatedly until they achieve fluency.

Fluency is highly correlated with **comprehension**. Jay Samuels developed the **automaticity theory** to explain this correlation. According to Samuels, students have limited mental attention, and the more reading functions—such as decoding—they can accomplish automatically the more attention they have to grasp the broader meanings of a text. In this view, fluency *is* automaticity.

Review Video: Fluency
Visit mometrix.com/academy and enter code: 531179

Pre-Reading, Reading, and Post-Reading

Research demonstrates that students who approach a text with a purpose comprehend it better than students who simply read it passively without any expectations or goals.

Teachers can promote reading comprehension in the **pre-reading phase** by explaining the **purpose** of the exercise and what the students will be doing with the text once they finish reading it. They can preview the format of the text so that students know what to expect as they read. They can solicit student background knowledge to build context and stimulate interest.

Teachers should encourage students to monitor their comprehension while they read with a variety of **self-questioning strategies**. For example, when reading a text with headings, students can stop at the end of a section and verify that they grasped the point anticipated by the heading. If they are reading a persuasive essay, they can stop periodically and ask themselves if they are convinced by the writer's argument and evidence.

Finally, students should **assess and summarize** once they have finished reading. If they find that they don't understand part of the narrative or the author's argument, they should return to the text to improve their comprehension.

A Text's Features, Structures, and Rhetorical Devices

An essential element of reading comprehension is the ability to predict how a text will be structured and how its author will present information or construct a narrative. Students who can successfully anticipate and identify these aspects of a text will have an advantage in overall comprehension because they can use what they already know to infer further meanings and evaluate the credibility of the author or the quality of his or her argument.

Students can be taught the general **features** of fiction, non-fiction, and academic texts. Given the nature of the text, certain **structures** can be expected. Fiction, for example, will likely contain a lot of dialogue composed of informal (social) language; academic texts, in contrast, will eschew dialogue and likely use only objective adjectives, such as those indicating size or number. Different types of texts incorporate different **rhetorical devices** as well: fiction may depend heavily on metaphor, while academic texts may rely on inductive and deductive arguments.

Teaching Writing

English Language Conventions

Modern approaches to writing treat the proper use of **English conventions** as one of several components of good writing, along with word choice, organization, voice, fluency, and message or content. Thus, while ESOL teachers may choose to teach some conventions explicitly, they must take care not to let a focus on grammar, punctuation, or error correction impede the overall writing process.

Process writing breaks the writing task into **five phases**: prewriting, drafting, revising, editing, and publishing. In this framework, students focus on the correct use of conventions in the editing phase (though the teacher or peers may point out errors in the revising phase), well after the creative and expansive portions of the task.

Main Genres of Academic Writing

- **Expository writing** is used to inform the reader by presenting information in an objective manner. It is written almost exclusively in the third person, uses complex sentences, and often utilizes the specialized vocabulary of an academic or technical field.

- **Descriptive writing** is used to portray an event, place, or person, usually with depth and detail. It may rely heavily on adjectives and adverbs to provide vivid descriptions of sensory images. Descriptive prose is common in fiction but may also be found in advertising and journalism.
- **Persuasive writing** is used to advance an argument or point of view. It often begins with the statement of a thesis, presentation of evidence, and a restatement of the thesis as a conclusion. The author may explicitly state his or her own opinions and likely will not pretend to be offering a balanced account of the subject.
- **Narrative writing** is used to tell a story, either fictional or factual. Narrations usually proceed in chronological order, often use literary devices (metaphors, etc.), and may make heavy use of description and dialogue.

Some typologies of academic writing consider poetry, letter, and journal writing to be separate genres.

Content-Area English Instruction

Integrating English Instruction into Content Areas

In addition to learning to use the English language proficiently, ELLs are required to learn the same **content knowledge** as native English speakers. Usually, this is done in an **integrated classroom**, including both native and non-native English speakers, and not always with a teacher who is trained specifically for teaching English. Many times, a school or district has a specialist present to support English language learners and their teachers in **modifying** or **developing curriculum** and instruction. To succeed in teaching ELLs in content areas, the teacher must determine which language skills are necessary to learn and perform well in the content objectives. For instance, when teaching a physics lesson on kinetics, the language features of prepositions and sequencing may be necessary to understand object placement and order of events, but students can still succeed if they make mistakes on plurals or struggle with their tense conjugations. In this content area, language-based corrective feedback may be counter-productive to the student learning the content knowledge. Focusing too much on unrelated language goals may take time away from the objectives at hand and may even artificially increase the students' cognitive load.

Specific Goals for Content-Area English Instruction

The primary goal when supporting ELLs in content areas is to make sure that the input they receive is **comprehensible**. The major factors of an ELL's ability to comprehend subject matter are **general academic English fluency** for the level and a foundation in the **content-specific vocabulary** and concepts involved. Specific strategies that content teachers may employ to ensure their instruction is effective for ELLs in their class are to **pre-test** to determine students' current knowledge levels, **pre-teach vocabulary** to ensure students are primed for the focal points of lessons, and to use frequent **comprehension checks** to ensure students are not lost. All students, not just ELLs, need a certain level of academic knowledge before being able to learn new and more complex ideas. Pre-tests can give a teacher a strong baseline for where to begin instruction if students do not demonstrate readiness in the foundational knowledge. If a comprehension check shows that students are not sure of the material, the teacher should try rewording with simpler, but still accurate, language or elaborating to clarify the point. Pre-teaching vocabulary is one of the most helpful ways of priming ELLs on new topics. Furthermore, cognates, or words that are shared between languages, are abundant in content areas and should be easy for the students to learn and retain with less effort.

Scaffolding Considerations for Content-Area Instruction

As with other types of English learning, employing a combination of instructional time and application time should help with retention of content knowledge. In instructional periods, the teacher should employ verbal scaffolding techniques, including prompting, questioning, and elaborating to ensure comprehension. Teaching should include **explicit teaching**, such as lecturing, but should also include modeling and opportunities for **practice and application** of ideas, especially discussion with classmates, as this helps with both expressive and receptive language skills. When using **modeling** to scaffold instruction, it is helpful to employ visuals and realia, or real-life objects, to help communicate ideas in a more concrete manner. In science, this may be a model or experiment. Mathematics instruction may benefit from using manipulatives or charts and graphs. In social science instruction, tables, timelines, and other types of visual representations of the information are helpful reinforcements of the concepts that may redirect the focus of the lesson to the visual and kinesthetic aspects of the materials, hopefully **reducing the language load** involved.

Discourse Complexity and Adaptation Techniques

It is important to note that different content areas may require distinct types and levels of scaffolding due to the language load involved in each subject. For instance, mathematics and science are inevitably going to have a lower **language load** than history or theatre instruction, but they do have a higher load of **specialized vocabulary** and processes. For instance, the names of laboratory equipment such as beakers, goggles, and microscopes are examples of specialized vocabulary that need to be understood to participate in activities safely. On the other hand, many history lessons may require reading passages that are several pages long to understand the narrative. The language may be less specialized, but the language load is certainly higher due to the volume of reading required. Depending on the circumstances, teachers may need to employ various types of adaptation techniques, including allowing time extensions on work, allowing the use of extra resources (e.g., a bilingual glossary or dictionary), or using excerpts from a reading instead of full-length passages.

Chapter Quiz

Ready to see how well you retained what you just read? Scan the QR code to go directly to the chapter quiz interface for this study guide. If you're using a computer, simply visit the online resources page at **mometrix.com/resources719/csetenglandev** and click the Chapter Quizzes link.

Principles of ELD Instruction and Assessment

Teaching Academic English

Jim Cummins and Cognitive Complexity

In 1981, Jim Cummins published a paper that modeled ELL communication experiences as falling in one of four quadrants created by sketching one axis measuring the **relative cognitive complexity** of the experience and the other measuring the **degree to which the experience occurred** in a context. Cummins outlined four resulting quadrants of experience: (I) cognitively undemanding, context-embedded; (II) cognitively undemanding, context-reduced; (III) cognitively demanding, context-embedded; and (IV) cognitively demanding, context-reduced.

	Cognitively Undemanding	**Cognitively Demanding**
Content-Embedded	I	III
Context Reduced	II	IV

This model built on his earlier distinction between **social (BICS)** and **academic (CALP) language**. Face-to-face social conversations generally fell in quadrant I, whereas learning activities with high academic language content fell in either quadrant III or quadrant IV. Cummins' main point was to underscore that ELLs needed more time to become proficient in academic-language activities, especially those largely free of context, such as standardized tests. Another insight to gain from the quadrants is that emerging ELLs need context support to learn academic language, at least early in their language development. ELL students who are challenged with cognitively-demanding tasks but given little or no support are unlikely to succeed and may become discouraged.

Vocabulary Acquisition Is Dynamic in Process

It is well known that language learners typically need to be exposed to a new word multiple times in order to learn it. This fact is particularly salient in the **acquisition of academic language** because, unlike common words in their social language vocabularies, students may rarely encounter academic language outside of the classroom. Thus, teachers should return repeatedly to academic vocabulary and attempt to situate new words in contexts which each add a new layer to student comprehension.

The idea that vocabulary acquisition is a **dynamic process** refers to the fact that student *understanding* of new words, and their ability to *use* those words, typically progresses over time—

students seldom learn a word and then effectively use it as the result of a single encounter. When they encounter a word repeatedly, they might first simply be aware that they have heard the word before, then later have a vague sense of what *kind* of word it is ("I know we use it to describe people…"). They will likely *comprehend* it long before they learn to *use* it, let alone understand its related forms and how it fits in a network of synonyms, antonyms, and associated words.

Summary Frames

A summary frame is a series of questions, often provided in an outline form, that help students understand the way in which a reading passage is organized or the way their own writing should be organized. **Summary frames** can be created to illustrate a range of **rhetorical forms**. For example, to introduce students to reading or writing texts that compare and contrast, the teacher might provide this framework: "___ and ___ are alike in some ways and different in others. They are alike because ____, ____, and ____. They are different because ____ and ____."

Summary frames are useful for teaching rhetorical forms, for illustrating how to combine sentences to form logical and orderly paragraphs, and for providing examples of transition words.

Activating Students' Prior Knowledge

Students learn new content most easily when it relates to the **knowledge they already have**. This is a central tenet of constructivist theories of learning and is widely accepted. Student background knowledge can range from isolated facts or impressions to full-blown **schema**—a mental framework for ordering and integrating knowledge. Background knowledge also has affective value—students who can relate what they are learning to their own past experiences are more enthusiastic and ultimately successful.

There are abundant techniques for **activating student prior knowledge**. One of the more common is an anticipation guide that poses a series of engaging questions to students about the unit to come. Good anticipation guides provide teachers with insight into student background knowledge and also stimulate students to think and talk about what they already know. Another common technique is to have the students fill out a know-want to know-learned (KWL) chart, which lists student prior knowledge explicitly in the first column.

Benjamin Bloom's Taxonomy of Educational Objectives

In 1956, the educational psychologist Benjamin Bloom created a **taxonomy of human cognitive skills** ranging from the concrete to the abstract and postulated that students progress in learning by mastering progressively more abstract cognitive skills. Bloom's original taxonomy included the following categories of cognitive skill, ranging from the most concrete to the most abstract: knowledge, comprehension, application, analysis, synthesis, and evaluation. Bloom also elaborated a **taxonomy of action verbs** that he argued were indicative of each of the cognitive activities—for example, when students *compare and contrast*, they are undertaking *analysis*.

Students of any language background need explicit instruction and practice in order to learn how to understand and produce academic language structured using cognitively complex verbs such as *analyze, persuade, differentiate*, or *evaluate*. Standardized exams typically test student familiarity with these concepts, increasing their importance for student success. However, research shows that classroom teachers typically prompt their students for responses on the lower end of the scale of cognitive demand—asking them to provide facts, for example, rather than analysis. ESOL teachers must consciously frame their inquiries to spur their students to formulate cognitively complex responses.

Review Video: Bloom's Taxonomy
Visit mometrix.com/academy and enter code: 755020

Literal, Inferential, and Evaluative Comprehension

As ESOL students progress in their language development, the ways in which they can respond to a written text will grow. At an early age, or at a beginning language level, students will strive for **literal comprehension**—an accurate understanding of the facts and events recounted in a text. By asking basic questions of early readers, teachers can check their understanding of vocabulary and syntax. Students with more reading experience achieve **inferential comprehension**—that is, using context clues and outside experiences to discover implied meanings in a text. Asking students about inferential meaning is a good way to bring their background knowledge into a classroom discussion and to get them to discuss ways in which the text relates to the real world. Students engage in **evaluative comprehension** when they offer an assessment of a claim in a text or use a text as a basis for expressing an opinion. Teachers can extend evaluative conversations by asking students for justifications or evidence for their claims and use them as a forum for putting targeted test vocabulary to use, such as *analyze, persuade*, and *contrast*.

Explicit Instruction

In order to effectively understand and use academic language, students must learn new, specialized vocabulary and develop strategies for deciphering complex and compound sentences. In addition to these basic skills, students also need to understand the different forms and functions of academic language and the basic conventions of each. Research suggests that students benefit from **explicit instruction** in these areas and benefit from repeated exposure to exemplary texts. Students will likely benefit from explicit instruction on how the form of a text follows its function, differences between persuasive and objective arguments, when to write from a third-person and a first-person point-of-view, and how to structure arguments with an appropriate balance of assertion and evidence.

Modify Rather Than Simplify

When teaching academic language to emerging ELLs, teachers should be careful not to **simplify** that language to the point where it ceases to be academic language at all. Given that ELLs develop proficiency in social language more rapidly than in academic language, resorting to restatements of essential ideas in social language might serve in the short-term to communicate a concept, but it will do nothing to advance the students' academic language proficiency. Instead, teachers should **repeat** their statements more slowly, and/or use **different intonations or stress** to call student attention to the aspects of the sentence that cause confusion or are critical to understanding. Teachers can **paraphrase** using synonyms for unknown words but should then revert to using the original word to demonstrate that the paraphrase was not for purposes of eliminating the new word from use. If teachers cannot help understanding by repeating their words more slowly or with indicative stress or tone changes, then they should aim at explanations that *elaborate* rather than *simplify* the original statement.

Standards-Based Instruction and Assessment for ELLs

Standards-Based Assessment

Recent educational reform in the United States has focused on establishing grade-level content and skill **standards** to guide both instruction and assessment. This approach provides greater transparency—all stakeholders can view the learning objectives in advance—and gives teachers the means to develop integrated, proportional lesson plans.

One reason policymakers advocated for a **standards-based curriculum**, and in particular for standardized assessments, was to narrow the gap in academic achievement that exists between both states and the districts and schools within states. Standardized assessment rates would allow policymakers to identify districts and schools in need of more resources or educational reform.

Standards-based assessment is also popular among those who see the need for greater teacher accountability, as student performance on standardized assessments arguably serves as a basis for measuring teacher performance. Critics of standards-based assessment focused less on the *nature* of standards-based assessment than on the *number* and *assigned importance* of these assessments, arguing that these factors force teachers to teach toward the exam. In response to these undesired effects, the 2015 Every Student Succeeds Act (ESSA) scaled back the schedule of standardized exams prescribed by the previous No Child Left Behind (NCLB) legislation.

Backward Lesson Planning

Backwards lesson planning is a lesson planning process in which a teacher begins with a specific **learning objective**—often excerpted from the state learning standards—and then works backward to develop lesson plans and activities that will help students achieve that objective. The authors Grant Wiggins and Jay McTighe popularized the concept in their 1998 book *Understanding By Design*.

The **backwards lesson planning method** is meant to rationalize classroom activities to ensure that each makes a clear contribution to the learning process. In a common description, the process is meant to focus attention on *learning* rather than *teaching*. The method is associated with the focus on standardized testing that arose in the No Child Left Behind era, but it has broader application as a method of systematizing instruction and ensuring that the various elements in a lesson plan fit together and build on one another toward clearly articulated objectives.

Curriculum Mapping

Curriculum mapping is the process of ensuring that what is taught corresponds to the **expected learning standards**. In longer terms, it is a process that ensures that there are no gaps or redundancies in what is taught and that a course covers in a thorough and systematic way the corresponding learning objectives. **Curriculum mapping** usually involves allocating instructional time to the various topics to be taught, often in proportion to the topics' relative weight on standardized exams.

Curriculum mapping is used not only to align the content of a course to a set of standards, but also to ensure **consistency** in teaching from one grade to another, in multiple classrooms teaching the same grade-level subject, and to maximize the extent to which the curriculum in one course reinforces the curriculum in another. The latter aspect of curriculum mapping is particularly useful for ESOL teachers who are striving to teach content (especially vocabulary) that their students will use in content classes.

The term "**curriculum calibration**" is also used to describe the process of aligning curriculum to standardized learning objectives.

Federal Requirements for ELL Participation

Federal law (Title VI of the Civil Rights Act of 1964 and the Equal Educational Opportunities Act of 1974) stipulates that public schools must provide the means for ELLs to **participate** "meaningfully and equally" in educational programs. The law requires that ELLs be provided **language services** to achieve English proficiency. States and school districts have measures in place to identify ELLs upon intake, they must monitor ELL progress toward achieving proficiency in English and content areas, and they must ensure that ELLs do not exit language service programs until they have demonstrated proficiency in reading, writing, speaking, and listening. The law also stipulates that ELLs be provided with needed **special education services**. Federal law does not prescribe what type of educational program be provided to ELLs—it leaves discretion to state and local authorities—but it does require the authorities to monitor the success of the programs and make adjustments if necessary. The **Every Student Succeeds Act (2015)** specified that ELL progress in English be assessed annually.

ELA vs. ELD

In 2010, a majority of states adopted a common set of standards (the Common Core) outlining what students should be expected to know in mathematics and language arts at each grade level. States that did not adopt the Common Core standards created their own standards designed to be comparable. The **ELA standards** set benchmarks for student literacy skills in the various subject matter areas.

English language development (ELD) programs utilize second-language instructional practices to assist students with limited English proficiency. When the Common Core was developed, many states with ELD programs, such as California, took steps to integrate the two sets of standards. In these settings, an ELD can be seen as a type of scaffolding program designed to help ELLs reach the same standards of literacy as native speakers. Other states and the WIDA (World-Class Instructional Design and Assessment) Consortium have also developed ELD programs to support ELA and similar standards.

Providing Differentiated Assessment and Instruction

ELD standards are designed to help educators identify and meet the specific needs of ELLs, recognizing that they are at a disadvantage in relation to native speakers in meeting the Common Core or other standardized benchmarks. ELD standards identify a range of **English proficiency levels**, such as beginner, intermediate, and advanced, thus providing a beginning framework for differentiation. Many ELD frameworks develop further categories that **subdivide** the primary proficiency levels—for example, California's ELD framework specifies learners in each of the three proficiency levels as needing substantial, moderate, or light support. The prescribed level of instructional support may vary by specific English skill, activity, or task. These categories provide teachers with a basis for providing differentiated instruction.

Many ELD frameworks recognize long-term English learners (students who have been enrolled for more than six years and are not progressing toward proficiency) as a separate proficiency level and design differentiated lessons to meet their needs.

Differentiation

A teacher employs differentiation when he or she modifies instruction to meet individual student needs. Teachers may **differentiate** their instruction by (a) modifying the content of the lesson, (b) modifying how the lesson is taught or learned, or (c) modifying how students demonstrate their learning.

One way for teachers to think about differentiation in an ESOL context is as the merger of a **content framework** (such as the Common Core) with an **ELD framework** (such as those developed by the WIDA Consortium or the state of California). ELD frameworks define proficiency levels for ELLs—for example, WIDA defines five levels, ranging from entering to bridging. The ELD framework also suggests ways in which teachers might differentiate various learning activities for students at different proficiency levels. For example, an entering student might follow an explicit, minimal writing model, and be given other activities to demonstrate the content knowledge, while a bridging student might be expected to organize his or her own lengthier, content-filled written response.

Using Student Assessment Results for Modification

Good teachers make a habit of **analyzing assessment results** in order to modify and differentiate their instruction. Teachers should attempt to determine whether cases of poor student performance were caused by language deficits or a lack of content understanding. Often teachers can determine this by looking at a student's response to other, similar questions, by assessing how well-written the student's responses are, or by consulting with a content instructor.

If the teacher discovers that a large number of students scored badly on a certain question or group of related questions, they should **reteach** that subject to the entire class. The teacher should try to identify the **core issue**—perhaps the lesson is too complex and needs to be divided into smaller, more manageable chunks; or perhaps success in the lesson was predicated on vocabulary that the students never grasped, in which case the teacher can begin anew with vocabulary instruction.

If the problem is a lack of content knowledge rather than language knowledge, an ESOL teacher can plan more content-related tasks in consultation with the content instructor. If the problem is language related and affects only one student or a group of students, the teacher can use scaffolding and differentiated teaching to address the deficits.

Using Student Assessment Results for Reteaching

When assessment results show that a significant portion of the class lack specific knowledge or a specific skill, teachers should consider **reteaching** that subject. It is important to remember that assessment results might be as formal as student scores on an exam, or as informal as students signaling their understanding with a thumbs-up or thumbs-down gesture.

Reteaching strategies include re-explaining the subject more slowly and using simplified vocabulary; using visual aids; relying on students who understand the concept to peer coach the students who do not; providing more background knowledge or calling on student experience to situate the new material in context; and focusing instruction on the suspected problem area, such as new vocabulary or a particular grammatical form.

Granting ELLs Accommodations

The Every Student Succeeds Act (ESSA) of 2015 renewed the federal government's commitment to ensuring that states provide appropriate accommodation to ESOL students taking state-level content exams. The ESSA leaves it to the states to define appropriate accommodation, and many variations exist. However, many states have joined multi-state consortia (the Partnership for Assessment of Reading of College and Careers and the Smarter Balanced Assessment Consortium are the two largest) for **assessment development**, leading to gradual harmonization of the accommodation standards.

Examples of the **accommodations** include allowing ESOL students additional time to complete the tests, allowing the use of bilingual dictionaries, and allowing a native speaker to read a translated version of the test instructions.

Separate legislation (the Individuals with Disabilities Education Act) mandates accommodations for students (including ELLs) with **disabilities**.

ADAPTING CLASSROOM ASSESSMENTS ELLS

English language learners are at a disadvantage relative to their English-speaking peers when faced with **content assessments**. Researchers often say that they face doubling the cognitive load, as they must process both language and content in both their comprehension of the task and their production of a response. In order to get a clear sense of an ESOL student's content knowledge, a teacher often must make adjustments to the test to render the language component more transparent and less taxing. Teachers can **modify** written exams by giving ESOL students fewer questions; questions and/or instructions in simpler, more literal language; or questions with embedded cues and prompts. Teachers may also allow ESOL students to exhibit their knowledge in different formats—for example, by means of an oral question-and-answer session, or by means of projects or presentations.

PORTFOLIO ASSESSMENTS FOR ELLS

Portfolio assessments, in which either a student or a teacher collects a student's work over time for eventual formative or summative assessment, is a valuable assessment tool for ESOL writing proficiency. Portfolios can be highly individualized or differentiated, allowing each student to be evaluated in terms of progress rather than by comparison with peers. By definition, a portfolio will contain a time-series of a student's work, making his or her progress over time evident. This quality is highly motivational. Finally, a well-constructed portfolio can help remind an ELL of the various *processes* involved in writing (by including various drafts) or the various traits of good writing (by including writing that focuses on vocabulary, voice, organization, etc.). **Portfolio assessments** share many of the weaknesses of other subjective assessments. To be effective, they should be accompanied by clear **rubrics** and frequent **student-teacher conversations** that clarify expectations.

ESOL AND ITS RELATION TO ELA STANDARDS

MEETING ELA STANDARDS

The Common Core State Standards hold ELLs to the same **standards of English language arts (ELA) proficiency** as native English speakers, while recognizing that ELLs may need more time and more support to reach those objectives. In response, both the WIDA consortium and several states (such as California) developed **English language development (ELD) frameworks** to give teachers and parents a detailed roadmap of how ELLs could meet the ELA standards.

The various ELD frameworks define **scales** of student English proficiency (for example, WIDA's ranges from entering to bridging). The frameworks then elaborate **benchmarks** by grade and proficiency level (e.g., in the third grade, a student at the developing stage of proficiency should be able to...) and offer teachers curriculum guidance and provide instructional suggestions for the various grade and English proficiency combinations. In circumstances where ELLs are grouped by language proficiency, teachers can use the ELD frameworks to guide their classroom-level plans and instructional delivery; when faced with a class composed of students with varying levels of proficiency, teachers can use the frameworks to plan differentiated lessons and activities.

Using Formative Assessments

Modern education theory recognizes the value of using **formative assessments** in every classroom context. Teachers achieve the best outcomes when they utilize frequent, varied, and non-intrusive assessments that address clearly-articulated learning objectives and transparent state standards. Modern theory also suggests that grades should primarily reflect whether a student has attained an educational objective and not whether he or she struggled along the way. This insight is particularly important when teaching ELLs: while under the **Common Core**, they are held to the same English language arts standards as native speakers, so they enter the school system at a language disadvantage. In this context, ESOL teachers need to make maximal use of formative assessments to identify what needs to be taught (or re-taught) and how.

Teachers should use formative assessments prior to launching an instructional unit in order to gauge student knowledge and needs; during instruction to check for understanding, identify needed lesson modifications, and detect students in need of help; and after instruction to ensure student comprehension with an eye toward modifying subsequent instruction.

Review Video: Learning Objectives
Visit mometrix.com/academy and enter code: 528458

Effective Resources for Language Learning

Selecting Materials and Resources

Teachers must take care that the **resources** they choose for the classroom are age-appropriate, culturally inclusive, language-accessible, affordable, varied, and easily accessible. One challenge ESOL teachers face is that resources that are language-appropriate for older ELLs may not be age-appropriate—that is, students may perceive them as childish or demeaning. When assigning **online language tasks**, teachers need to make sure students have time to complete the work in class rather than assume the students have access to technology or the Internet at home. Teachers should invite students to bring **realia and written texts** from their native cultures for discussion but shouldn't make the presentation of a home culture mandatory. Teachers should strive to provide resources in **different media** (audio, visual, performative guides, etc.) in order to appeal to different learning preferences and to provide reinforcement of learning through multiple media.

Authentic, Meaningful, and Purposeful Communicative Interactions

Meaningful and purposeful classroom activities are those that achieve a specific learning goal while engaging the students with a topic or a process that is interesting to them. The phrase "**communicative interactions**" points to the sociocultural aspect of language learning—students learn best when they are engaged in authentic communicative acts rather than simply listening to a lecture or practicing repetitive worksheet exercises.

In order to make lessons meaningful, teachers should use **authentic texts and realia**, examples and scenarios from the students' original cultures, and scenarios that reproduce scenes and activities that the students actually experience. Texts should include sympathetic characters facing familiar challenges.

In order to promote communicative interactions, teachers should stage activities that draw students into **conversations**, such as small-group discussions, problem-solving tasks, skits, or dialogue journals. In guiding the conversation, teachers should ask open-ended, exploratory questions that avoid right/wrong answers and invite elaboration. Students should assess and discuss what they read and should write in order to be read—whether it be a product like a classroom newsletter or a journal to be read by a classmate or a parent.

David Ausubel's Subsumption Theory

The educational psychologist David Ausubel's work underscored the importance of **context** for learning. In his view, students learn best when the new material relates to what they already know. He labeled this kind of learning **meaningful** and contrasted it with rote learning, in which students learn isolated information that they can only relate to other information in an arbitrary way. With meaningful learning, new information is **subsumed** under existing cognitive structures and knowledge. Ausubel suggested that the most important factor determining whether students will remember what they learn is not repetition but rather the **integration** of that knowledge in a system of meaning. Even information earned by means of an artificial mnemonic device will eventually be lost, Ausubel argued, unless it is used and, thus, anchored in a broader network of meaning.

Many of Ausubel's insights are now accepted as established principles, and his work is a useful reminder of the importance of activating students' prior knowledge, pre-teaching concepts, and in general providing students with a context for what is to be taught.

Use of Technology

The use of technology in the classroom—and indeed, to blur the line between the inside and outside of a classroom—is widespread, limited in most cases only by funding and teacher unfamiliarity with emerging platforms. The adoption of **technology** is leading to the growth of blended learning, in which online learning replaces a portion of the face-to-face instruction time. Technology plays a key role in many classroom differentiation strategies, as students using software can learn at their own pace and using different learning styles. Technologies that are of particular value in ESOL classrooms include **document cameras**, which can easily provide a visual accompaniment to a spoken lesson, and **online voice recorders**, which allow teachers and students to record specific lessons for targeted speaking practice. Any technology that gives quick access to pictures provides essential scaffolding for early ELLs. Anonymous chat and collaboration sites are particularly useful for ELLs who are not comfortable participating in class.

ESOL teachers need to be careful not to require technologies that their students cannot afford or to assume that students have internet connectivity at home.

Review Video: Benefits of Technology in the Classroom
Visit mometrix.com/academy and enter code: 536375

Computer Assisted Language Learning (CALL)

Computer assisted language learning (CALL) is the use of computer technology to learn languages. Discussions of CALL often distinguish between the use of computers as a tutor and their use as a tool for communicating with others. The most commonly used tutoring applications in ESOL classrooms include **pronunciation tutorials**, in which students listen to native English speakers and record their own speech; **reading tutorials**, in which electronic glossaries provide definitions and draw connections between related texts; and programs that provide outlines and graphic organizers to assist in the **writing process**.

The use of computers as a communication tool is often called **computer-mediated communication (CMC)**. CMC may either be synchronous (real-time interaction with a teacher or other students) or asynchronous (in which students post work for later review or augmentation by other users).

CALL is widely used to differentiate instruction and learning, as individual students can use CALL to learn different lessons at different rates. When used responsibly by self-motivated learners, CALL can provide unique opportunities for self-guided learning. As a communication tool, CALL expands the possibilities for distance learning and collaboration beyond the physical classroom. And finally, computer-based assessments can automate much of the grading and feedback functions of teaching.

Technology and Differentiated Instruction

The single greatest advantage of technology use in the classroom is the opportunities it provides for **differentiated instruction**. Using computer technology, a teacher can differentiate a lesson by content and degree of difficulty, by the amount or nature of scaffolding provided, by learner-style preference, and by a student's preferred method of demonstrating learning. If students have access to the learning technologies at home, they can listen to or read a lesson multiple times, gaining the critical advantages of time and repetition. The same technologies can be used to **differentiate assessments**. With the right technologies, students can listen to questions multiple times or access hyperlinks to contextual information.

Review Video: Differentiated Instruction
Visit mometrix.com/academy and enter code: 100342

School use of technology varies greatly, as does student access to technologies at home. Teachers must be mindful of these limitations and careful not to disadvantage students who lack access. While technology-based learning is great for differentiation and for autonomous learning, students who lack direction may waste their time or pursue inappropriate goals. Finally, even a well-equipped classroom may lack bandwidth or suffer technology failures—teachers have to be prepared with alternative lesson plans.

New Literacies of Online Research and Comprehension

The concept of new literacies of online research and comprehension (often simply called "new literacies") is based on the assertion that online reading and research require a different set of literacy skills than do traditional, paper-based reading, and research. According to this still-emerging body of research, success in traditional reading does not automatically translate to success in online reading. Further, students are likely to have significant advantages in online literacy over their teachers. And online literacy is **deictic**, or ever-changing, in ways that traditional literacy is not, making online literacy an ongoing, dynamic engagement.

Donald Leu has outlined **five functions** critical to online literacy. The first is **identifying the problem**. Students must initiate online research by accurately formulating a question or a search phrase—a skill seldom, if ever, needed in traditional reading. Second, students must know how to **locate information online**, skimming and choosing from search engine results. Third, students must be able to **evaluate sources for reliability and bias**. Fourth, they must be able to **synthesize information drawn from different sources**. (As the number of sources has grown, so has the likelihood that relevant information will be spread among multiple locations.) Finally, students may be called upon to **communicate their results in multiple new formats**, requiring a different range of rhetorical skills.

Corpus and Concordance

A corpus (plural: corpora) is a collection of texts gathered by linguists for purposes of **research**. Today, linguists use computers to search and analyze textual data for insights into language use. Corpora are used, for example, to compile dictionaries and to juxtapose prescriptive and descriptive grammars.

A **concordance** is a list of the ways in which a word is used in **context**. It can be very useful for an ESOL student trying to understand idiosyncratic constructions—for example, which prepositions go with which verbs—or to see how an unfamiliar word is actually used in discourse.

Simple search engines will return some of the information available from a concordance, but intermediate and advanced ESOL students may benefit from a **concordance program** that provides more information than a dictionary about actual usage. Concordances can also show which words are typically used in association with one another—a useful tool when building subject-matter vocabulary.

Assessments Designed for ELLs

First, Second, and Third Generation Test Questions

Education theorists have identified three different types of test questions given historically to assess English language learner aptitude. Though each generation of test question has its strengths and drawbacks, the schema is meant to demonstrate a progression in the quality of assessment.

The **first-generation test question** was typically a single essay question which a teacher graded subjectively on a full spectrum of language criteria: syntax, content, organization, spelling, and penmanship. Alternatively, a series of unrelated short-answer questions were given without supporting context. The **second-generation test** was composed of multiple-choice or true/false questions, a format that solved the problem of subjective grading but left each question devoid of context. In addition, each question could only assess one skill or concept, necessitating long or incomplete exams. The **third-generation test** attempted to test language used in authentic contexts, often by having students analyze a real-life text or perform an authentic writing task. Though these tests were once again subjective in nature, teachers began to use rubrics to reduce the uncertainty involved in grading.

Placement Tests

The purpose of a **placement test** is to identify a student's level of proficiency in the target language in order to guide his or her placement in a program or school. In order to be effective, a placement test should test an appropriate **range of language skills**—a multiple-choice test, for example, might offer insight into a student's knowledge of grammar or vocabulary, but will not test language production or reception. Ideally, a placement test will be tailored to a specific language program or school by including a sample of the actual material taught so that the results provide for unambiguous placements. However, programs can also adapt or interpret the results of standardized exams. Ideally, a placement exam will also offer an initial diagnosis of student strength or weakness in order to help teachers provide early efficacious instruction.

Identification Assessments

An identification assessment is used to identify students in need of **English language assistance**. By federal law (Title VI of the Civil Rights Act of 1964 and the Equal Educational Opportunities Act of 1974), school districts must have procedures in place to screen newly arriving students for potential language assistance. Districts typically begin this process by conducting a **home language**

survey, a series of questions that seek to identify households in which a language other than English is spoken. In these cases, an expert will typically assess the student's educational history and, if there is little or no evidence of previous academic experience in English, refer him or her to take an identification assessment. Different states and consortia use different identification tests—in California, the ELPAC (English Language Proficiency Assessments for California) is used, whereas school districts in Texas may choose from a series of state-approved exams. A minority of states do not use an identification assessment at all but rely instead on a human screener to make ESOL identifications.

Review Video: Developmental Screening Strategies
Visit mometrix.com/academy and enter code: 100353

Reclassification

Reclassification (or redesignation) assessments are used to determine whether an ESOL student has reached sufficient proficiency to be classified as a fluent English speaker and effectively exit the ESOL program.

Federal law requires that states assess ESOL student proficiency every year, but it does not specify the criteria that a state must use in making reclassification decisions. Most states consider additional factors beyond test results, including teacher and parental input, when making reclassification decisions. However, overall **criteria for reclassification** differ widely by state—even states which use the same annual proficiency exam may set different thresholds for exit from an ESOL program. Critics suggest that the reclassification process is often biased toward basic English proficiency but does not effectively measure student English proficiency in the content areas.

Diagnostic Assessments

A diagnostic assessment is designed to reveal a student's strengths and weaknesses. Unlike a placement exam, a **diagnostic exam** is not used to determine the appropriate level of instruction for a student, but the results can be used to tailor instruction or provide the student with an awareness of areas in need of improvement. Unlike an achievement test, a diagnostic test doesn't measure whether students have learned what has already been taught, but instead focuses on the direction of **future instruction**. Diagnostic tests are often detailed and comprehensive within a certain area of instruction (punctuation and capitalization, for example). ESOL teachers often employ diagnostic exams at the beginning of an academic year, particularly if they have new or unfamiliar students in class, in order to get a sharper sense of what they should teach during the academic year.

Proficiency vs. Achievement Tests

Achievement tests are used to measure whether students have learned what has been taught—or, in other words, whether the student has gained the skills and knowledge targeted by instruction. **Achievement tests** are typically summative by nature, as they are usually administered at the end of a learning cycle.

Language proficiency tests are used to evaluate a student's overall language ability at a given moment in time rather than their mastery of recent classroom lessons. Proficiency tests (such as the TOEFL or IELTS exams) are often used to control access to schools or universities or to control the exit from ESOL programs.

Using Assessment Results for Evaluation

ESOL programs rely heavily on assessments to measure **individual student progress**. This same aggregated data can and should be used to evaluate the **overall ESOL program** and to identify areas of improvement. It is important to remember, however, that not all measures of ESOL program success are easily quantifiable—the degree to which ELLs are integrated socially at school is one example—and thus assessment results should not be the *only* basis for program evaluation.

Evaluators must be sure to use assessment data that pinpoints student success in both basic English proficiency and in use of English in the content areas. **Longitudinal (or historic) data** is also important: a school might be meeting regional or national benchmarks, but if its performance has declined over time, a responsible administrator will want to know why. Evaluators should also look at the assessment data from both **peer groups**—a school or district may be achieving consistent benchmarks but be lagging behind peers with similar students—and **high-performing groups**, which can serve as an inspiration for reform or renewal.

Review Video: Assessment Reliability and Validity
Visit mometrix.com/academy and enter code: 424680

Bias in Assessments

Assessments are prone to biases in design. Biases in assessment refer to any sort of advantage or disadvantage that distorts the accurate reporting of the assessment. In other words, an academic assessment attempts to demonstrate how proficient someone is at particular competencies, but if the assessment is not designed appropriately, other factors can impact how well students perform and can give preference to one group of students over another. Common factors that affect ELLs in assessment include language biases and cultural biases. **Language biases** can include factors such as the use of advanced vocabulary, idioms, or complex sentence structures that can throw off and confuse a student who might otherwise be able to answer the questions. For instance, a student taking a math test may fail to answer a question correctly because the *language* elements hurt his ability to read the question correctly. **Cultural biases** similarly might help or harm a student's ability to answer a question correctly if the question assumes knowledge of certain phenomenon. For instance, a history question might require some knowledge of a sport, such as baseball, to understand the question. A student lacking that piece of cultural capital might be unable to answer certain questions. It is important for teachers to be aware of these biases, especially when working with ELLs, and work to design assessments that do not inhibit or advantage students in unfair ways.

Professional Development and Collaboration for Teachers of ELLs

Content Instructors and ESOL Instructors

While content teachers in states with high numbers of ELLs are likely to receive **professional development courses** to help them understand how to work with ELLs, a minority of states mandate such training, even though a majority of content classrooms contain at least one ELL.

ESOL teachers are often called upon—either formally or informally—to **help their colleagues** effectively reach their ELLs. ESOL teachers might help by identifying an ELL's language proficiency level or go further to suggest appropriate teaching supports, reasonable expectations, and teaching methods. They might organize multi-teacher conferences to ensure that ELL students receive consistent instruction throughout the day. ESOL teachers might usefully join parent-teacher conferences to address language concerns. Finally, ESOL teachers might either recommend ESOL-oriented professional development activities to their colleagues or, in the absence of such activities, volunteer to lead periodic training seminars.

Furthering Professional Development

The best professional development provides a teacher with new ideas and the knowledge of how to implement them in the classroom. The simplest—and likely most effective—form of professional development is **networking** with other experienced ESOL teachers, either as a peer or as a mentee. **ESOL conferences** provide the best intersection of networking with learning about ESOL research. The latter can also be accessed through professional journals and the websites of informational clearinghouses such as the Center for Applied Linguistics or the Centre for Educational Research on Languages and Literacies. **Websites** such as Colorin Colorado and Brown University's Education Alliance can be invaluable, and ESOL teachers have established numerous useful blogs, online discussion groups, and Twitter feeds. Though they are potentially expensive in terms of both cost and time, **summer workshops** often offer more systematic training and a resume credential. Finally, committed career professionals should consider doing their own **research for publication**, particularly in an aspect of ESOL that they are passionate about.

TESOL, CAL, ACTFL, NCELA, and NABE

Teachers and prospective teachers of ESOL have a number of organizations they can turn to for information and professional development.

- **TESOL (Teachers of English to Speakers of Other Languages)**: the preeminent organization in the field, offering virtual seminars, online courses, certificate programs, and meetings and conventions dedicated to the field. www.TESOL.org
- **CAL (Center for Applied Linguistics)**: a nonprofit that conducts research into language and culture, develops assessment and curriculum material, and offers training and educational resources for teachers. www.CAL.org
- **ACTFL (American Council on the Teaching of Foreign Languages)**: a membership organization promoting language teaching, with particular expertise in language testing, including for teachers pursuing bilingual certifications. www.ACTFL.org
- **NCELA (National Clearinghouse for English Language Acquisition)**: a resource site run by the US Department of Education, providing data, research, and the English Learner Toolkit, which provides guidance to state and local educators on how to fulfill federal civil rights mandates in the area of English language acquisition. www.ncela.ed.gov
- **NABE (National Association for Bilingual Education)**: a nonprofit that advocates for educational equity and provides professional development and instructional resources for ESOL teachers. www.NABE.org

Assessment Methodology

Assessment Methods

Effective teaching requires multiple methods of assessment to evaluate student comprehension and instructional effectiveness. Assessments are typically categorized as diagnostic, formative, summative, and benchmark and are applicable at varying stages of instruction. **Diagnostic** assessments are administered before instruction and indicate students' prior knowledge and areas of misunderstanding to determine the path of instruction. **Formative** assessments occur continuously to measure student engagement, comprehension, and instructional effectiveness. These assessments indicate instructional strategies that require adjustment to meet students' needs in facilitating successful learning and include strategies like checking for understanding, observations, total participation activities, and exit tickets. **Summative** assessments are given at the end of a lesson or unit to evaluate student progress in reaching learning targets and identify areas of misconception for reteaching. Such assessments can be given in the form of exams and quizzes or be project-based activities in which students demonstrate their learning through hands-on, personalized methods. Additionally, portfolios serve as valuable summative assessments in allowing students to demonstrate their progress over time and provide insight regarding individual achievement. **Benchmark** assessments occur less frequently and encompass large portions of curriculum. These assessments are intended to evaluate the progress of groups of students in achieving state and district academic standards.

Assessment Types

- **Diagnostic:** These assessments can either be formal or informal and are intended to provide teachers with information regarding students' level of understanding prior to beginning a unit of instruction. Examples include pretests, KWL charts, anticipation guides, and brainstorming activities. Digital resources, such as online polls, surveys, and quizzes are also valuable resources for gathering diagnostic feedback.
- **Formative:** These assessments occur throughout instruction to provide the teacher with feedback regarding student understanding. Examples include warm-up and closure activities, checking frequently for understanding, student reflection activities, and providing students with color-coded cards to indicate their level of understanding. Short quizzes and total participation activities, such as four corners, are also valuable formative assessments. Numerous digital resources, including polls, surveys, and review games, are also beneficial in providing teachers with formative feedback to indicate instructional effectiveness.
- **Summative:** Summative assessments are intended to indicate students' levels of mastery and progress toward reaching academic learning standards. These assessments may take the form of written or digital exams and include multiple choice, short answer, or long answer questions. Examples also include projects, final essays, presentations, or portfolios to demonstrate student progress over time.
- **Benchmark:** Benchmark assessments measure students' progress in achieving academic standards. These assessments are typically standardized to ensure uniformity, objectivity, and accuracy. Benchmark assessments are typically given as a written multiple choice or short answer exam, or as a digital exam in which students answer questions on the computer.

Review Video: Formative and Summative Assessments
Visit mometrix.com/academy and enter code: 804991

Determining Appropriate Assessment Strategies

As varying assessment methods provide different information regarding student performance and achievement, the teacher must consider the most applicable and effective assessment strategy in each stage of instruction. This includes determining the **desired outcomes** of assessment as well as the information the teacher intends to ascertain and how they will apply the results to further instruction. **Age-** and **grade-level-**appropriateness must be considered when selecting which assessment strategies will enable students to successfully demonstrate their learning. Additionally, the teacher must be cognizant of students' individual differences and learning needs to determine which assessment model is most **accommodating** and reflective of their progress. It is also important that teachers consider the practicality of assessment strategies and methods they will use to implement the assessment for maximized feedback regarding individual and whole-class progress in achieving learning goals.

Assessments That Reflect Real-World Applications

Assessments that reflect **real-world applications** enhance relevancy and students' ability to establish personal connections to learning that deepen understanding. Implementing such assessments provides authenticity and enhances engagement by defining a clear and practical purpose for learning. These assessments often allow for hands-on opportunities for demonstrating learning and can be adjusted to accommodate students' varying learning styles and needs while measuring individual progress; however, assessments that focus on real-world applications can be subjective, thus making it difficult to extract concrete data and quantify student progress to guide future instructional decisions. In addition, teachers may have difficulty analyzing assessment results on a large scale and comparing student performance with other schools and districts, as individual assessments may vary.

Diagnostic Tests

Diagnostic tests are integral to planning and delivering effective instruction. These tests are typically administered prior to beginning a unit or lesson and provide valuable feedback for guiding and planning instruction. Diagnostic tests provide **preliminary information** regarding students' levels of understanding and prior knowledge. This serves as a baseline for instructional planning that connects and builds upon students' background knowledge and experiences to enhance success in learning. Diagnostic tests allow the teacher to identify and clarify areas of student misconception prior to engaging in instruction to ensure continued comprehension and avoid the need for remediation. They indicate areas of student strength and need as well as individual instructional aids that may need to be incorporated into lessons to support student achievement. In addition, these tests enable the teacher to determine which instructional strategies, activities, groupings, and materials will be most valuable in maximizing engagement and learning. Diagnostic tests can be **formal** or **informal** and include pre-tests, pre-reading activities, surveys, vocabulary inventories, and graphic organizers (such as KWL charts). These tests are used to assess student understanding prior to engaging in learning. Diagnostic tests are generally not graded, as there is little expectation that all students in a class possess the same baseline of proficiency at the start of a unit.

Formative Assessments

Formative assessments are any assessments that take place in the **middle of a unit of instruction**. The goals of formative assessments are to help teachers understand where a student is in his or her progress toward **mastering** the current unit's content and to provide the students with **ongoing feedback** throughout the unit. The advantage of relying heavily on formative assessments in instruction is that it allows the teacher to continuously **check for comprehension** and adjust instruction as needed to ensure that the whole class is adequately prepared to proceed at the end of the unit. To understand formative assessments well, teachers need to understand that any interaction that can provide information about the student's comprehension is a type of formative assessment which can be used to inform future instruction.

Formative assessments are often a mixture of formal and informal assessments. **Formal formative assessments** often include classwork, homework, and quizzes. Examples of **informal formative assessments** include simple comprehension checks during instruction, class-wide discussions of the current topic, and exit slips, which are written questions posed by teachers at the end of class, which helps the teacher quickly review which students are struggling with the concepts.

Summative Assessments

Summative assessment refers to an evaluation at the end of a discrete unit of instruction, such as the end of a course, unit, or semester. Classic examples of summative assessments include end-of-course assessments, final exams, or even qualifying standardized tests such as the SAT or ACT. Most summative assessments are created to measure student mastery of particular **academic standards**. Whereas formative assessment generally informs current instruction, summative assessments are used to objectively demonstrate that each individual has achieved adequate mastery of the standards in question. If a student has not met the benchmark, he or she may need extra instruction or may need to repeat the course.

These assessments usually take the form of **tests** or formal portfolios with rubrics and clearly defined goals. Summative assessments are usually high-stakes, heavily-weighted, and they should always be formally graded. These types of assessments often feature a narrower range of question types, such as multiple choice, short answer, and essay questions to help with systematic grading.

Project-based assessments are beneficial in evaluating achievement, as they incorporate several elements of instruction and highlight real-world applications of learning. This allows students to demonstrate understanding through a hands-on, individualized approach that reinforces connections to learning and increases retainment. **Portfolios** of student work over time serve as a valuable method for assessing individual progress toward reaching learning targets. Summative assessments provide insight regarding overall instructional effectiveness and are necessary for guiding future instruction in subsequent years but are not usually used to modify current instruction.

Review Video: Assessment Reliability and Validity
Visit mometrix.com/academy and enter code: 424680

Benchmark Assessments

Benchmark assessments are intended to quantify, evaluate, and compare individual and groups of students' achievement of school-wide, district, and state **academic standards.** They are typically administered in specific intervals throughout the school year and encompass entire or large units of curriculum to determine student mastery and readiness for academic advancement. Benchmark assessments provide data that enable the teacher to determine students' progress toward reaching academic goals to guide current and continued instruction. This data can be utilized by the school and individual teachers to create learning goals and objectives aligned with academic standards. It can also be used to plan instructional strategies, activities, and assessments to support students in achieving these academic standards. In addition, benchmark assessments provide feedback regarding understanding and the potential need for remediation to allow the teacher to instill necessary supports in future instruction that prepare students for success in achieving learning targets.

Alignment of Assessments with Instructional Goals and Objectives

To effectively monitor student progress, assessments must align with **instructional goals** and **objectives**. This allows the teacher to determine whether students are advancing at an appropriate pace to achieve state and district academic standards. When assessments are aligned with specific learning targets, the teacher ensures that students are learning relevant material to establish a foundation of knowledge necessary for growth and academic achievement. To achieve this, teachers must determine which instructional goals and objectives their students must achieve and derive instruction, content, and activities from these specifications. Instruction must reflect and reinforce learning targets, and the teacher must select the most effective strategies for addressing students' needs as they work to achieve them. Assessments must be reflective of content instruction to ensure they are aligned with learning goals and objectives, as well as to enable the teacher to evaluate student progress in mastering them. The teacher must clearly communicate learning goals and objectives throughout all stages of instruction to provide students with clarity on expectations. This establishes a clear purpose and focus for learning that enhances relevancy and strengthens connections to support student achievement.

Clearly Communicating Assessment Criteria and Standards

Students must be clear on the purpose of learning throughout all stages of instruction to enhance understanding and facilitate success. When assessment **criteria** and **standards** are clearly communicated, the purpose of learning is established, and students are able to effectively connect instructional activities to learning goals and criteria for assessment. Communicating assessment criteria and standards provides students with clarity on tasks and learning goals they are expected to accomplish as they prepare themselves for assessment. This allows for more **focused instruction** and engagement in learning, as it enhances relevancy and student motivation. Utilizing appropriate forms of **rubrics** is an effective strategy in specifying assessment criteria and standards, as it informs students about learning goals they are working toward, the quality of work they are expected to achieve, and skills they must master to succeed on the assessment. Rubrics indicate to students exactly how they will be evaluated, thus supporting their understanding and focus as they engage in learning to promote academic success.

Rubrics for Communicating Standards

The following are varying styles of rubrics that can be used to communicate criteria and standards:

- **Analytic:** Analytic rubrics break down criteria for an assignment into several categories and provide an explanation of the varying levels of performance in each one. This style of rubric is beneficial for detailing the characteristics of quality work as well as providing students with feedback regarding specific components of their performance. Analytic rubrics are most effective when used for summative assessments, such as long-term projects or essays.
- **Holistic:** Holistic rubrics evaluate the quality of the student's assignment as a whole rather than scoring individual components. Students' scores are determined based upon their performance across multiple performance indicators. This style of rubric is beneficial for providing a comprehensive evaluation but limits the amount of feedback that students receive regarding their performance in specific areas.

- **Single-point:** Single-point rubrics outline criteria for assignments into several categories. Rather than providing a numeric score to each category, however, the teacher provides written feedback regarding the students' strengths and ways in which they can improve their performance. This style of rubric is beneficial in providing student-centered feedback that focuses on their overall progress.
- **Checklist:** Checklists typically outline a set of criteria that is scored using a binary approach based upon completion of each component. This style increases the efficiency of grading assignments and is often easy for students to comprehend but does not provide detailed feedback. This method of grading should generally be reserved for shorter assignments.

Communicating High Academic Expectations in Assessments

The attitudes and behaviors exhibited by the teacher are highly influential on students' attitudes toward learning. Teachers demonstrate belief in students' abilities to be successful in learning when they communicate **high academic expectations**. This promotes students' **self-concept** and establishes a **growth mindset** to create confident, empowered learners that are motivated to achieve. High expectations for assessments and reaching academic standards communicates to students the quality of work that is expected of them and encourages them to overcome obstacles as they engage in learning. When communicating expectations for student achievement, it is important that the teacher is aware of students' individual learning needs to provide the necessary support that establishes equitable opportunities for success in meeting assessment criteria and standards. Setting high expectations through assessment criteria and standards while supporting students in their learning enhances overall achievement and establishes a foundation for continuous academic success.

Effective Communication and Impact on Student Learning

Communicating high academic expectations enhances students' self-concept and increases personal motivation for success in learning. To maximize student achievement, it is important that the teacher set high academic expectations that are **clearly** communicated through **age-appropriate** terms and consistently reinforced. Expectations must be reflected through learning goals and objectives and must be **visible** at all times to ensure student awareness. Teachers must be **specific** in communicating what they want students to accomplish and clearly detail necessary steps for achievement while assuming the role of facilitator to guide learning and provide support. Providing constructive **feedback** throughout instruction is integral in reminding students of academic expectations and ensuring they are making adequate progress toward reaching learning goals. When high academic expectations are communicated and reinforced, students are empowered with a sense of confidence and self-responsibility for their own learning that promotes their desire to learn. This ultimately enhances achievement and equips them with the tools necessary for future academic success.

Analyzing and Interpreting Assessment Data

Teachers can utilize multiple techniques to effectively analyze and interpret assessment data. This typically involves creating charts and graphs outlining different data subsets. They can list each learning standard that was assessed, determine how many students overall demonstrated proficiency on the standard, and identify individual students who did not demonstrate proficiency on each standard. This information can be used to differentiate instruction. Additionally, they can track individual student performance and progress on each standard over time.

Teachers can take note of overall patterns and trends in assessment data. For example, they can determine if any subgroups of students did not meet expectations. They can consider whether the data confirms or challenges any existing beliefs, implications this may have on instructional planning and what, if any, conclusions can be drawn from this data.

Analyzing and interpreting assessment data may raise new questions for educators, so they can also determine if additional data collection is needed.

Using Assessment Data to Differentiate Instruction for Individual Learners

By analyzing and interpreting assessment data, teachers can determine if there are any specific learning standards that need to be retaught to their entire classes. This may be necessary if the data shows that all students struggled in these specific areas. Teachers may consider reteaching these standards using different methods if the initial methods were unsuccessful.

Teachers can also form groups of students who did not demonstrate proficiency on the same learning standards. Targeted instruction can be planned for these groups to help them make progress in these areas. Interventions can also be planned for individual students who did not show proficiency in certain areas. If interventions have already been in place and have not led to increased learning outcomes, the interventions may be redesigned. If interventions have been in place and assessment data now shows proficiency, the interventions may be discontinued.

If assessment data shows that certain students have met or exceeded expectations in certain areas, enrichment activities can be planned to challenge these students and meet their learning needs.

Aligning Assessments with Instructional Goals and Objectives

Assessments that are congruent to instructional goals and objectives provide a **clear purpose** for learning that enhances student understanding and motivation. When learning targets are reflected in assessments, instructional activities and materials become more **relevant**, as they are derived from these specifications. Such clarity in purpose allows for more focus and productivity as students engage in instruction and fosters connections that strengthen overall understanding for maximized success in learning. Aligning assessments with instructional goals and objectives ensures that students are learning material that is relevant to the curriculum and academic standards to ensure **preparedness** as they advance in their academic careers. In addition, it enables the teacher to evaluate and monitor student progress to determine whether they are progressing at an ideal pace for achieving academic standards. With this information, the teacher can effectively modify instruction as necessary to support students' needs in reaching desired learning outcomes.

Norm-Referenced Tests

On **norm-referenced tests**, students' performances are compared to the performances of sample groups of similar students. Norm-referenced tests identify students who score above and below the average. To ensure reliability, the tests must be given in a standardized manner to all students.

Norm-referenced tests usually cover a broad range of skills, such as the entire grade-level curriculum for a subject. They typically contain a few questions per skill. Whereas scores in component areas of the tests may be calculated, usually overall test scores are reported. Scores are often reported using percentile ranks, which indicate what percentage of test takers scored lower than the student being assessed. For example, a student's score in the 75th percentile means the student scored better than 75% of other test takers. Other times, scores may be reported using grade-level equivalency.

One advantage of norm-referenced tests is their objectivity. They also allow educators to compare large groups of students at once. This may be helpful for making decisions regarding class placements and groupings. A disadvantage of norm-referenced tests is that they only indicate how well students perform in comparison to one another. They do not indicate whether or not students have mastered certain skills.

Criterion-Referenced Tests

Criterion-referenced tests measure how well students perform on certain skills or standards. The goal of these tests is to indicate whether or not students have mastered certain skills and which skills require additional instruction. Scores are typically reported using the percentage of questions answered correctly or students' performance levels. Performance levels are outlined using terms such as *below expectations*, *met expectations*, and *exceeded expectations*.

One advantage of criterion-referenced tests is that they provide teachers with useful information to guide instruction. They can identify which specific skills students have mastered and which skills need additional practice. Teachers can use this information to plan whole-class, small-group, and individualized instruction. Analyzing results of criterion-referenced tests over time can also help teachers track student progress on certain skills. A disadvantage of criterion-referenced tests is that they do not allow educators to compare students' performances to samples of their peers.

Ways That Standardized Test Results Are Reported

- **Raw scores** are sometimes reported and indicate how many questions students answered correctly on a test. By themselves, they do not provide much useful information. They do not indicate how students performed in comparison to other students or to grade-level expectations.
- **Grade-level equivalents** are also sometimes reported. A grade-level equivalent score of 3.4 indicates that a student performed as well as an average third grader in the fourth month of school. It can indicate whether a student is performing above or below grade-level expectations, but it does not indicate that the student should be moved to a different grade level.
- **Standard scores** are used to compare students' performances on tests to standardized samples of their peers. Standard deviation refers to the amount that a set of scores differs from the mean score on a test.
- **Percentile ranks** are used on criterion-referenced tests to indicate what percentage of test takers scored lower than the student whose score is being reported.
- **Cutoff scores** refer to predetermined scores students must obtain in order to be considered proficient in certain areas. Scores below the cutoff level indicate improvement is needed and may result in interventions or instructional changes.

Formal and Informal Assessments

Assessments are any method a teacher uses to gather information about student comprehension of curriculum, including improvised questions for the class and highly-structured tests. **Formal assessments** are assessments that have **clearly defined standards and methodology** and which are applied consistently to all students. Formal tests should be objective and scrutinized for validity and reliability since they tend to carry higher weight for the student. Summative assessments, such as end-of-unit tests, lend themselves to being formal tests because it is necessary that a teacher test the comprehension of all students in a consistent and thorough way.

Although formal assessments can provide useful data about student performance and progress, they can be costly and time-consuming to implement. Administering formal assessments often interrupts classroom instruction and may cause testing anxiety.

Informal assessments are assessments that do not adhere to formal objectives, and they do not have to be administered consistently to all students. As a result, they do not have to be scored or recorded as a grade and generally act as a **subjective measure** of class comprehension. Informal assessments can be as simple as asking the students to raise their hands if they are ready to proceed to the next step or asking a particular question of an individual student.

Informal assessments do not provide objective data for analysis, but they can be implemented quickly and inexpensively. Informal assessments can also be incorporated into regular classroom instruction and activities, making them more authentic and less stressful for students.

Using Various Assessments

The goal of **assessment** in education is to gather data that, when evaluated, can be used to further student learning and achievement. **Standardized tests** are helpful for placement purposes and to reflect student progress toward goals set by a school district or state. If a textbook is chosen to align with district learning standards, the textbook assessments can provide teachers with convenient, small-scale, regular checks of student knowledge against the target standard.

In order be effective, teachers must know where their students are in the learning process. Teachers use a multitude of **formal and informal assessment methods** to do this. Posing differentiated discussion questions is an example of an informal assessment method that allows teachers to gauge individual student progress rather than their standing in relation to a universal benchmark.

Effective teachers employ a variety of assessments, as different formats assess different skills, promote different learning experiences, and appeal to different learners. A portfolio is an example of an assessment that gauges student progress in multiple skills and through multiple media. Teachers can use authentic or performance-based assessments to stimulate student interest and provide visible connections between language-learning and the real world.

Assessment Reliability

Assessment reliability refers to how well an assessment is constructed and is made up of a variety of measures. An assessment is generally considered **reliable** if it yields similar results across multiple administrations of the assessment. A test should perform similarly with different test administrators, graders, test-takers, and over multiple iterations. Factors that affect reliability include the day-to-day wellbeing of the student (students can sometimes underperform), the physical environment of the test, the way it is administered, and the subjectivity of the scorer (with written-response assessments).

Perhaps the most important threat to assessment reliability is the nature of the **exam questions** themselves. An assessment question is designed to test knowledge of a certain construct. A question is reliable in this sense if students who understand the content answer the question correctly. Statisticians look for patterns in student marks, both within the single test and over multiple tests, as a way of measuring reliability. Teachers should watch out for circumstances in which a student or students answer correctly a series of questions about a given concept (demonstrating their understanding) but then answer a related question incorrectly. The latter question may be an unreliable indicator of concept knowledge.

Measures of Assessment Reliability

- **Test-retest reliability** refers to an assessment's consistency of results with the same test-taker over multiple retests. If one student shows inconsistent results over time, the test is not considered to have test-retest reliability.

- **Intertester reliability** refers to an assessment's consistency of results between multiple test-takers at the same level. Students at similar levels of proficiency should show similar results.
- **Inter-rater reliability** refers to an assessment's consistency of results between different administrators of the test. This plays an especially critical role in tests with interactive or subjective responses, such as Likert-scales, cloze tests, and short answer tests. Different raters of the same test need to have a consistent means of evaluating the test-takers' performance. Clear rubrics can help keep two or more raters consistent in scoring.
- **Intra-rater reliability** refers to an assessment's consistency of results with one rater over time. One test rater should be able to score different students objectively to rate subjective test formats fairly.
- **Parallel-forms reliability** refers to an assessment's consistency between multiple different forms. For instance, end-of-course assessments may have many distinctive test forms, with different questions or question orders. If the different forms of a test do not provide the same results, the test is said to be lacking in parallel-forms reliability.
- **Internal consistency reliability** refers to the consistency of results of similar questions on a particular assessment. If there are two or more questions targeted at the same standard and at the same level, they should show the same results across each question.

Assessment Validity

Assessment validity is a measure of the relevancy that an assessment has to the skill or ability being evaluated and the degree to which students' performance is representative of their mastery of the topic of assessment. In other words, a teacher should ask how well an assessment's results correlate to what it is looking to assess. Assessments should be evaluated for validity on both the **individual question** level and as a **test overall**. This can be especially helpful in refining tests for future classes. The overall validity of an assessment is determined by several types of validity measures.

An assessment is considered **valid** if it measures what it is intended to measure. One common error that can reduce the validity of a test (or a question on a test) occurs if the instructions are written at a reading level the students can't understand. In this case, it is not valid to take the student's failed answer as a true indication of his or her knowledge of the subject. Factors internal to the student might also affect exam validity: anxiety and a lack of self-esteem often lower assessments results, reducing their validity as a measure of student knowledge.

An assessment has content validity if it includes all the **relevant aspects** of the subject being tested—if it is comprehensive, in other words. An assessment has **predictive validity** if a score on the test is an accurate predictor of future success in the same domain. For example, SAT exams purport to have validity in predicting student success in a college. An assessment has construct validity if it accurately measures student knowledge of the subject being tested.

Measures of Assessment Validity

- **Face validity** refers to the initial impression of whether an assessment seems to be fit for the task. As this method is subjective to interpretation and unquantifiable, it should not be used singularly as a measurement of validity.

- **Construct validity** asks if an assessment actually assesses what it is intended to assess. Some topics are more straightforward, such as assessing if a student can perform two-digit multiplication. This can be directly tested, which gives the assessment a strong content validity. Other measures, such as a person's overall happiness, must be measured indirectly. If an assessment asserted that a person is generally happy if he or she smiles frequently, it would be fair to question the construct validity of that assessment because smiling is unlikely to be a consistent measure of all peoples' general happiness.
- **Content validity** indicates whether the assessment is comprehensive of all aspects of the content being assessed. If a test leaves out an important topic, then the teacher will not have a full picture as a result of the assessment.
- **Criterion validity** refers to whether the results of an assessment can be used to **predict** a related value, known as **criterion**. An example of this is the hypothesis that IQ tests would predict a person's success later in life, but many critics believe that IQ tests are not valid predictors of success because intelligence is not the only predictor of success in life. IQ tests have shown validity toward predicting academic success, however. The measure of an assessment's criterion validity depends on how closely related the criterion is.
- **Discriminant validity** refers to how well an assessment tests only that which it is intended to test and successfully discriminates one piece of information from another. For instance, a student who is exceptional in mathematics should not be able to put that information into use on a science test and gain an unfair advantage. If the student is able to score well due to his or her mathematics knowledge, the science test did not adequately discriminate science knowledge from mathematics knowledge.
- **Convergent validity** is related to discriminant validity, but takes into account that two measures may be distinct but correlated. For instance, a personality test should distinguish self-esteem from extraversion so that they can be measured independently, but if an assessment has convergent validity, it should show a correlation between related measures.

Practicality

An assessment is **practical** if it uses an appropriate amount of human and budgetary resources. A practical exam doesn't take very long to design or score, nor does it take students very long to complete in relation to other learning objectives and priorities. Teachers often need to balance a desire to construct comprehensive or content-valid tests with a need for practicality: lengthy exams consume large amounts of instruction time and may return unreliable results if students become tired and lose focus.

Assessment Bias

An assessment is considered biased if it disadvantages a certain group of students, such as students of a certain gender, race, cultural background, or socioeconomic class. A **content bias** exists when the subject matter of a question or assessment is familiar to one group and not another. For example, a reading comprehension passage that discusses an event in American history would be biased against students new to the country. An **attitudinal bias** exists when a teacher has a pre-conceived idea about the likely success of an assessment of a particular individual or group. A **method bias** arises when the format of an assessment is unfamiliar to a given group of students. **Language bias** occurs when an assessment utilizes idioms, collocations, or cultural references unfamiliar to a group of students. Finally, **translation bias** may arise when educators attempt to translate content-area assessments into a student's native language—rough or hurried translations often result in a loss of nuance important for accurate assessment.

Authentic Assessments

An authentic assessment is an assessment designed to closely resemble something that a student does, or will do, in the real world. For example, students will never encounter a multiple-choice test requiring them to choose the right tense of a verb, but they will encounter contexts in which they have to write a narration of an event that has antecedents and consequents spread out in time—like narrating their version of what caused a traffic accident. The latter is an example of a potential **authentic assessment**.

Well-designed authentic assessments require a student to exercise **advanced cognitive skills** (e.g., solving problems, integrating information, performing deductions), integrate **background knowledge**, and confront **ambiguity**. Research has demonstrated that mere language proficiency is not predictive of future language success—learning how to utilize knowledge in a complex context is an essential additional skill.

The terms "authentic" and "performance-based" are often used interchangeably when describing assessments; however, a performance-based assessment doesn't necessarily have to be grounded in a possible authentic experience.

Performance-Based Assessments

A performance-based assessment is one in which students demonstrate their learning by performing a **task** rather than by answering questions in a traditional test format. Proponents of **performance-based assessments** argue that they lead students to use **high-level cognitive skills** since they focus on how to put their knowledge to use and plan a sequence of stages in an activity or presentation. They also allow students more opportunities to individualize their presentations or responses based on preferred learning styles. Research suggests that students welcome the chance to put their knowledge to use in real-world scenarios.

Advocates of performance-based assessments suggest that they avoid many of the problems of language or cultural bias present in traditional assessments, allowing more accurate assessment of how well students learned the underlying concepts. In discussions regarding English as a second language, they argue that performance assessments come closer to replicating what should be the true goal of language learning—the effective use of language in real contexts—than do more traditional exams. Critics point out that performance assessments are difficult and time-consuming for teachers to construct and for students to perform. Finally, performative assessments are difficult to grade in the absence of a well-constructed and detailed rubric.

Technology-Based Assessments

Technology-based assessments provide teachers with multiple resources for evaluating student progress to guide instruction. They are applicable in most formal and informal instructional settings and can be utilized as formative and summative assessments. Technology-based assessments simplify and enhance the efficiency of determining comprehension and instructional effectiveness, as they quickly present the teacher with information regarding student progress. This data enables the teacher to make necessary adjustments to facilitate student learning and growth. Implementing this assessment format simplifies the process of aligning them to school and district academic standards. This establishes objectivity and uniformity for comparing results and progress among students. It also helps ensure that all students are held to the same academic expectations. While technology-based assessments are beneficial, there are some shortcomings to consider. This format may not be entirely effective for all learning styles in demonstrating understanding, as individualization in technology-based assessment can be limited. These assessments may not illustrate individual students' growth over time but rather their mastery of an academic standard, thus hindering the ability to evaluate overall achievement. As technology-based evaluation limits hands-on opportunities, the real-world application and relevancy of the assessment may be unapparent to students.

Advantages and Disadvantages of Technology-Based Assessments

Technology-based assessments can have many advantages. They can be given to large numbers of students at once, limited only by the amounts of technological equipment schools possess. Many types of technology-based assessments are instantly scored, and feedback is provided quickly. Students are sometimes able to view their results and feedback at the conclusion of their testing sessions. Data can be quickly compiled and reported in easy-to-understand formats. Technology-based assessments can also often track student progress over time.

Technology-based assessments can have some disadvantages as well. Glitches and system errors can interfere with the assessment process or score reporting. Students must also have the necessary prerequisite technological skills to take the assessments, or the results may not measure the content they are designed to measure. For example, if students take timed, computer-based writing tests, they should have proficient typing skills. Otherwise, they may perform poorly on the tests despite strong writing abilities. Other prerequisite skills include knowing how to use a keyboard and mouse and understanding how to locate necessary information on the screen.

Portfolio Assessments

A **portfolio** is a collection of student work in multiple forms and media gathered over time. Teachers may assess the portfolio both for evidence of progress over time or in its end state as a demonstration of the achievement of certain proficiency levels.

One advantage of **portfolio assessments** is their breadth. Unlike traditional assessments, which focus on one or two language skills, portfolios may contain work in multiple forms, such as writing samples, pictures, and graphs designed for content courses, video and audio clips, student reflections, teacher observations, and student exams. A second advantage is that they allow a student to develop work in authentic contexts, including in other classrooms and at home.

In order for portfolios to function as an objective assessment tool, teachers should negotiate with students in advance of what genres of work will be included and outline a grading rubric that makes clear what will be assessed, such as linguistic proficiency, use of English in academic contexts, and demonstrated use of target cognitive skills.

Curriculum-Based Assessments

Curriculum-based assessments, also known as **curriculum-based measurements (CBM)**, are short, frequent assessments designed to measure student progress toward meeting curriculum **benchmarks**.

Teachers implement CBMs by designing **probes**, or short assessments that target specific skills. For example, a teacher might design a spelling probe, administered weekly, that requires students to spell 10 unfamiliar but level-appropriate words. The data from these assessments can be tracked over time to measure student progress toward defined grade-level goals.

CBM has several clear advantages. If structured well, the probes have high reliability and validity. Furthermore, they provide clear and objective evidence of student progress—a welcome outcome for students and parents who often grapple with less-clear and subjective evidence. Used correctly, CBMs also motivate students and provide them with evidence of their own progress; however, while CBMs are helpful in identifying areas of student weaknesses, they do not identify the causes of those weaknesses or provide teachers with strategies for improving instruction.

Textbook Assessments

Textbook assessments are the assessments provided at the end of a chapter or unit in an approved textbook. **Textbook assessments** present several advantages for a teacher: they are already made; they are likely to be accurate representations of the chapter or unit materials; and, if the textbook has been prescribed or recommended by the state, it is likely to correspond closely to Common Core or other tested standards.

Textbook assessments can be limiting for students who lag in the comprehension of academic English or whose preferred learning style is not verbal. While textbooks may come with DVDs or recommended audio links, ESOL teachers will likely need to supplement these assessment materials with some of their own findings. Finally, textbook assessments are unlikely to represent the range of assessment types used in the modern classroom, such as a portfolio or performance-based assessments.

Peer Assessment

A peer assessment is when students grade one another's work based on a teacher-provided framework. **Peer assessments** are promoted as a means of saving teacher time and building student metacognitive skills. They are typically used as **formative** rather than summative assessments, given concerns about the reliability of student scoring and the tensions that can result if student scores contribute to overall grades. Peer assessments are used most often to grade essay-type written work or presentations. Proponents point out that peer assessments require students to apply metacognition, build cooperative work and interpersonal skills, and broaden the sense that the student is accountable to peers and not just the teacher. Even advocates of the practice agree that students need detailed rubrics in order to succeed. Critics often argue that low-performing students have little to offer high-performing students in terms of valuable feedback—and this disparity may be more pronounced in ESOL classrooms or special education environments than in mainstream ones. One way to overcome this weakness is for the teacher to lead the evaluation exercise, guiding the students through a point-by-point framework of evaluation.

Chapter Quiz

Ready to see how well you retained what you just read? Scan the QR code to go directly to the chapter quiz interface for this study guide. If you're using a computer, simply visit the online resources page at **mometrix.com/resources719/csetenglandev** and click the Chapter Quizzes link.

CSET Practice Test #1

Want to take this practice test in an online interactive format?
Check out the online resources page, which includes interactive practice questions and much more: **mometrix.com/resources719/csetenglandev**

1. According to research, what is a common outcome when teachers interpret oral language proficiency assessments, such as the Language Assessment Scales-Oral, the Woodcock-Muñoz Language Survey, and the IDEA Proficiency Test, in terms of an ELL's general scholastic performance?

a. The student is more likely to receive the help he or she needs, both in terms of language learning and in terms of academic achievement.
b. The student is more likely to be held back a grade.
c. The student is more likely to be placed in a special education program.
d. The student is more likely to be placed at a level higher than his or her language abilities can support.

2. Is acculturation or assimilation more likely to produce second language learners who are successful at both BICS and CALP thresholds?

a. Assimilation: when learners feel their own culture is respected, their affective filter will rise, motivating them to learn.
b. Acculturation: adapting to a new culture, which includes understanding cultural expectations, semiotics, values, and beliefs, is essential to second language acquisition in that it provides appropriate context.
c. Acculturation: when language learners prioritize the demands of their new culture over their culture of origin, with time they abandon their prior cultural values and expectations and become a tabula rasa upon which the adopted culture can more fully write itself.
d. Assimilation: when language learners prioritize the demands of their new culture over their culture of origin, with time they abandon their prior cultural values and expectations and become a tabula rasa upon which the adopted culture can more fully write itself.

3. Research indicates that the Silent/Receptive stage of second language acquisition typically lasts up to ______, during which time a learner understands and can respond to roughly ________ words.

a. Two years; 1,000
b. Six months; 500
c. One month; 100
d. 18 months; 1,000

4. The Cognitive Academic Language Learning Approach (CALLA) and Specially Designed Academic Instruction in English (SDAIE) are examples of which of the following?

a. English for a Specific Purpose (ESP)
b. Content-based ESL models
c. Direct Instruction
d. Total Physical Response (TPR) approach

5. Which of the following statements is true?

a. ELLs are typically more proficient at expressing themselves verbally than they are at listening and then interpreting what is being said by someone else.
b. ELLs who are not literate in their first language have a better chance at becoming literate in their second language.
c. ELLs often understand more in terms of vocabulary and correct syntax than they demonstrate in their own speaking.
d. Once an ELL has achieved BICS competency, CALP competency will soon follow.

6. Second language acquisition research suggests L2s tend to do what to acquire linguistic rules?

a. Integrate formulaic expressions and apply new uses to them.
b. Learn grammar rules and progressively apply them.
c. Learn words and phrases as chunks and use them in repetitive ways.
d. Try to apply phrases from L1 and bridge them into L2.

7. Canale and Swain define communicative competence as consisting what four elements?

a. Competence in grammar, vocabulary, semantics, and phonetics
b. Reading, writing, listening, and speaking
c. Reading, writing, math, and science
d. Competence in grammar, sociolinguistics, discourse, and communication strategies

8. A second-grade teacher is planning a unit on measurements in his math unit. Which Specially Designed Academic Instruction in English (SDAIE) strategy would best support his English language learners in their English language development?

a. Using rulers and scales to measure actual objects that the teacher collected
b. Shortening the language being used in word problems so learners grasp the concepts faster
c. Activating prior knowledge by asking students about how their parents cook at home using measurements
d. Asking students to deduce how each unit of measurement is used based on their own research

9. Which of the following presents the most effective way a third-grade teacher can help students expand their vocabularies?

a. Give them a word-a-day to memorize. They must use the word five times in conversation and once in writing. Then at the end of the week, give them the opportunity to write a creative story or poem using all five of the week's words.
b. Play a game in which one student selects a word from the dictionary that is complex and unknown. Next, singly or in groups, have students take a risk and try to guess the definition.
c. Teach a unit on prefixes and suffixes. Offer some examples of each. Next, group the students into teams and see which team comes up with the most words that use prefixes and suffixes. Challenge them by asking for a word with both a prefix and a suffix.
d. Have students find words in newspapers, magazines, and elsewhere that they do not understand. Give them the definitions, and have them write them down in a word book or put them on the word wall.

10. The new ESL teacher is compiling a file of information for each of her students. Her files include level of L1 education and literacy; level of L2 competency in the four modalities of speaking, writing, listening, and reading; the type and depth of English study the student has undertaken; the student's interests and personality type; and the most effective learning styles for the particular student. What does the teacher most likely intend to use these files for?

a. She will use the information they contain to vary her lessons to meet each student's specific needs.
b. She will send them home periodically so that parents can read her notes and sign off on them.
c. She will use the information to separate the students into their respective levels in future classes.
d. She will share the students' files with classmates so they can get to know one another on a more intimate, personal level.

11. An ESL teacher is using dialogue journals with her students. The students write in the journals three times a week on any subject they choose. What is the purpose of such journals?

a. The teacher will discover what is important to the students and can modify her instruction accordingly.
b. This will give students ample time to practice writing dialogue, including grammatical practice, such as use of quotation marks, and content practice, such as writing dialogue that is dynamic, interesting, and characterizes the speakers.
c. The teacher will use these journals to correct student misconceptions about rules of grammar and semantics. Because the students are invested in their own words, they will be more open to such correction than in highly-systematized classroom instruction.
d. The teacher will write comments and questions in response, modeling correct English usage.

12. What is the BSM, and what is it designed to establish?

a. The Bilingual Strategies Method establishes effective instructional methods for mainstreamed bilingual students.
b. The Bilingual Syntax Measure is a tool designed to assess oral language proficiency and dominance between two languages.
c. The Burke-Stanley Milestone establishes points along the continuum from little English to full fluency.
d. The Babcock Statistical Model establishes a measurable baseline for bilingual educators.

13. Which of the following is a common criticism that has been leveled at oral proficiency assessments, such as the Language Assessment Scales-Oral, the Woodcock-Muñoz Language Survey, and the IDEA Proficiency Test?

a. They are biased toward native English speakers.
b. They are biased toward non-native English speakers.
c. They do not accurately reflect native speakers' academic performance and therefore cannot accurately reflect non-native speakers' performance.
d. They do not accurately reflect native speakers' proficiency and therefore cannot accurately reflect non-native speakers' proficiency.

14. In terms of models, which program model does research indicate is least effective?

a. Two-way immersion
b. Sheltered English
c. Transitional bilingual education
d. Pull-out ESL classes

15. What 1982 Supreme Court case established the right to a free education for undocumented immigrant children?

a. Plyler v. Doe
b. Lau v. Nichols
c. Meyer v. Nebraska
d. Castaneda v. Pickard

16. A student is capable of speaking relatively easily, but slowly and makes periodic errors in speech. Which level of capability is the student most likely in?

a. Intermediate Fluency
b. Advanced Fluency
c. Early Production
d. Speech Emergence

17. An upper-elementary school teacher is developing a rubric for a science project she will conduct with her fifth-grade students. What is the first question she should ask herself when developing this rubric?

a. What type of task am I asking students to complete?
b. What is the level of language I should use when considering my English language learners?
c. How will I break up the rubric into categories such as hypothesis, observations, and results?
d. What should students be able to do and know at the end of the project?

18. Which of the following classroom practices is LEAST effective with regard to second language acquisition:

a. Presenting sufficient and meaningful reading and writing experiences for students to practice strategies
b. Keeping all reading and writing activities at the student's current reading level
c. Reviewing and re-teaching as required to ensure that students have integrated essential content
d. Daily introduction of a few new words or concepts

19. That tiny red car is a <u>Smart car</u>. In this statement, the underlined words are:

a. A predicate adjective
b. Predicate adjectives
c. A predicate nominative
d. Predicate nominatives

20. An eleventh-grade anatomy teacher is administering a test for his unit on the bones in the body. Several of his essay questions require extensive writing to demonstrate knowledge of the skeletal system. What are ways he can ensure that for the English learners in his class, his assessment measures content knowledge rather than language skills?

a. Allow students to answer questions orally to the teacher.
b. Administer only half of the exam, so that they have time to write
c. Develop an alternative assessment that asks the student to draw pictures
d. Translate the test into the students' home language, and allow them to answer in that language

21. The parents of a first-grade LEP student do not want her placed in a special education classroom; they feel that she is better off in a regular classroom at her grade level. The classroom teacher, ESL teacher, school counselor, and diagnostician are all certain that she has several interrelated learning disabilities, as well as some emotional issues. Given that she is unlikely to thrive in a regular classroom, will cause an extra burden of work to the teacher, and will without doubt be disruptive and cause problems for other students, can she be placed in special education classes?

a. No; parental permission is required.
b. Yes; parental permission is required, but in its absence a building can, with requests from four or more professionals, be overridden.
c. Possibly; the school must refer the case to Children's Protective Services, which will make the final decision.
d. Temporarily, while the district takes the parents to court to force the issue. If the court rules in favor of the parents, the district must place the student in a regular classroom, pay the parents' legal costs, and pay a fine if the judge so orders. If the court rules in favor of the district, the parents must pay all court costs, but no fine can be assigned.

22. Which of the following describes the Self-Contained Model for teaching?

a. Emphasis on technological aids and a single teacher who provides support as issues come up.
b. Students attend typical coursework with the general population of a school and receive adaptive help from a specialist at the end of the day
c. A single teacher has students in a self-contained classroom and is responsible for both language and academic performance
d. Students are given one day out of their five-day week to spend in an ESL class while the rest of the days, they attend traditional classes.

23. Basic Interpersonal Communicative Skills (BICS) and Cognitive Academic Language Proficiency (CALP) describe two distinct thresholds of language proficiency attained by a language learner. What are these two thresholds?

a. BICS skills are necessary for academic communication, require content-specific vocabularies and more sophisticated syntax, and do not rely upon external contextual information, while CALP skills permit social communications that are face-to-face and include contextual information, informal vocabulary, and relatively simple syntax.
b. BICS skills are limited to single-word responses in oral communication, include a very limited vocabulary in L2, and permit some interface with L1, while CALP skills require external contextual clues in order to be interpreted.
c. CALP skills are limited to single-word responses in oral communication, include a very limited vocabulary in L2, and permit some interface with L1, while BICS skills depend heavily upon prior knowledge.
d. BICS skills permit social communications that are face-to-face and include contextual information, informal vocabulary, and relatively simple syntax, while CALP skills are necessary for academic communication, require content-specific vocabularies and more sophisticated syntax, and do not rely upon external contextual information.

24. When does special education law apply to LEPs?

a. Never; the two are distinct and share no overlap.
b. Only when an LEP student also has learning, emotional, or physical disabilities as well
c. Always
d. It has not been definitively decided.

25. A student whose L1 is Basque is displaying certain problems. The ESL teacher is uncertain whether he has one or more learning disabilities or if it could be a problem with his language development. She is uncertain what to do. She knows that if she refers him for assessment, he might be inaccurately labeled as learning impaired and placed in a special education class. If his problems are language-based, such a move could be detrimental. She knows that there are no assessments available in Basque in her district, and she feels strongly that he needs to be presented with certain questions and allowed to answer in his own words before a decision is made. The boy's adult aunt, a fluent English speaker and the teacher's neighbor and friend, has offered to help as an informal translator. Is this a suitable fix?

a. No. The friendship between the teacher and aunt precludes using her as a translator. Both her friendship with the teacher and her familial relationship with the student could affect her objectivity.
b. No. She is not a trained translator, and, for this reason alone, the aunt is not suitable for this task. The school is legally responsible for providing a trained translator or materials in Basque, if they are available. The teacher must advocate on behalf of the student and try to find a trained translator or the materials in Basque.
c. Yes. The student needs to be assessed one way or another to determine whether he has learning disabilities or whether his problem is in the area of language development. It is unreasonable for the school to expect the teacher to devote hours to tracking down a translator, and the aunt will do the job for free. There's really no reason not to take her up on it!
d. Yes. The student will likely feel very comfortable with his aunt translating. There is the added bonus that if he doesn't understand a question or wants to ask what the purpose of it is, they can privately share a conversation about the test out loud, while simultaneously protecting the student's privacy.

26. According to Banks's Four Approaches to Multicultural Curriculum Reform, which of the following describes an additive multicultural education approach?

a. Including novels and other works in the curriculum to demonstrate the works of diverse contributors
b. Following the traditional curriculum while including alternate concepts and perspectives
c. Modifying the traditional curriculum to focus on diverse views in place of the original focus
d. Having students create a petition to support equity in the community as it pertains to the curriculum

27. Which of the following is NOT required for an LEP's permanent record?

a. The student's level of language proficiency designated
b. A writing sample
c. Parental approval
d. Program entry and exit dates and notification of same to parents

28. An upper-level elementary school teacher is developing a unit on American history. How can he use formative assessments to support his students' English language and literacy development?

a. Create versions of the unit test to support learners with different linguistic needs.
b. Have English learners complete an alternative project that does not require essay writing such as a visual display of American history.
c. Administer a unit-end assessment to determine mastery.
d. Conduct informal checks on the daily language objective of the lesson, so the teacher can incorporate his observations into the next day's lesson.

29. What should a teacher working with an ESL student who is at the preproduction stage do?

a. Devise role-playing games and activities.
b. Offer ample opportunity for face-to-face dialogue.
c. Encourage silent students to speak; this is especially important for introverted students.
d. Incorporate gesture, pictures, manipulatives, and other extra-verbal tools into her teaching.

Refer to the following for questions 30–31:

A high school art teacher has assigned biographical readings on different artists to her students, including several beginning-level and intermediate-level English learners.

30. Which assignment is MOST appropriate for her English learners to complete to help them comprehend the texts?

a. Assigning an alternative activity in which they look at artwork created by the artists
b. Using an organizer with fill in the blanks for key words to aid comprehension
c. Scrambling the text and asking students to put the biographical information in order
d. Asking students to paraphrase and summarize what they have read

31. How can the teacher best simplify a text for ELLs at the beginning and intermediate stages?

a. Substitute one-syllable words for two-syllable words; delete as much text as possible and provide illustrations instead; have students keep reader response journals.
b. Shorten the text by putting more words on each page; delete illustrations that will distract the reader; provide a glossary of terms at the end of the book.
c. Shorten the text; abbreviate sentences; replace abstract language with concrete language; break complex sentences into two or three simpler, more direct sentences; omit detail that enhances the text but doesn't change or clarify meaning.
d. Clarify the text by offering interpretations at the bottom of each page; provide a Spanish-English glossary of terms at the end of the book; omit illustrations that will distract the reader.

32. Lau v. Nichols (US Supreme Court, 1974) determined that ELLs must be given what right?

a. To the same educational opportunities as all students
b. To receive private tutoring until they are working at grade level or above
c. To instruction that they have the skills to understand
d. To unbiased, fair grading practices

33. Because the United States began as a melting pot of people from many different nationalities and ethnic groups, bilingual communities and education were a matter of course. It was essential for business people who served members of a particular culture to know that language, and immigrant children who did not speak English were often taught in their language of origin. By WWI, the United States began to develop a strong sense of itself as a nation, and English emerged as the "national" language. Non-English-speaking children were no longer taught in any language other than English. When did this trend begin to reverse, and why?

a. After WWII, as Americans began to see themselves as part of a "world nation" consisting of a vast and diverse group of individuals with cultural ties worthy of respect.
b. In the 1960s, Cuban immigrants established a successful bilingual program, and the Civil Rights movement put attention on correcting educational and social agendas that were prejudiced in favor of the white middle class.
c. The late 1950s, the influence of early hippies and beatniks, who preached the idea of loving one another and living in peace had a strong, immediate impact on the field of education.
d. The 1990s, with the Clinton administration, saw bilingual education as an essential step toward leading the nation into the 21st century.

34. Realia means:

a. Real-world experiences
b. Reliable and, therefore, trustworthy methods of instruction
c. Concrete objects used in demonstrations to develop vocabulary and encourage discourse
d. Manifested, or "realized," concepts.

35. In the early production stage of language acquisition, an L2 learner typically:

a. Understands 1,000 words and can respond to instructions involving up to three requests
b. Begins to speak in sentences of one-to-two clauses
c. Understands up to 5,000 words, but uses only a handful
d. Understands and uses roughly 1,000 words

36. A sixth-grade English language arts teacher is considering how to scaffold a reading activity with several short stories. Which of the following would be an appropriate pre-reading scaffolding activity to support her early-advanced English learners?

a. Activating prior knowledge through writing a creative piece in the perspective of one of the characters once the teacher has read the story aloud
b. Creating or selecting visuals to go along with the short stories to aid comprehension
c. Using a video to summarize what the story is about before reading the text
d. Selecting short passages from the reading to build student interest and have them predict what will happen in the text

37. Which answer best describes the stages of language acquisition?

a. Letter recognition stage; vocabulary development stage; listening stage; contextually predictive stage
b. Recognition of primary syntactical patterning stage; articulation stage; contextual referencing stage; BICS stage; CALP stage
c. Pre-production stage; early production stage; speech emergence stage; intermediate fluency stage
d. Listening stage; copying stage; single-word response stage; multiple-word response stage; confidence stage

38. The Texas English Language Proficiency Assessment System (TELPAS) is used for _____ students in grades__________

a. All students; K–5th
b. EB students; K–5th
c. EB students; K–12th
d. All students; K–12th

39. An ESL teacher has asked a group of high school students to visit her classroom and work individually with her students. The teacher has given the high school volunteers tape recorders, paper, and pencils and asked them to begin with a brief conversation with their respective L2s that will lead the L2s to a memory of a personal experience. The volunteers then take dictation, writing down exactly what the non-native speakers say. Next, the volunteers read their stories back to the authors. Following that, the authors read their own stories silently or aloud. This method is designed to simultaneously model encoding, develop sight word vocabulary, and motivate the ESL students to work toward fluency. This approach is known as:

a. Two-way immersion
b. Language Experience Approach
c. The Silent Way
d. Audiolingual Approach

40. How are traditional ESL programs and Content-Based ESL Curriculum (CBEC) different?

a. Traditional programs are immersion programs in which LEPs are taught only in L2 and must “sink or swim.” CBEC offers instruction in a two-way immersion format, given in both L2 and L1.
b. Traditional ESL programs prioritize social language skills. CBEC offers instruction in content areas that are age-appropriate to the LEPs’ mainstreamed peers.
c. Traditional ESL programs focus on grammar; CBEC focuses on phonetics.
d. Traditional ESL programs prioritize a high level of CALP and do not find BICS to be central to communication.

41. My neighbor’s pit bull puppy is <u>protective</u>. In this statement, the underlined word is:

a. A predicate adjective
b. A predicate nominative
c. A prepositional phrase
d. The object of a preposition

42. Cooperative Learning is a teaching approach that combines students at varying scholastic levels and with various learning styles into small groups for learning activities that encourage interaction. All students have ample opportunity to speak, and groups foster a sense of mutual respect. Additionally, students at different levels and with different learning styles observe one another and expand their learning skills and strategies. This approach is most effective when:

a. The small groups are observed and monitored.
b. The groups are organized homogeneously.
c. Students work with the same classmates over the course of an entire school year.
d. Learning tasks are authentic, challenging, and meaningful.

43. An English Language Development (ELD) teacher noticed that when she had administered a listening test to her students twice, the scores were not reliable. What would indicate to her that the test is not reliable?

a. The scores were drastically different among all of the students.
b. The test took too long for students to complete the first and second time.
c. The test did not ask questions relevant to the topic that was being taught.
d. The scores were different the first and second time students took the test.

44. What impact did the No Child Left Behind Act of 2001 have on school funding and English learners?

a. Schools must measure and share student results, including those of English learners, on state standardized tests to receive federal funds.
b. Schools should not include English learners in their school results for state standardized tests to receive funding.
c. All classes must have English learners to receive federal funding so that they are integrated into mainstream classes.
d. Schools must offer all state standardized tests to English learners in the language of their choice and report that to the state.

45. According to Cummins' Threshold Hypothesis, cognitive and academic growth in L2 is largely dependent upon:

a. Development of CALP in L1
b. Research-based, high quality instruction
c. Development of BICS
d. L2 immersion

46. An age equivalent score is used to tell whether a student is:

a. Working at an appropriate grade level in a particular content area
b. Working at an IQ level normal for equal aged students
c. Working at a level that is below or above others his or her age
d. Working at a specific standard level for a subject

47. A teacher is having difficulty with her fifth grade ESL students. She pre-teaches lessons by giving students specialized vocabulary they will need, reminds them of prior knowledge, and writes important information on the board in her clearest cursive handwriting. She asks the ESL students if they understand; the students nearly always nod and smile in agreement. She speaks very slowly and loudly and is careful to use a few of the most current slang expressions to make the students feel that she "speaks their language." Nonetheless, the students demonstrate little understanding of the material when tested in an essay format. They do only a little better when asked to choose the correct answer on tests. What is the teacher doing wrong?

a. Some ESL students may not be able to interpret cursive handwriting.
b. When asked a question directly, many students will agree whether or not they understand what is being asked. Moreover, students may agree in order to avoid the embarrassment of admitting in public that they do not understand.
c. The teacher's use of slang that has not been taught as idiom is more likely to confuse the students than to clarify their English.
d. All the above

48. A middle school English Language Development (ELD) teacher notices that her students have difficulty reviewing for their social studies tests because their notes are incomplete. They explain that the teacher talks too quickly during class when they are writing notes, so they often miss some of the key words or ideas as they try to write everything down. Which strategy would best support these learners?

a. Give them all of the class notes so they don't need to worry about taking notes.
b. Teach them how to take better notes such as only writing key words, organizing based on topic, and underlining or highlighting main ideas.
c. Ask the teacher to record the lessons so they can listen to the lessons again at home.
d. Tell the teacher that she must talk much more slowly.

49. A teacher has decided to incorporate Total Physical Response strategies into her classroom instruction. She will:

a. Break from academic instruction every hour for 10 minutes of organized exercise.
b. Involve her students in a series of physical activities in response to her instructions and requests.
c. Break for academic instruction every hour for five minutes of independent exercise.
d. Break from academic instruction two times a day (excluding lunch) for guided meditation practice and Brilliant Mind exercises.

50. The primary approach to teaching English to non-native speakers until the late 1960s was:

a. Two-way immersion
b. Sheltered English
c. Immersion
d. ESL

51. A classroom teacher with several mainstreamed ESL students is frustrated. She has noted that few of their parents come to parent-teacher conferences, and those who do, come inconsistently and have little to say. She is aware that many of them have limited English skills and also that several have very young children at home. What can she do to encourage the parents to increase their participation in their children's education?

a. Drop in unexpectedly at their homes with a gift of freshly baked bread or cookies.
b. Send home an announcement about a Foreign Parents' night, in which foods from many lands will be featured and for which they will be the featured speakers.
c. Invite several parents from the same or similar cultures to work with their children and a translator if one is available, and create a classroom presentation on some cultural aspect that will be of interest to the students. For example, Mexican and other Central American parents might present a slideshow on the Day of the Dead, followed by a show-and-tell of objects used in that celebration.
d. Nothing. They have made it clear to her that they have priorities that do not include the needs of her student, their child. It's best if she simply expects less of them and takes it upon herself to provide additional academic and emotional support to the poor child, who is clearly being neglected.

52. What are the characteristics of an additive educational program?

a. It works with students who come from families with a history of drug or alcohol abuse. By starting therapy at a young age, the hope is that these children won't grow up to become addicts as well.
b. It is a social studies program that primarily focuses on the positive. It means that only those characteristics of a social group that are joyful, exuberant, or peace-loving will be taught.
c. It is a program that uses a student's culture of origin as a scaffold to teach her about her new culture.
d. It is a program that explores all the ways advertisements exploit cultures by furthering stereotypes and prejudices.

53. A previously happy and affectionate ELL has suddenly become tearful and withdrawn. She reacts very strongly to any kind of unexpected touch, and she has abruptly stopped giving hugs to the teacher or to her friends. She will not tell the teacher what is causing her sadness or hurt, but the teacher is aware that the girl's mother has a new boyfriend who has recently moved in with the family. The student, who used to love writing in her journal both in Spanish and in English, now uses it only for drawings. The teacher has not violated the student's privacy by looking at the journal without permission, but she has noticed that during journal time the girl angrily scribbles what appear to be pictures of a man (or someone wearing a hat and pants) being shot, stabbed, or otherwise tortured. What should the teacher do?

a. Read the journal without permission; the girl is obviously disturbed, and if she is being abused in some way, the teacher has the responsibility to find out in any way possible.
b. Nothing at the moment; she should continue to observe the student and offer her an ear. Until the girl asks for help, she can legally do nothing.
c. Refer the student to the school counselor, who is trained to help in situations such as this.
d. Get the mother's permission to refer the student to the school counselor. She cannot be referred without parental permission.

54. In 1981, the United States Court of Appeals for the Fifth Circuit reversed a 1978 ruling in the case of Castaneda v. Pickard. As a result, a three-pronged assessment was established to ensure that English learner programs met requirements established by what act?

a. No Child Left Behind (2001)
b. Equal Educational Opportunities Act (1974)
c. The Bilingual Education Act (1968)
d. The Civil Rights Act (1964)

55. What is the best way that teachers can build rapport with families to increase family involvement in the school?

a. Learn the languages spoken by students, and greet parents in their native tongue.
b. Phone calls with the family to understand the student's culture and get a sense of the student's life.
c. Read about the culture that the student comes from in ethnographic and anthropological studies.
d. Send newsletters home in English with the child.

56. Developing a student's capacity for independent academic study and task completion through an approach known as __________ is achieved through the combined efforts of strategies, such as hands-on activities, accessing prior knowledge, pre-teaching content-area vocabulary, and putting the lesson into context with visual aids and modeling.

a. Native Language Support
b. ESL
c. Scaffolding
d. Direct Experience

57. A kindergarten student new to the United States speaks almost no English. His teacher, who is a fluent Spanish speaker, has noted that both his vocabulary and mastery of underlying grammatical rules in Spanish are also weak. The student depends upon a shared external context to convey a disproportionate amount of his intended meaning in oral communication or he withdraws entirely. What should the teacher expect from this student in terms of his relative ability to learn English?

a. Because his first language is not developed, he will most likely obtain English vocabulary and skills more rapidly, both because he is hungry for language and because there are fewer prior linguistic assumptions that could impede L2 development.
b. Because his first language is not developed, he will most likely obtain English vocabulary and skills much more slowly; the speed with which L2 learners develop proficiency can be anticipated by the degree of richness L1 exhibits.
c. It is too early to anticipate; each child is a unique being and to base assumptions of future learning on evidence of past learning is a fallacy.
d. It is too early to anticipate; because the child is so young, is new to the United States, and must therefore be experiencing culture shock and because at this point little is known about his family/social situation, the teacher must remain open and curious about the student's ability to absorb L2 or the teacher will risk doing him an injustice by labeling him and teaching him accordingly.

58. Cummins' Common Underlying Proficiency theory holds that using one language encourages proficiency in both L1 and L2. What is the opposing theory?

a. Opposing Underlying Proficiency
b. Separate Underlying Proficiency
c. Anti-Underlying Proficiency
d. Opposite Underlying Proficiency

59. Which example of a classroom display best describes a language-rich environment for English learners?

a. Posters of age-appropriate books that have a diversity of characters
b. Bulletin boards with exemplary student work to promote excellence
c. Labels of classroom items in both the primary language and English
d. Pictures of the many different cultures represented in the school

60. Who is always required by law to follow a student's IEP?

a. The school nurse
b. All school staff
c. Teachers who work with the student
d. No one is strictly required.

61. An ESL teacher offers her students the following question to test their understanding of proper English grammar: Which of the following sentences is correct?

a. Both my dog and my husband thinks I am a servant.
b. Both my dogs and my husbands think I am a servant.
c. Both my dogs and my husband thinks I am a servant.
d. Both my dog and my husband think I am a servant.

62. An SDAIE approach can be problematic for an individual ESL teacher because it requires specialized training and is most effective when the program is adopted system wide. What strategy can such a teacher use to provide CBEC to her students without receiving that specialized training or having system wide support?

a. Determine the content areas that ESL students will be taught in the following semester and begin preparing them well in advance through a variety of approaches.
b. Teach concepts essential to a core understanding of the material that reach beyond just specialized vocabulary.
c. Organize learning thematically, and teach a series of interrelated, in-depth lessons related to that theme.
d. All the above

63. TPR stands for:

a. Teaching-Productive Resources
b. Total Physical Response
c. Typical Production Register
d. Theory of Psychological Reference

64. An approach to language learning that begins with practical communicative usage and that over time incorporates grammar, vocabulary, phonemic awareness, etc. is known as a(n) ______approach.

a. top-down
b. functional
c. total physical response
d. natural

65. Two young women are at a coffee shop. They are having an animated conversation about three young men sitting at a table across the room. Much of their conversation seems cryptic, either because they do not want others to understand or because most of what they are talking about is fully present in the room, allowing them to use a verbal shorthand—or both. They don't realize a linguist is sitting at the next table, observing them and noting the relationship between orally manifested meaning (language) and contextual information conveyed through gesture, facial expression, inference, etc. In what area of linguistic study is the eavesdropper engaging?

a. Pragmatics
b. Contextual linguistics
c. Sociolinguistics
d. Etiquette orality

66. A student who is new to the United States understands some English, but his vocabulary is limited, and his grasp of syntax is weak. Although he is 11, his previous education was very limited, so he has been placed in a fourth grade classroom. For the first few weeks, he was very quiet and kept to himself. In an effort to bring him out of his shell, his teacher put him into a pod with several highly social students whose first language is English. The students tried to draw him in, talking loudly and gesturing to make him understand. When he ignored them, they left him alone. To her dismay, the teacher's previously quiet student grew sullen and very angry. He hit a child during recess one day and stormed out of class in the middle of a lesson the next day. What is most likely the problem with the boy?

a. Since he started out quiet and rapidly became angry, it's probable that he is undergoing some kind of trauma at home.
b. He is experiencing a high affective filter due possibly to culture shock, which is heightened by being placed with younger students, as well as by his inability to freely communicate. He may feel shame, insecurity, embarrassment, frustration, or a combination of these, which he compensates for and covers up with anger.
c. He is simply undisciplined. Because he has spent little time in a school, he doesn't clearly understand the dynamics, rules, and regulations, and he must be treated with firm kindness.
d. He is simply undisciplined. He has probably gotten away with this type of behavior before, and he likely feels that it is a normal way to express pent-up frustration. The teacher must move swiftly to punish him for outbursts or striking others, as such behavior cannot be allowed.

67. A teacher is having fun with her students. She has created numerous sentences that are ridiculous in their "meaning." She has asked her students to tell her which of the sentences are possible in English, regardless of how odd the meaning is, and which sentences cannot make any sense whatsoever. An example of one of these possible sentences is: The grandfather clock and my grandmother are secretly in love. An impossible sentence might be: The shy giggling would not choo-choo the quickly goose. What is the teacher using the assignment to evaluate?

a. Students' semantic understanding
b. Students' syntactic understanding
c. Students' phonemic understanding
d. Students' morphemic understanding

68. Phonemic awareness is a type of:

a. Phonological awareness. Phonemic awareness is the ability to recognize sounds within words.
b. Phonics. It is a teaching technique whereby readers learn the relationship between letters and sounds.
c. Alphabetization. Unless a reader knows the alphabet, phonemic awareness is useless.
d. Syntactical awareness. Understanding the underlying structure of a sentence is key to understanding meaning.

69. Communicative competence consists of grammatical, sociolinguistic, discourse, and strategic competence and is currently the objective of many language education programs. To whom can the spread of its ideas best be attributed?

a. Canale and Swain
b. Chomsky
c. Hull
d. Krashen

70. The ESL teacher has a goal of increasing interaction among her students. She has studied Swain's theory of comprehensible output, and is basing her instruction accordingly. Which of the following would be an appropriate strategy for her to employ?

a. Project-based learning
b. Manipulatives
c. Rubrics
d. All the above

71. A 10th-grade British literature teacher has several intermediate-level English learners in his class. He has students give presentations on different British poets. Which approach aligns with Specially Designed Academic Instruction in English (SDAIE) in supporting students' listening skills?

a. Encouraging students to ask questions to clarify any information they did not understand during the presentation
b. Asking students to compare and contrast two different poets that were presented in a short essay after watching the presentations
c. Giving students a list of the poets being presented before the class presentations so they can do research on one of the poets
d. Reminding speakers to pace their speaking, speak clearly during the presentation, and use slides that highlight the key ideas

72. What is one difference between ESL and bilingual models?

a. ESL models are pull-out or push-in. Bilingual models are self-contained.
b. ESL models primarily use English and employ a specific methodology to teach English and continue to develop L1. Bilingual models introduce instruction concepts first in L1 and over time transfer them into English.
c. Bilingual models are pull-out or push-in; ESL models are self-contained.
d. Bilingual models are English-only and employ specific methodology to teach English and continue to develop L1. ESL models introduce instruction concepts first in L1 and over time transfer them into English.

73. A class is doing a project about a kitchen they have been in. The project can be based on a grandparent's kitchen or that of a friend; an outdoor "kitchen," such as at a campground or on a deck; a play kitchen that they recall from pre-school; or any other type of kitchen. The students can work individually or in a small group of their choosing. Some students are drawing and painting, while others are creating three-dimensional models. One group is creating a play that takes place in a kitchen. One child is writing about her grandmother, who cooks tortillas on a hot rock. Another is creating a shoe-box diorama that depicts a fisherman smoking a fish in a temporary smokehouse. After producing their projects, the students are required to give a two-minute presentation describing all of the elements they chose to include. The teacher has reviewed vocabulary with the students, but a number of them approach her for help with English words. What has the teacher created this project to do?

a. Expand the specialized vocabulary of her students.
b. Determine each student's preferred learning style.
c. Encourage students to be curious about and respectful of differences in culture.
d. Teach students about different cooking methods.

74. How are language acquisition and language learning distinct?

a. Language learning refers to learning a second language, where language acquisition refers to a primary language.
b. Language acquisition develops unconsciously through use, while language learning requires instruction.
c. Language learning precedes and is required for language acquisition.
d. All the above.

75. A new middle school English language learner from another country is often late for class and seems to think this is acceptable. He is hardworking otherwise. The teacher is frustrated but considers why this may be the case. Which is the MOST likely reason for this behavior?

a. The student doesn't value school and doesn't care about being late.
b. The student comes from a culture in which a strict schedule is not valued as highly as in American culture.
c. The student doesn't know the time that the class begins.
d. The student focuses on his friendships more than his schoolwork because of his age and maturity.

Refer to the following for questions 76–77:

A teacher's third grade class includes students from Costa Rica, Chile, Peru, Mexico, Korea, Vietnam, India, Iraq, and the United States, with students speaking a total of six different languages. Over the course of several months, the class has explored the cultures of each country. The teacher has been careful to include lessons that demonstrate how different cultures have different values and beliefs about behavior, relationships, religion, and education. She has placed each of her students in small, homogeneous groups and asked them to create some kind of presentation that will teach the class about different cultural expectations and the emotions that can arise when there is cultural confusion.

76. Of the following presentations, which is most likely to be the most effective?

a. A game the group creates that explores the foods of various cultures
b. Oral reports given by group members on how they celebrate Christmas
c. A play in which a Korean student, a Hispanic student, and an American-born student perform a series of skits demonstrating how different cultures greet acquaintances and the confusion that can arise when people from two distinct cultures meet
d. A fairy tale orally presented in English, Spanish, and Korean

77. How else can she encourage mutual cultural respect?

a. Label objects in the room with all six languages; invite speakers from each of the countries to visit the classroom and talk about one or two aspects of their cultures; break the class into culturally diverse smaller groups for class projects and study; and invite students to teach the class songs from their cultures.
b. Organize field trips to local museums to view the works of painters from other lands; show students photographs of types of clothing from the various countries; and announce a "language day" once a month, on which only the teacher is allowed to speak English, and everyone but the English speakers are allowed to speak in their native tongue.
c. Give each child a journal, and ask them to use it to write down memories and information about their countries of origin. They may show their journals to one another, but two rules apply: 1) If you share with one, you must share with all and 2) Anyone you show your journal to must, in turn, show you theirs.
d. Hang flags representing all the different cultures the classroom contains; teach the class to greet one another in all of the languages and require them to do so before class starts each day; and group children by language/cultural group for projects and group study to strengthen their bond.

78. Which takes longer to develop, BICS or CALP?

a. BICS
b. CALP
c. They are interrelated and therefore develop at the same pace
d. They are not interrelated, but they take approximately the same time to develop

79. What is Krashen's Monitor Hypothesis concerned with?

a. The importance of frequent assessment and adjustment of teaching methods according to the results
b. The degree to which an ESL teacher is monitored and advised by a mentor
c. Monitoring learning by using computer programs specifically designed for ELLs to offer a stable and consistent model of learning achievement
d. The ways in which language learning influences acquisition

80. In second language acquisition, what is Stage II also called?

a. Speech Emergence Stage
b. Receptive Stage
c. Intermediate Proficiency Stage
d. Early Production Stage

Answer Key and Explanations for Test #1

1. C: The student is more likely to be placed in a special education program. Oral-language proficiency assessments should not be used as an overall indicator of a student's academic performance, as research has demonstrated that ELLs with little English are very likely to be inappropriately placed in special education classes.

2. B: Acculturation involves adapting to a new culture, which includes understanding cultural expectations, semiotics, values, and beliefs; it is essential to second language acquisition in that it provides appropriate context. Acculturation permits ELLs to adapt to new cultural expectations without the loss of the culture of origin. Success with BICS and CALP in L2 is dependent on a degree of success in L1.

3. B: The Silent/Receptive (Pre-Production Stage) is a brief stage that typically lasts up to six months in which language learners develop a bank of approximately 500 words they understand but do not use verbally. Newly introduced words that are explained so that the student can understand them are readily added to this bank. It is important that teachers not force or push a student in this stage to speak. They may communicate by pointing or gesturing, can follow commands, and may answer questions with a nod or a single word.

4. B: The Cognitive Academic Language Learning Approach (CALLA) and Specially Designed Academic Instruction in English (SDAIE) and other sheltered-English approaches feature using content-area instruction as a vehicle for language instruction. English for a specific purpose (ESP) is a very specialized branch of English instruction, which is focused less on generalized English skills and more on acquiring vocabulary and other useful language for particular purposes like business, science, or a particular vocation. ESP is more specialized than just academic language. Direct instruction refers to teaching English directly without use of the first language as a platform. Direct Instruction is a highly structured, teacher-centered model that emphasizes explicit teaching and guided practice of skills, and it is not organized around content-area instruction as the vehicle for language development. Total physical response (TPR) is an approach that involves adding action into the instruction, including movement and application of actions to help with grounding the language in the real world. CALLA and SDAIE are both types of approaches to language learning that focus on academic content as the primary driver for language learning opportunities. While they are both content-based, they do also address generalized English skills to promote accurate, formal uses of language, and not just practical skills which are applied to a narrow subject.

5. C: ELLs often understand more in terms of vocabulary and correct syntax than they demonstrate in their own speaking. The other statements contain information that is false.

6. A: Second language acquisition research suggests that L2s tend to integrate formulaic expressions and then apply them to understand linguistic rules. Research shows early second language learners integrate a limited number of formulaic expressions that are perceived less as individual words than as functional phrases. These phrases are memorized as global wholes. Phrases such as "Where is the library?" or "Would you like to go with me?" later become templates for discovering the rules of the language. "Where is the library?" becomes the formula for "Where is the airport (Laundromat, etc.)?" "Would you like to go with me?" becomes the template for "Would you like to eat dinner with me (like to see a movie with me, etc.)?" Over time, the learner realizes that the subject can change and that the verb must then change to be in agreement.

7. D: Competence in grammar, sociolinguistics, discourse, and communication strategies. Competence in grammar requires mastery of the rules of language; sociolinguistic competence requires an understanding of what is appropriate; competence in discourse requires the ability to organize messages into a coherent and cohesive whole; strategic competence refers to the use of communication strategies in ways that are appropriate.

8. A: Using real, physical materials is often a scaffolding strategy used for English learners to help support their learning and understanding. Shortening word problems can be helpful depending on how they are modified, but mere simplification is not a successful strategy because students will need to develop their language skills. Although activating prior knowledge is a key strategy, some families may cook with exact measurements, whereas others do not. Deduction is also a great learning tool with the appropriate supports, but individual research for English learners at this young age can be overwhelming without scaffolding.

9. C: The teacher should teach a unit on prefixes and suffixes and then offer some examples of each. Next, the teacher should group the students into teams and see which team comes up with the most words that use prefixes and suffixes. Then, the teacher should challenge them by asking for a word with both a prefix and a suffix. By understanding prefixes and suffixes, students will be able to independently figure out the meaning on many words, building their morphological awareness.

10. A: She will use the information they contain to vary her lessons to meet each student's specific needs. Because all students are individuals with unique abilities, experiences, and personalities, the most effective teaching methods must allow for modifying lessons to specific, individual needs. Parents don't benefit from having these notes sent home to them. Separating the students into groups based on language levels would not be the likely intent of these files, as each student likely has differing needs and interests that would make similar groupings difficult. Finally, it would be unethical to share a student's files with their classmates.

11. D: The teacher will write comments and questions in response, modeling correct English usage. Dialogue or interactive journals offer teachers the opportunity to engage students in the writing process. The teacher responds to a student's entry with questions or comments about the topic introduced by the students. The teacher doesn't correct errors but instead models correct usage.

12. B: The Bilingual Syntax Measure is a tool designed to assess bilingual students for oral language proficiency and dominance between two languages. Its reliability has been debated since its development.

13. D: They do not accurately reflect native speakers' proficiency and therefore cannot accurately reflect non-native speakers' proficiency. A study examined the efficacy of the Language Assessment Scales-Oral, the Woodcock-Muñoz Language Survey, and the IDEA Proficiency Test by giving all three to both native English-speaking non-Hispanic Caucasian and Hispanic students from all socioeconomic levels. Interestingly, these L1 English speakers did not receive similar results from the three tests, which ostensibly assessed for the same information. In fact, none of the native English speakers who were given the Woodcock-Muñoz Language Survey were assigned fluent status. On the other hand, all students scored as fluent in the Language Assessment Scales-Oral, while 87% were described by IDEA Proficiency Test results as being fluent. L1 English speakers who do not uniformly score in the fluent range throw into doubt the assessment's ability to accurately reflect an L2's proficiency.

14. D: Pull-out ESL classes. Of the program choices given, pull-out models consistently prove to be less effective. Given plenty of support from a teacher, mainstreamed classes show better results than pull-out ESL classes.

15. A: Plyler v. Doe was the 1982 Supreme Court case that established the right to a free education for undocumented immigrant children. In 1975, Texas laws were revised, permitting districts to refuse to enroll illegal alien children. The Supreme Court used this case to strike down the Texas law, finding it in violation of the 14th Amendment, which gives equal rights to all people.

16. A: Intermediate Fluency. This stage is marked by an increased level of complexity in speech, though some grammatical features and pronunciation aren't well set. Complex speech is starting to emerge, but errors do take place. Early production is a stage in which beginning language learners start to speak and have a relatively small vocabulary. Advanced fluency follows intermediate fluency and begins the process of naturalizing speech.

17. D: The first question a teacher should ask herself is what specific standards she would like students to demonstrate. This includes the knowledge as well as the skills. Remember, backwards planning starts with the objectives in mind rather than the task or activity. Although all of these questions are important to ask oneself as a teacher developing a rubric, the first should be an alignment of the rubric and the standards or objectives.

18. B: Presenting sufficient and meaningful reading and writing experiences for students to practice strategies and reviewing and re-teaching as required to ensure that students have integrated essential content are part of scientifically-based, quality classroom instruction. Daily introduction to new concepts, words, and materials can be okay as long as they are integrated a little at a time. Students require multiple exposures to a word before recognition begins to happen automatically. This relies on Krashen's input hypothesis, which states that learners benefit from exposure to slightly more difficult language than their current level. This renders answer choice B as the least effective, since it implies only using a level of language that the student is comfortable with.

19. C: The underlined words represent a predicate nominative. A predicate nominative is a noun phrase which defines or clarifies the subject, and it typically follows a linking verb. Multiple words do not make multiple predicate nominatives. In this case, "tiny red car" is a singular noun; therefore, "Smart car" is a singular predicate nominative, not multiple.

20. A: Allowing students to give oral answers rather than written ones allows them to share their knowledge without having to write in English. Often, English learners' writing abilities develop slower than speaking skills, so it is easier to explain something orally than through writing. Although translating the test may assess the content knowledge of students, it would require the teacher to then be able to understand the primary language of the students. Furthermore, administering only half of the exam or offering an alternative exam may turn out to not assess the same skills as the original exam.

21. A: No; parental permission is required. Under no circumstances can a student be placed in a special education classroom without the permission of a parent or a legal guardian.

22. C: Self-Contained Model. The One Teacher Approach is one in which a single teacher working in a self-contained classroom carries the responsibility for her students' linguistic and academic achievement. This allows for integration of language skills on a progressive scale while learning academic English.

23. D: BICS skills permit social communications that are face-to-face and include contextual information, informal vocabulary, and relatively simple syntax, while CALP skills are necessary for academic communication, require content-specific vocabularies and more sophisticated syntax, and do not rely upon external contextual information.

24. B: Special education law applies to LEPs only when the student also has learning, emotional, or physical disabilities. Under IDEA, only students with learning disabilities, emotional and/or behavioral disabilities, physical disabilities, and developmental disabilities are eligible for special services. LEP students typically experience challenges in communication, but unless they have qualifying disability, they will not be eligible for special education.

25. B: No. She is not a trained translator, and, for this reason alone, is not suitable for this task. The school is legally responsible for providing a trained translator or materials in Basque, if they are available. The teacher must advocate on behalf of the student and try to find a trained translator or the materials in Basque. The fact that the volunteer translator is both the boy's aunt and the teacher's friend compounds the problem, in that her objectivity could be affected by her feelings and desire to help.

26. B: Banks's four approaches include the contributions approach, the additive approach, the transformation approach, and the social action approach. The additive approach attempts to maintain the traditional curriculum while including concepts and perspectives from a variety of viewpoints. Choice A represents the contributions approach, which focuses on particular holidays, heroes, and events from diverse cultures. The transformation approach, as seen in choice C, is a more aggressive approach, as it completely changes the instructional objectives to focus directly on cultural issues. Finally, choice D relates to the social action approach, which focuses on getting students involved in responding to cultural issues as part of the curriculum.

27. B: A writing sample is not required for an LEP's permanent record. The permanent record must contain parental approval; program entry dates, exit dates, and notifications; designation of language proficiency level; recommendation for placement; LEP identification; criterion-referenced test exemption dates, as well as all pertaining documents; and ongoing monitoring results.

28. D: Formative assessments are given throughout the unit for teachers to keep track of what concepts and ideas need to be retaught to students. Unit tests and projects are often thought of as summative rather than formative assessments. Informing teaching with assessments is one of the most important components of formative assessments. English language and literacy development can be tracked through things like testing knowledge of vocabulary and academic language use. Sentence frames can also be used within the assessments.

29. D: A teacher working with an ESL student who is at the preproduction stage should incorporate gesture, pictures, manipulatives, and other extra-verbal tools into her teaching. The preproduction, or silent/receptive, stage of language acquisition is the first stage in which a learner must break into unfamiliar language that offers no easy entry. Visual images, coupled with the appropriate name, gestures indicating type or quality of movement, and other extra-verbal tools, will allow learners to begin to piece together the meanings that their first words carry.

30. B: Considering the language level of learners is essential when planning learning activities that are appropriate. For beginning-level learners, fill-in-the-blank activities are appropriate. Although summarizing and paraphrasing may be an appropriate activity for intermediate or advanced-level learners, it would not be appropriate for beginning-level students. Similarly, scrambling the text and asking students to put the biographical information in order may be too advanced for beginning-level learners. It is important to ensure that the activity also matches the purpose, which is to comprehend the text. Alternate activities should still achieve the same objective. Answer A does not fulfil the same objective of reading comprehension.

31. C: The teacher should shorten the text; abbreviate sentences; replace abstract language with concrete language; break complex sentences into two or three simpler, more direct sentences; omit detail that enhances the text but doesn't change or clarify meaning. Beginning/intermediate stage ELLs will be able to understand ideas, theories, and other forms of meaning when they are offered in the context of a language the ELL can understand.

32. C: Lau v. Nichols determined that ELLs must be given the right to instruction that they have the skills to understand. The 1974 Supreme Court decision as a result of Lau v. Nichols established that school districts must provide ELL students the tools necessary to understand instruction.

33. B: In the 1960s, Cuban immigrants established a successful bilingual program, and the Civil Rights movement put attention on correcting educational and social agendas that were prejudiced in favor of the white middle class.

34. C: Realia are concrete objects used in demonstrations, to develop vocabulary and encourage discourse. The use of realia during instruction offers students the chance to involve a range of senses. Objects that can be handled, carefully examined, smelled, tasted, or listened to offer a richer learning experience.

35. D: In the early production stage of language acquisition, an L2 learner typically understands and uses roughly 1,000 words. The early production stage lasts approximately six months beyond the pre-production stage and is characterized by an understanding and use of approximately 1,000 words in one-to-two-word phrases or by responding to questions with appropriate action.

36. D: Early-advanced English learners can be challenged more than beginning-level students. Pre-reading activities should build interest and background knowledge rather than simply giving away the entire story before reading. Visuals can do that, but pre-reading activities should come before the reading, not during. Activating prior knowledge is key to pre-reading; however, a writing activity after reading does not constitute pre-reading.

37. C: The stages of language acquisition are the pre-production stage, early production stage, speech emergence stage, and intermediate fluency stage. During the pre-production stage, language is being absorbed and its meanings learned, but it is not being verbally produced. The early production stage features a willingness to initiate conversation with gesture or a single word and to answer questions with one or two words. Yes and no become commonly used. The speech emergence stage is characterized by developing comprehension and fewer errors in speech. By the intermediate fluency stage, a speaker exhibits greater comprehension, more complex sentence structures, a richer vocabulary, and more sophisticated errors.

38. C: The Texas English Language Proficiency Assessment System (TELPAS) is used for emergent bilingual (EB) students in grades K–12th.

39. B: The Language Experience Approach, also called Dictated Stories, enlists the aid of volunteers who take down a story being dictated by a student verbatim. The stories are next read to the authors, and then each author reads her story silently or aloud. This approach utilizes several essential elements of literacy; encoding is modeled, sight word vocabulary developed, and the ownership a young author feels produces motivation.

40. B: Traditional ESL programs prioritize social language skills. CBEC offers instruction in content areas that are age-appropriate to the LEPs' mainstreamed peers. Traditional ESL programs make the rapid absorption of social language skills a priority and, to that end, teach streamlined, socially necessary vocabulary and simple syntactical structures that enable students to communicate their basic needs. CBEC instruction is more deeply grounded in the same content that non-ESL students receive in order to prepare them for mainstreaming.

41. A: A predicate adjective. A predicate adjective is an adjective that comes after a linking verb (such as the verb "to be") and modifies or describes the subject. In this example, "puppy" is the subject, "is" is the linking verb, and "protective" is the adjective.

42. D: Learning tasks are authentic, challenging, and meaningful. Shared learning activities give students the opportunity to absorb learning strategies employed by other students. Students involved in a shared learning activity will speak, discuss, argue, and consider quite naturally. The opportunity for authentic dialogue is especially useful for ELLs. The more meaningful the task, the more involved and motivated the students—and the more authentic their dialogue—will be.

43. D: A test is reliable when it offers a relatively stable measure of the test taker's skills. This means that if the test is taken twice by the same person, the scores between the two should be similar. When an assessment is valid, this means that it measures what it should be measuring. For example, a test on reading comprehension should include questions regarding aspects of the passage rather than writing or speaking skills. An invalid test is demonstrated in Answer C. A practical assessment means that it does not take too much time or resources to administer. Answer B may be describing a test that is impractical.

44. A: The No Child Left Behind Act of 2001 required that for schools to receive federal funding, they must measure and report student achievement on standardized tests for all students, including English learners. This includes state assessments. The Every Student Succeeds Act (ESSA), passed in 2015, gave states flexibility in how to measure and report achievement rather than using a prescribed measure from the federal government.

45. A: According to Cummins' Threshold Hypothesis, cognitive and academic growth in L2 is largely dependent upon development of CALP in L1. The Threshold Hypothesis (Cummins & Swain, 1986) finds that a higher proficiency threshold in the first language is a core contributor to the learner's acquisition of a second language. A speaker who did not achieve Cognitive Academic Language Proficiency in L1 will have more difficulty doing so in L2.

46. C: An age equivalent score is used in a norm-referenced assessment to determine whether a student is working at, above, or below a level similar to his or her peers by studying the average age of others who got the same score as he or she did.

47. D: The teacher is likely doing multiple wrong actions. Some ESL students may not be able to interpret cursive handwriting. When asked a question directly, many students will agree, whether or not they understand what is being asked. Moreover, students may agree in order to avoid the embarrassment of admitting in public that they do not understand. The teacher's use of slang that has not been taught as idiom is also more likely to confuse the students than clarify meaning for them.

48. B: Although offering notes can support students in the immediate situation, the best long-term solution is to help students learn how to take notes. Research has shown that strong note-taking skills promote academic achievement. Asking the teacher to slow down is an important accommodation, but even if the teacher does slow down, English learners must still know how to identify key words and ideas being shared by any teacher. Recording the lesson may provide a short-term solution, but it will require an extensive amount of time for the learner, and it is possible that the students may not have access to technology that would allow them to listen to the recording.

49. B: The teacher should involve her students in a series of physical activities in response to her instructions and requests. Total Physical Response (TPR) employs physical involvement to make learning more meaningful and easier to retain. A sequence of instructions given by the teacher prompts a succession of detailed actions. Advocates recommend special hands-on training with a trained senior instructor.

50. C: Immersion. Until the late 1960s, immersion was the primary language instruction model. Typically, immigrant students—many of whom had little or no English—were mainstreamed into a classroom where they received language and content instruction in English only. This approach is also referred to as submersion or a 'sink or swim' model, in which students are mainstreamed with no specialized language support. Research has shown that this method is not as efficient or effective.

51. C: The teacher should invite several parents from the same or similar cultures to work with their children and a translator if one is available. and she should create a classroom presentation on some cultural aspect that will be of interest to the students. For example, Mexican and other Central American parents might present a slideshow on the Day of the Dead, followed by a show-and-tell of objects used in that celebration.

52. C: It is a program that uses a student's culture of origin as a scaffold to teach her about her new culture. An Additive Educational Program is one that supports and celebrates bicultural identity and encourages acculturation, rather than assimilation.

53. C: Refer the student to the school counselor, who is trained to help in situations such as this. It is essential that the teacher not violate the child's trust by reading the journal or showing it to anyone else. Such a violation of trust at this time could be very damaging. While the teacher should certainly monitor the situation and give close attention to the student's moods and behavior, she should not delay bringing the situation to the attention of the counselor.

54. B: The Equal Educational Opportunities Act (1974) is a federal law prohibiting discrimination against students based on race, color, sex, or national origin. This act requires school districts to actively work to resolve situations in which students are denied equal participation.

55. B: Conducting conferences and phone calls is the best way to understand the student's culture and build a relationship with the family, though home visits are often infeasible with teaching schedules. Any consistent method that builds an ongoing relationship of two-way communication with a student's family and shows an interest in the student's life is great for building rapport. While learning basic greetings or key phrases in families' home languages can positively impact rapport, relying on full language learning for multiple languages is often impractical compared with direct, ongoing two-way communication (as in choice B). Reading about the student's culture can be helpful as well, but it is important not to generalize findings when applying them to specific students or families. Newsletters are useful for communicating about what is going on in the student's class, but they are a means of one-way communication and is not very well correlated with building rapport with a family.

56. C: Scaffolding. Scaffolding provides a student with a combination of strategies to support independent learning, including hands-on activities; accessing prior knowledge; pre-teaching content-area vocabulary; and putting the lesson into context with visual aids and modeling.

57. B: Because his first language is not developed, he will most likely obtain English vocabulary and skills much more slowly; the speed with which L2 learners develop proficiency can be anticipated by the degree of richness L1 exhibits. Research has demonstrated that the degree to which an L2 is obtained is related to the speaker's mastery of L1.

58. B: According to the Separate Underlying Proficiency theory (SUP), no relationship between L1 and L2 language acquisition exists, because each language is treated as its own separate system with no overlap of skills or proficiency. Currently, this theory is generally disregarded.

59. C: A language-rich environment refers to classrooms that have a large amount of text and language present physically in the classroom. This includes posters, word walls, and student writing; however, the goal of a language-rich environment is to expose students to language rather than promote excellence, as is stated in Answer B. Therefore, including labels in the classroom in the students' primary languages as well as in English best helps to create a language-rich environment. Pictures of different cultures and books with diverse characters are not the best examples of language-rich environments, although they can support cultural inclusion.

60. C: By law, all teachers working with a particular student must follow that student's Individualized Education Plan. Information contained within an IEP is confidential and is only available to faculty and staff who have a valid educational interest in the student. Therefore, the school nurse and other school staff are not necessarily required to follow an IEP, only those who are directly responsible for implementing any part of the student's IEP.

61. D: Both my dog and my husband think I am a servant. My dog thinks I am a servant, and my husband also thinks I am a servant. The third person singular form of to think, is "thinks." However, the use of the word "both" links the two singular subjects into a plural subject; hence, the verb form must change to "think" to be in agreement.

62. D: The teacher should use all of the above strategies. By consulting with mainstream teachers to determine what content the students will be learning in upcoming months, she can choose or modify appropriate and understandable texts. The ESL teacher should only teach the content that she feels confident with, and she should emphasize deeper understanding of limited content over a glancing familiarity with a wider range of content.

63. B: Total Physical Response. TPR is an approach pioneered by James J. Asher in the late 1960s, which emphasizes physical activity as a means to increase language retention. It involves a set of detailed instructions or commands, which then require appropriate physical actions.

64. A: A Top-down approach to language learning begins with practical communicative usage that, over time, incorporates grammar, vocabulary, phonemic awareness, and other essential elements of speech. The top-down approach emphasizes meaningful use of language over accurate use of language elements. The functional approach also emphasizes practical use of language but emphasizes spoken language over written language, whereas the top-down method may use both written and spoken language together. Total physical response pairs physical action with learning to build solid associations with concepts. The natural approach tends to follow the pattern of first language acquisition, giving learners time to listen without speaking and slowly emerge into speech.

65. A: The eavesdropper is likely engaging in pragmatics. Pragmatics examines how speakers' linguistic understanding depends upon external context, how meaning can be found in the confluence of the rules of a language—its grammar, vocabulary, idioms, and so forth—and contextual information that is not embedded in the language itself, such as inferences, spatial relationships, and so forth.

66. B: He is experiencing a high affective filter due possibly to culture shock, which is heightened by being placed with younger students, as well as by his inability to freely communicate. He may feel shame, insecurity, embarrassment, frustration, or a combination of these, which he compensates for and covers up with anger.

67. B: Students' syntactic understanding. The teacher wants her students to understand the types of syntactical arrangements (grammatical structures) that are not allowed. For example, a sentence like "The quickly telephone and lonely" would not be possible because "quickly," an adverb, is modifying "telephone," a noun. In addition, "lonely" is an adjective, but has no noun to modify. Finally, the sentence has no verb. However, a silly sentence like "The quick telephone and forlorn toothbrush waltzed to the music of the moon" is grammatically possible, albeit absurd.

68. A: Phonemic awareness is the ability to recognize sounds within words, so it is a type of phonological awareness. Segmenting words and blending sounds are components of phonemic awareness. Phonological awareness includes an understanding of multiple components of spoken language. The ability to hear individual words within a vocalized stream and the ability to identify spoken syllables are types of phonological awareness.

69. A: Canale and Swain. This theory determines that communicative competence consists of both organizational competence (competence with grammar and discourse) and pragmatic competence (sociolinguistic and speech acts) and is currently the objective of many language education programs.

70. A: Project-based learning. Swain's theory of comprehensible output has resulted in practitioners who have developed strategies that are designed to create opportunities for face-to-face communication that requires authentic negotiation to arrive at shared meanings. In addition to project-based learning, other suggested strategies include cooperative learning, student-teacher individualized communications, and working with a partner to study selected materials.

71. D: Asking presenters to speak clearly not only supports listening but also can enhance the speaker's speaking abilities. In addition, adding visual supports aids comprehension for English language learners as well as other classmates during a presentation. Although encouraging asking questions allows students to support their listening skills, teachers need to be mindful of students feeling self-conscious asking questions. Writing an essay may be an effective activity done after the presentations, but it assesses rather than supports listening skills. Research prior to the presentations may help build background knowledge, but if only done for one poet, students may still struggle with other presentations on others.

72. B: ESL models primarily use English and employ specific methodologies to teach English. Bilingual models introduce instructional concepts first in L1, continue to develop L1, and over time transfer them into English.

73. C: This project is helpful for encouraging students to be curious about and respectful of differences in culture. While the project preparation aspect is focused on one's own memories, the collaborative aspects and the presentation element requires the whole class to be exposed to other cultures and experiences. For many people, the memory of a kitchen is especially evocative and suggests warmth, love, and nurturing. As the place where meals are prepared, kitchens are also very much cultural reflections—from the food chosen to the methods used to prepare it. By encouraging each student to share a memory of a particular kitchen, the teacher is encouraging wide cultural respect. This project may incidentally help students with specialized kitchen vocabulary, but it does not seem to be a primary focus because each student's project will have its own vocabulary such that the class would not be able to focus in on a unified set of terms together.

74. B: Language acquisition develops unconsciously through use, while language learning requires instruction. Language acquisition is natural, subconscious, and concerned with message content. Language learning is formal, concerned with grammatical rules, and conscious.

75. B: Differences in family or cultural values and school values are most likely at play in this scenario. Teachers should be aware of differences between a student's home culture and the dominant culture. American schools often value timeliness, efficient use of time, competition, order, and respect toward authority. This is not always the same in all cultures. Some schools in other countries may value humility, cooperation, and family. Since the student in question is hardworking and doesn't seem to mind being late for class, it is less likely that he doesn't value school, is focusing more on friendships, or doesn't know the time that the class begins.

76. C: A play in which a Korean student, a Hispanic student, and an American-born student perform a series of skits demonstrating how different cultures greet acquaintances and the confusion that can arise when people from two distinct cultures meet will best demonstrate the types of misinterpretation and confusion that can arise when two cultures bring different expectations to the same experience.

77. A: To encourage mutual cultural respect, the teacher can label objects in the room with all six languages; invite speakers from each of the countries to visit the classroom and talk about one or two aspects of their cultures; break the class into culturally-diverse, smaller groups for class projects and study; and invite students to teach the class songs from their cultures.

78. B: CALP. On average, research shows that it takes five years or more from first exposure to gain grade-level Cognitive Academic Language Proficiency (CALP). Basic Interpersonal Communication Skills (BICS) can be achieved within two years of first exposure.

79. D: The ways in which language learning influences acquisition. The Monitor hypothesis examines how language acquisition and language learning are related. Krashen sees acquisition as the utterance initiator, while learning is the monitor/editor. The monitor plans, edits, and corrects language acts when the ELL is not rushed. It also follows the rules of the language and fully integrates the rule under consideration. The monitor role should be a minor one, since it is conscious of itself and, therefore, is not intuitive. Interestingly, research indicates that extroverts tend to be under-users who are much more concerned with the immediacy of communication in the moment; introverts and perfectionists are over-users and are determined to speak correctly or not speak at all. Optimal users apply the monitor in a limited but appropriate way and exhibit a balanced personality that is neither extroverted nor introverted.

80. D: In the Early Production Stage, ELLs begin to use words that they learned in the Pre-production Stage. One word and yes/no responses are common. Conversation is initiated with gesture or one or two words. Children in this stage will verbally respond to an increasingly wider variety of linguistic stimuli.

CSET Practice Test #2

To take this additional CSET practice test, visit our online resources page:
mometrix.com/resources719/csetenglandev

How to Overcome Test Anxiety

Just the thought of taking a test is enough to make most people a little nervous. A test is an important event that can have a long-term impact on your future, so it's important to take it seriously and it's natural to feel anxious about performing well. But just because anxiety is normal, that doesn't mean that it's helpful in test taking, or that you should simply accept it as part of your life. Anxiety can have a variety of effects. These effects can be mild, like making you feel slightly nervous, or severe, like blocking your ability to focus or remember even a simple detail.

If you experience test anxiety—whether severe or mild—it's important to know how to beat it. To discover this, first you need to understand what causes test anxiety.

Causes of Test Anxiety

While we often think of anxiety as an uncontrollable emotional state, it can actually be caused by simple, practical things. One of the most common causes of test anxiety is that a person does not feel adequately prepared for their test. This feeling can be the result of many different issues such as poor study habits or lack of organization, but the most common culprit is time management. Starting to study too late, failing to organize your study time to cover all of the material, or being distracted while you study will mean that you're not well prepared for the test. This may lead to cramming the night before, which will cause you to be physically and mentally exhausted for the test. Poor time management also contributes to feelings of stress, fear, and hopelessness as you realize you are not well prepared but don't know what to do about it.

Other times, test anxiety is not related to your preparation for the test but comes from unresolved fear. This may be a past failure on a test, or poor performance on tests in general. It may come from comparing yourself to others who seem to be performing better or from the stress of living up to expectations. Anxiety may be driven by fears of the future—how failure on this test would affect your educational and career goals. These fears are often completely irrational, but they can still negatively impact your test performance.

Elements of Test Anxiety

As mentioned earlier, test anxiety is considered to be an emotional state, but it has physical and mental components as well. Sometimes you may not even realize that you are suffering from test anxiety until you notice the physical symptoms. These can include trembling hands, rapid heartbeat, sweating, nausea, and tense muscles. Extreme anxiety may lead to fainting or vomiting. Obviously, any of these symptoms can have a negative impact on testing. It is important to recognize them as soon as they begin to occur so that you can address the problem before it damages your performance.

The mental components of test anxiety include trouble focusing and inability to remember learned information. During a test, your mind is on high alert, which can help you recall information and stay focused for an extended period of time. However, anxiety interferes with your mind's natural processes, causing you to blank out, even on the questions you know well. The strain of testing during anxiety makes it difficult to stay focused, especially on a test that may take several hours. Extreme anxiety can take a huge mental toll, making it difficult not only to recall test information but even to understand the test questions or pull your thoughts together.

Effects of Test Anxiety

Test anxiety is like a disease—if left untreated, it will get progressively worse. Anxiety leads to poor performance, and this reinforces the feelings of fear and failure, which in turn lead to poor performances on subsequent tests. It can grow from a mild nervousness to a crippling condition. If allowed to progress, test anxiety can have a big impact on your schooling, and consequently on your future.

Test anxiety can spread to other parts of your life. Anxiety on tests can become anxiety in any stressful situation, and blanking on a test can turn into panicking in a job situation. But fortunately, you don't have to let anxiety rule your testing and determine your grades. There are a number of relatively simple steps you can take to move past anxiety and function normally on a test and in the rest of life.

Physical Steps for Beating Test Anxiety

While test anxiety is a serious problem, the good news is that it can be overcome. It doesn't have to control your ability to think and remember information. While it may take time, you can begin taking steps today to beat anxiety.

Just as your first hint that you may be struggling with anxiety comes from the physical symptoms, the first step to treating it is also physical. Rest is crucial for having a clear, strong mind. If you are tired, it is much easier to give in to anxiety. But if you establish good sleep habits, your body and mind will be ready to perform optimally, without the strain of exhaustion. Additionally, sleeping well helps you to retain information better, so you're more likely to recall the answers when you see the test questions.

Getting good sleep means more than going to bed on time. It's important to allow your brain time to relax. Take study breaks from time to time so it doesn't get overworked, and don't study right before bed. Take time to rest your mind before trying to rest your body, or you may find it difficult to fall asleep.

Along with sleep, other aspects of physical health are important in preparing for a test. Good nutrition is vital for good brain function. Sugary foods and drinks may give a burst of energy but this burst is followed by a crash, both physically and emotionally. Instead, fuel your body with protein and vitamin-rich foods.

Also, drink plenty of water. Dehydration can lead to headaches and exhaustion, especially if your brain is already under stress from the rigors of the test. Particularly if your test is a long one, drink water during the breaks. And if possible, take an energy-boosting snack to eat between sections.

Along with sleep and diet, a third important part of physical health is exercise. Maintaining a steady workout schedule is helpful, but even taking 5-minute study breaks to walk can help get your blood pumping faster and clear your head. Exercise also releases endorphins, which contribute to a positive feeling and can help combat test anxiety.

When you nurture your physical health, you are also contributing to your mental health. If your body is healthy, your mind is much more likely to be healthy as well. So take time to rest, nourish your body with healthy food and water, and get moving as much as possible. Taking these physical steps will make you stronger and more able to take the mental steps necessary to overcome test anxiety.

Mental Steps for Beating Test Anxiety

Working on the mental side of test anxiety can be more challenging, but as with the physical side, there are clear steps you can take to overcome it. As mentioned earlier, test anxiety often stems from lack of preparation, so the obvious solution is to prepare for the test. Effective studying may be the most important weapon you have for beating test anxiety, but you can and should employ several other mental tools to combat fear.

First, boost your confidence by reminding yourself of past success—tests or projects that you aced. If you're putting as much effort into preparing for this test as you did for those, there's no reason you should expect to fail here. Work hard to prepare; then trust your preparation.

Second, surround yourself with encouraging people. It can be helpful to find a study group, but be sure that the people you're around will encourage a positive attitude. If you spend time with others who are anxious or cynical, this will only contribute to your own anxiety. Look for others who are motivated to study hard from a desire to succeed, not from a fear of failure.

Third, reward yourself. A test is physically and mentally tiring, even without anxiety, and it can be helpful to have something to look forward to. Plan an activity following the test, regardless of the outcome, such as going to a movie or getting ice cream.

When you are taking the test, if you find yourself beginning to feel anxious, remind yourself that you know the material. Visualize successfully completing the test. Then take a few deep, relaxing breaths and return to it. Work through the questions carefully but with confidence, knowing that you are capable of succeeding.

Developing a healthy mental approach to test taking will also aid in other areas of life. Test anxiety affects more than just the actual test—it can be damaging to your mental health and even contribute to depression. It's important to beat test anxiety before it becomes a problem for more than testing.

Study Strategy

Being prepared for the test is necessary to combat anxiety, but what does being prepared look like? You may study for hours on end and still not feel prepared. What you need is a strategy for test prep. The next few pages outline our recommended steps to help you plan out and conquer the challenge of preparation.

Step 1: Scope Out the Test

Learn everything you can about the format (multiple choice, essay, etc.) and what will be on the test. Gather any study materials, course outlines, or sample exams that may be available. Not only will this help you to prepare, but knowing what to expect can help to alleviate test anxiety.

Step 2: Map Out the Material

Look through the textbook or study guide and make note of how many chapters or sections it has. Then divide these over the time you have. For example, if a book has 15 chapters and you have five days to study, you need to cover three chapters each day. Even better, if you have the time, leave an extra day at the end for overall review after you have gone through the material in depth.

If time is limited, you may need to prioritize the material. Look through it and make note of which sections you think you already have a good grasp on, and which need review. While you are studying, skim quickly through the familiar sections and take more time on the challenging parts.

Write out your plan so you don't get lost as you go. Having a written plan also helps you feel more in control of the study, so anxiety is less likely to arise from feeling overwhelmed at the amount to cover.

Step 3: Gather Your Tools

Decide what study method works best for you. Do you prefer to highlight in the book as you study and then go back over the highlighted portions? Or do you type out notes of the important information? Or is it helpful to make flashcards that you can carry with you? Assemble the pens, index cards, highlighters, post-it notes, and any other materials you may need so you won't be distracted by getting up to find things while you study.

If you're having a hard time retaining the information or organizing your notes, experiment with different methods. For example, try color-coding by subject with colored pens, highlighters, or post-it notes. If you learn better by hearing, try recording yourself reading your notes so you can listen while in the car, working out, or simply sitting at your desk. Ask a friend to quiz you from your flashcards, or try teaching someone the material to solidify it in your mind.

Step 4: Create Your Environment

It's important to avoid distractions while you study. This includes both the obvious distractions like visitors and the subtle distractions like an uncomfortable chair (or a too-comfortable couch that makes you want to fall asleep). Set up the best study environment possible: good lighting and a comfortable work area. If background music helps you focus, you may want to turn it on, but otherwise keep the room quiet. If you are using a computer to take notes, be sure you don't have any other windows open, especially applications like social media, games, or anything else that could distract you. Silence your phone and turn off notifications. Be sure to keep water close by so you stay hydrated while you study (but avoid unhealthy drinks and snacks).

Also, take into account the best time of day to study. Are you freshest first thing in the morning? Try to set aside some time then to work through the material. Is your mind clearer in the afternoon or evening? Schedule your study session then. Another method is to study at the same time of day that you will take the test, so that your brain gets used to working on the material at that time and will be ready to focus at test time.

Step 5: Study!

Once you have done all the study preparation, it's time to settle into the actual studying. Sit down, take a few moments to settle your mind so you can focus, and begin to follow your study plan. Don't give in to distractions or let yourself procrastinate. This is your time to prepare so you'll be ready to fearlessly approach the test. Make the most of the time and stay focused.

Of course, you don't want to burn out. If you study too long you may find that you're not retaining the information very well. Take regular study breaks. For example, taking five minutes out of every hour to walk briskly, breathing deeply and swinging your arms, can help your mind stay fresh.

As you get to the end of each chapter or section, it's a good idea to do a quick review. Remind yourself of what you learned and work on any difficult parts. When you feel that you've mastered the material, move on to the next part. At the end of your study session, briefly skim through your notes again.

But while review is helpful, cramming last minute is NOT. If at all possible, work ahead so that you won't need to fit all your study into the last day. Cramming overloads your brain with more information than it can process and retain, and your tired mind may struggle to recall even previously learned information when it is overwhelmed with last-minute study. Also, the urgent nature of cramming and the stress placed on your brain contribute to anxiety. You'll be more likely to go to the test feeling unprepared and having trouble thinking clearly.

So don't cram, and don't stay up late before the test, even just to review your notes at a leisurely pace. Your brain needs rest more than it needs to go over the information again. In fact, plan to finish your studies by noon or early afternoon the day before the test. Give your brain the rest of the day to relax or focus on other things, and get a good night's sleep. Then you will be fresh for the test and better able to recall what you've studied.

Step 6: Take a Practice Test

Many courses offer sample tests, either online or in the study materials. This is an excellent resource to check whether you have mastered the material, as well as to prepare for the test format and environment.

Check the test format ahead of time: the number of questions, the type (multiple choice, free response, etc.), and the time limit. Then create a plan for working through them. For example, if you have 30 minutes to take a 60-question test, your limit is 30 seconds per question. Spend less time on the questions you know well so that you can take more time on the difficult ones.

If you have time to take several practice tests, take the first one open book, with no time limit. Work through the questions at your own pace and make sure you fully understand them. Gradually work up to taking a test under test conditions: sit at a desk with all study materials put away and set a timer. Pace yourself to make sure you finish the test with time to spare and go back to check your answers if you have time.

After each test, check your answers. On the questions you missed, be sure you understand why you missed them. Did you misread the question (tests can use tricky wording)? Did you forget the information? Or was it something you hadn't learned? Go back and study any shaky areas that the practice tests reveal.

Taking these tests not only helps with your grade, but also aids in combating test anxiety. If you're already used to the test conditions, you're less likely to worry about it, and working through tests until you're scoring well gives you a confidence boost. Go through the practice tests until you feel comfortable, and then you can go into the test knowing that you're ready for it.

Test Tips

On test day, you should be confident, knowing that you've prepared well and are ready to answer the questions. But aside from preparation, there are several test day strategies you can employ to maximize your performance.

First, as stated before, get a good night's sleep the night before the test (and for several nights before that, if possible). Go into the test with a fresh, alert mind rather than staying up late to study.

Try not to change too much about your normal routine on the day of the test. It's important to eat a nutritious breakfast, but if you normally don't eat breakfast at all, consider eating just a protein bar. If you're a coffee drinker, go ahead and have your normal coffee. Just make sure you time it so that the caffeine doesn't wear off right in the middle of your test. Avoid sugary beverages, and drink enough water to stay hydrated but not so much that you need a restroom break 10 minutes into the test. If your test isn't first thing in the morning, consider going for a walk or doing a light workout before the test to get your blood flowing.

Allow yourself enough time to get ready, and leave for the test with plenty of time to spare so you won't have the anxiety of scrambling to arrive in time. Another reason to be early is to select a good seat. It's helpful to sit away from doors and windows, which can be distracting. Find a good seat, get out your supplies, and settle your mind before the test begins.

When the test begins, start by going over the instructions carefully, even if you already know what to expect. Make sure you avoid any careless mistakes by following the directions.

Then begin working through the questions, pacing yourself as you've practiced. If you're not sure on an answer, don't spend too much time on it, and don't let it shake your confidence. Either skip it and come back later, or eliminate as many wrong answers as possible and guess among the remaining ones. Don't dwell on these questions as you continue—put them out of your mind and focus on what lies ahead.

Be sure to read all of the answer choices, even if you're sure the first one is the right answer. Sometimes you'll find a better one if you keep reading. But don't second-guess yourself if you do immediately know the answer. Your gut instinct is usually right. Don't let test anxiety rob you of the information you know.

If you have time at the end of the test (and if the test format allows), go back and review your answers. Be cautious about changing any, since your first instinct tends to be correct, but make sure you didn't misread any of the questions or accidentally mark the wrong answer choice. Look over any you skipped and make an educated guess.

At the end, leave the test feeling confident. You've done your best, so don't waste time worrying about your performance or wishing you could change anything. Instead, celebrate the successful completion of this test. And finally, use this test to learn how to deal with anxiety even better next time.

Review Video: Test Anxiety
Visit mometrix.com/academy and enter code: 100340

Important Qualification

Not all anxiety is created equal. If your test anxiety is causing major issues in your life beyond the classroom or testing center, or if you are experiencing troubling physical symptoms related to your anxiety, it may be a sign of a serious physiological or psychological condition. If this sounds like your situation, we strongly encourage you to seek professional help.

Online Resources

Due to our efforts to try to keep this book to a manageable length, we've created a link that will give you access to all of your online resources:

mometrix.com/resources719/csetenglandev

It's Your Moment, Let's Celebrate It!

Share your story @mometrixtestpreparation